The charm of Blithewold is its simplicity — and there are very few places like it. It will be hard, over the years, to keep it that way, the temptation being to add, add, add, exploit, exploit until it is one more tourist trap like so many others. Blithewold has it over so many other places because it was planned with taste and elegance instead of ostentation. Perhaps that is why, in this glittering old world, so many people love it so much.

Alice DeWolf Pardee

They were all part of such a gracious, peaceful, unhurried life...and in spite of personal difficulties they seemed as if they knew how to cope with the difficulties and put them in their place and make living calm and good in spite of everything.

Gertrude Keller Johnston, letter to Marjorie Lyon, 1946

A place consists of everything that has happened there; it is a reservoir of memories, and understanding those memories is not a trap but a liberation, a menu of possibilities. The richer the knowledge, the wider the options. Multiplicity is all. The only enemy is narrow, singular definition. And Sissinghurst, perhaps like any place that people have loved, is layered with these multiplicities. Even now, anyone who lives or works here soon develops an intense relationship to it, none of them quite the same, none quite distinct, none of them quite secure. ... It is a place drenched both in belonging and in the longing to belong.

Adam Nicolson, *Sissinghurst – An Unfinished History*

BLITHEWOLD

Legacy of
an American
Family

Margaret Whitehead

For Marjorie Shaw Jeffries

and

Mary C. Philbrick

Always the same – yet ever new.

Old, yet eternally young.

So it is with Blithewold, so it is with Aunt Marjorie.

A Spirit indwells the place, a Spirit indwells the person.

The same Spirit indwells each one of us.

That's why we recognize it

When we come, are nurtured, and depart in peace.

Reverend Boyd Lyon, Blithewold Guestbook, September 1975

TABLE OF CONTENTS

PREFACE

In September 1998, Blithewold Mansion, Gardens & Arboretum faced the very real threat of being closed to the public forever. The Trust that had owned Blithewold since Marjorie Van Wickle Lyon's death in 1976 could no longer afford the upkeep of the property, and had offered it for lease, inviting various organizations to submit proposals. Interested parties were an events-catering company, a local university, and an exclusive private club. All plans would severely restrict public access to the Blithewold mansion and grounds. I recognized then with sadness that the full story of this estate so rich in history might never be told. In a turn of events worthy of a novel, however, the mansion and gardens were rescued. Twenty dedicated members of Blithewold quickly formed themselves into a group they called Save Blithewold, Inc., and immediately went to work to make friends and neighbors aware of the crisis before it was too late. Within three weeks, they had gathered more than $650,000 in pledges and formed a proposal for managing Blithewold and its grounds, which they put before the Trust Board. The Board accepted their proposal, and Blithewold was saved.

I determined then that I would at some point put into a clear narrative everything I had learned during my years at Blithewold about the estate and its family while studying the vast amount of material in the archival collection. But, a great deal of research and documentation remained to be done. In 1999, a group of Archives volunteers embarked on the enormous task of systematically transcribing thousands of pages of letters and documents. Three years ago I finally found the voice and the passion to bring together the history of the family and the place, and I began writing the story of Blithewold — the story of how it evolved as a much-loved home and then a public place, one that was almost lost and then was regained.

Blithewold's rich archival collection reveals how two European colonial-era families — the Pardees and the Van Wickles — arrived in Connecticut and New Jersey, respectively, in the 1600s. Their narratives are documented in unusual detail in the Blithewold collection but are only briefly described in this book. The bulk of the book you hold covers the years 1810 to 2010, beginning with the birth of Ario Pardee — through the marriage of his daughter Bessie to Augustus Van Wickle (the founder of Blithewold), to their children and grandchildren — right down to the present day.

The Archives themselves are preserved in a protected environment, using modern-day conservation methods. Staff and Archives volunteers have spent years sorting, organizing, transcribing, and interpreting diaries, journals, travel itineraries, family correspondence, and business records. Thousands of photographs, cross-referenced with the written material, add to the depth of understanding. Present-day family members came to respect and have confidence in the "new" Blithewold's integrity after 1999, and they donated further treasures in the form of personal memoirs and essays describing life at Blithewold. They have also contributed letters and photographs that directly relate to this remarkable family — and the legacy it has bestowed for the enjoyment and education of the public.

Marjorie Shaw Jeffries, Bessie Pardee Van Wickle McKee's only surviving grandchild, stated in 2009 that her grandmother would be amazed to know of the passion and dedication of so many "strangers" who keep Blithewold alive and thriving. She said that Bessie McKee would be delighted to see the gardens that, more than seventy years after her death, have fulfilled her dream of *"an estate in which new beauties are constantly revealed, and the perfect accord between architecture and grounds is ever apparent."*[1] Little did Bessie know that the estate she began to create with her first husband Augustus Van Wickle in 1895 would flourish and give pleasure and inspiration to 35,000 visitors a year more than a century later.

---

[1] Quote from a wood-bound album describing Blithewold, with text and photographs, handwritten by Samuel Dean, in Bessie's voice. Ca. 1915. Blithewold Archives.

ACKNOWLEDGEMENTS AND READERS' NOTES

Most of the information used in this book is taken from three basic blocks of letters and diaries that, taken together, present a vivid picture of the life and times of one family from 1832 to 1976. The first block consists of family letters and diaries that had been saved by Bessie Pardee Van Wickle McKee and her daughter Marjorie Van Wickle Lyon and stored together in trunks and drawers at Blithewold. A second block, including sensitive information and business letters that had been kept at Marjorie Lyon's home office at 4 Acorn Street in Boston, was donated to Save Blithewold in 2000 by Marjorie Shaw Jeffries. The third block includes letters and documents that came from the personal files of Bessie's younger daughter, Augustine Van Wickle Shaw Toland. They were retrieved from her Whitemarsh, Pennsylvania, home after her death in 1977, by her daughter, Marjorie Shaw Jeffries. All three collections are preserved in the Blithewold Archives.

Other information sources are interviews over a ten-year period with family members Marjorie Shaw Jeffries and Nancy Pardee Abercrombie, and with long-time Blithewold resident, Eleanor Rae Gladding, whose father, Arthur Rae, worked at Blithewold as chauffeur and estate manager for more than 50 years. Mrs. Gladding offers a unique perspective and keen observation of life in service in the early 1900s.

Many of the letters in the first chapter (The Pardees) are the property of the descendants of Gertrude Keller Johnston, Ario Pardee's granddaughter and Bessie's niece. These family letters formed the basis for Gertrude Johnston's book *Dear Pa ... And So it Goes.* They are quoted here with kind permission of the family.

When Marjorie Lyon died in 1976 Blithewold became the property of the Rhode Island Heritage Foundation, but Mrs. Lyon's niece, Marjorie Shaw Jeffries, inherited the Lyons' house in Boston, as well as everything in it. Mrs. Jeffries stored all her aunt's papers, diaries, and photograph albums in her own attic. In 2000 she donated this large collection of material to Save Blithewold, Inc. Since this was all new information, a new era of research at Blithewold began — archivists could now fill in the details of the family's personal lives, the trials and misfortunes of the Depression years, family crises, the changes of ownership of the various properties, and records of what happened to the family after Bessie died in 1936.

Mrs. Jeffries has been extremely generous in sharing her memories of her life at Blithewold with me. Over the years, she has answered my searching, sometimes uncomfortable, questions with honesty and frankness. The story of Blithewold and its family has only been put into perspective through her generosity. She, in turn, insists that she owes peace of mind to Save Blithewold, Inc.

When Blithewold was taken over by the Heritage Foundation of Rhode Island in 1976, in accordance with Marjorie Lyon's last will and testament, Mrs. Jeffries thought her association with the estate was over, since she disapproved of the Trust's management of Blithewold. When the Trust announced in 1998 that it was no longer able to support Blithewold, we approached her and shared with her the dreams of the loyal group who had formed Save Blithewold, Inc. She immediately joined in the effort, offering financial, emotional, and material support. For twelve years she has encouraged my research and my writing, sharing stories of her family that would otherwise have remained unknown forever.

For my own part, the writing of this book has clarified in my mind the connections among different family members — their relationships to each other and to the outside world. Simply recording events in chronological order and matching those events with photographs from the archival collection has revealed new, previously concealed, significance. In the words of Frank Cabot of the Garden Conservancy in reference to his book *The Greater Perfection,* "*For those of you who have not yet done so I highly recommend the effort that goes into writing a book, if only for the unintended consequences that ensue."[1]*

For her generosity, her support, and her friendship, I dedicate this book to Marjorie Shaw Jeffries. I dedicate it, also, to Mary C. Philbrick, my partner in investigative research on the third floor of Blithewold for many, many years. Thanks are due, too, to Nancy Pardee Abercrombie, Bessie's great-niece, who, since the founding of Save Blithewold, Inc., has added her own family archives and personal reminiscences over the years. And great appreciation is due to my dear friend Julie Morris, whose retentive memory for all things Blithewold has added tremendously to this work.

The task of transcribing thousands of pages of personal correspondence and diaries has been undertaken by the author and a small group of Archives volunteers. We have struggled with almost indecipherable, spider-like handwriting on thin, aging onionskin paper, analyzing strange words and syntax until their meanings finally became clear and the stories unfolded and came into focus. We were always conscious of the fact that we were in a race against time — many of the letters were deteriorating rapidly due to the destructive effect of early acidic inks on the writing paper.

The dedication and devotion of the Archives volunteers have resulted in electronic and hard copies of every piece of correspondence in the Blithewold collection. For this work I would like to acknowledge and thank Jessica Abramson, Nicole Amaral, Elsa Bertsch, Martha Christina, Catherine Cummings, Betty Durfee, Mary Ellen Dwyer, Jean Erler, Patricia Ley, Amanda Martinson, Ruoxia Li Miller, Jeanne Nugent, Mary Philbrick, Nancy Scott, Cheryl Williams, and Sarah Vukovich. We all feel enriched and honored to have been given the opportunity to immerse ourselves into the narrative of this extraordinary family.

---

[1] From the narration by Frank Cabot, founder of the Garden Conservancy, in his DVD *Quatre Vents,* in which he discusses his book, *A Greater Perfection.*

I am also indebted to Sally Kijanka for her kind permission to freely use the material in her mother's book, *Dear Pa — And So It Goes.*

I deeply appreciate the advice, encouragement, and support given to me by landscape historian Karen L. Jessup, Ph.D., in the early manuscript phase. Her knowledge and guidance inspired my resolve.

Gratitude also goes to those who have read my work as it has evolved and have commented and advised and urged me on: my husband Duncan, Marjorie Jeffries, Karen Jessup, Julie Morris, Elsa Bertsch, Gioia Browne, Betty Durfee, Patricia Ley, Ruth Miller, and Sally Phillips. The contribution of my proofreader, Jean Erler, has been invaluable.

I wish to thank the countless people at Blithewold — staff, volunteers, and Board members — who have shown great interest in this project and have supported me in my mission.

Margaret Whitehead

June 2011

THE PARDEES

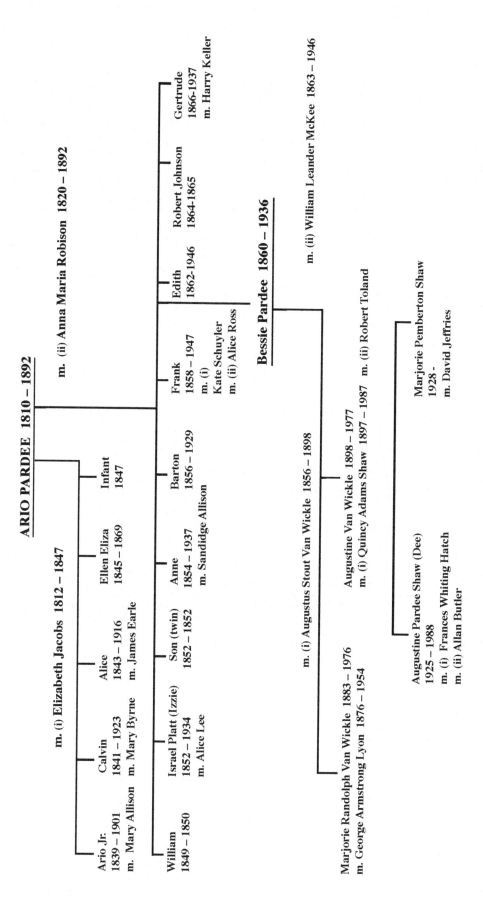

ARIO PARDEE 1810 – 1892

m. (i) Elizabeth Jacobs 1812 – 1847

m. (ii) Anna Maria Robison 1820 – 1892

Ario Jr.
1839 – 1901
m. Mary Allison

Calvin
1841 – 1923
m. Mary Byrne

Alice
1843 – 1916
m. James Earle

Ellen Eliza
1845 – 1869

Infant
1847

William
1849 – 1850

Israel Platt (Izzie)
1852 – 1934
m. Alice Lee

Son (twin)
1852 – 1852

Anne
1854 – 1937
m. Sandidge Allison

Barton
1856 – 1929

Frank
1858 – 1947
m. (i)
Kate Schuyler
m. (ii) Alice Ross

Edith
1862-1946

Robert Johnson
1864-1865

Gertrude
1866-1937
m. Harry Keller

Bessie Pardee 1860 – 1936

m. (i) Augustus Stout Van Wickle 1856 – 1898

m. (ii) William Leander McKee 1863 – 1946

Marjorie Randolph Van Wickle 1883 – 1976
m. George Armstrong Lyon 1876 – 1954

Augustine Van Wickle 1898 – 1977
m. (i) Quincy Adams Shaw 1897 – 1987   m. (ii) Robert Toland

Augustine Pardee Shaw (Dee)
1925 – 1988
m. (i) Frances Whiting Hatch
m. (ii) Allan Butler

Marjorie Pemberton Shaw
1928 -
m. David Jeffries

THE VAN WICKLES

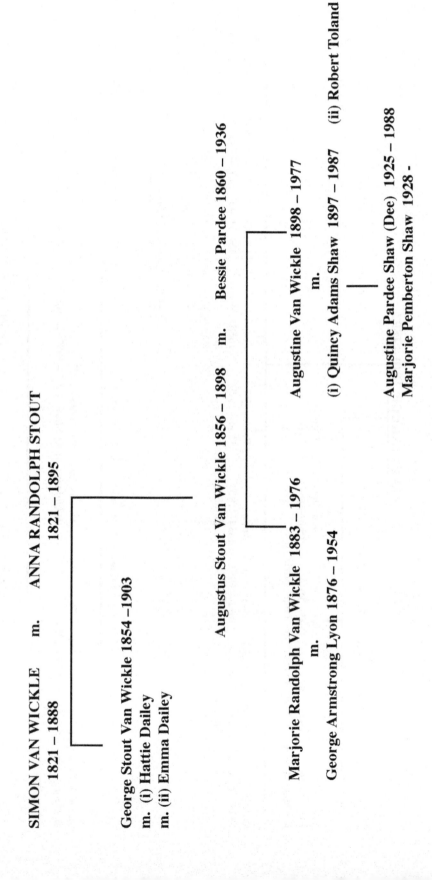

SIMON VAN WICKLE   m.   ANNA RANDOLPH STOUT
1821 – 1888   1821 – 1895

George Stout Van Wickle 1854 –1903
m. (i) Hattie Dailey
m. (ii) Emma Dailey

Augustus Stout Van Wickle 1856 – 1898   m.   Bessie Pardee 1860 – 1936

Augustine Van Wickle 1898 – 1977
m.
(i) Quincy Adams Shaw 1897 – 1987   (ii) Robert Toland

Marjorie Randolph Van Wickle 1883 – 1976
m.
George Armstrong Lyon 1876 – 1954

Augustine Pardee Shaw (Dee) 1925 – 1988
Marjorie Pemberton Shaw 1928 -

BLITHEWOLD TIME LINE

1810   ARIO PARDEE is born in Chatham, New York.

1820   ANNA MARIA ROBISON is born in Bloomsburg, Pennsylvania.

1821   SIMON VAN WICKLE is born in New Brunswick, New Jersey. ANNA RANDOLPH STOUT is born in New Jersey.

1856   AUGUSTUS STOUT VAN WICKLE is born in New Brunswick, New Jersey.

1860   BESSIE PARDEE is born in Hazleton, Pennsylvania.

1876   AUGUSTUS VAN WICKLE graduates from Brown University in Rhode Island. He is sent to work at the Van Wickle coal mines near Hazleton, Pennsylvania, and it is in Hazleton that he meets Bessie Pardee.

1882   AUGUSTUS marries BESSIE in Hazleton. They go to live in Cleveland, Ohio.

1883   Their daughter MARJORIE RANDOLPH VAN WICKLE is born in Cleveland.

1887   The Van Wickles move to Morristown, New Jersey.

1888   SIMON VAN WICKLE, Augustus's father, dies in New Brunswick, New Jersey.

1892   ARIO PARDEE dies in Hazleton.   ANNA MARIA PARDEE dies in Hazleton. The Van Wickles move to Hazleton.

1893   The Van Wickles visit the World's Columbian Exposition in Chicago.

1894   The Van Wickles visit Bristol, Rhode Island, and purchase a HERRESHOFF yacht that they name the

Marjorie. They purchase the Gardner estate on Ferry Road in Bristol, which they name BLITHEWOLD.

1895   ANNA VAN WICKLE, Augustus's mother, dies in New Brunswick, New Jersey. Bessie hires JOHN DEWOLF to design the landscape at Blithewold.

1896   The Van Wickles spend the first summer at Blithewold in their new Queen-Anne-style mansion. The architect is Francis Hoppin of Hoppin & Koen, Newport, Rhode Island.

1898   In June AUGUSTUS VAN WICKLE is killed in a skeet-shooting accident in Hazleton. In November Bessie gives birth to their second daughter, AUGUSTINE VAN WICKLE.

1901   BESSIE VAN WICKLE marries WILLIAM McKEE. MARJORIE VAN WICKLE attends the official opening of the Van Wickle Memorial Gates at Brown University.

1903   MARJORIE embarks on an eleven-month tour of Europe and Egypt with her cousin Dorothy Pardee, friend Gertrude Vaughan, and chaperone/guide Helen Macartnay.

1905   MARJORIE and BESSIE attend the official opening of the Fitz Randolph Gates at Princeton University, named for Augustus Van Wickle's ancestor. The ceremony is also attended by Woodrow Wilson and Grover Cleveland.

1906   In June, the first Blithewold mansion is totally destroyed by fire. All furniture and furnishings are saved. Plans are begun immediately to rebuild.

1907   Blithewold is rebuilt in an English Country Manor style, of stone and stucco, using some architectural features saved from the first house. The architect is Walter Kilham of Kilham & Hopkins, Boston, Massachusetts.

1908   The family spends its first summer in the new Blithewold. Furnishings from Blithewold I are used to decorate the new house.

1911   The Giant Sequoia is planted in the Enclosed Garden at Blithewold.

1914   MARJORIE VAN WICKLE marries GEORGE ARMSTRONG LYON in a ceremony in front of the Summerhouse in the Enclosed Garden at Blithewold.

1917   America enters the war in Europe. George Lyon goes for Officers' Training and is posted to Camp Jackson in Columbia, South Carolina. Marjorie joins the Red Cross of America there, an affiliation she will continue for almost forty years.

1918   GEORGE LYON goes to France as a Captain in the American Army.

1919   GEORGE LYON is awarded the prestigious Croix de Guerre by the French government for his wartime service in France. AUGUSTINE VAN WICKLE marries QUINCY ADAMS SHAW, JR. in Boston.

1925   AUGUSTINE gives birth to a daughter, AUGUSTINE PARDEE (DEE) SHAW.

1926   Ernest Wilson and Alfred Rehder of the Arnold Arboretum visit Blithewold and declare it an Arboretum.

1928   ESTELLE CLEMENTS, who had lived with the family for 30 years, dies in Greenville, Mississippi, at the age of 79, of pneumonia. AUGUSTINE gives birth to a second daughter, MARJORIE PEMBERTON SHAW.

1932   BESSIE transfers ownership of Blithewold to Marjorie and Augustine. The McKees' townhouse on Commonwealth Avenue is sold to offset debts from

William McKee's failing business. The McKees move permanently to Blithewold; 30 acres to the south is sold to the Columban Fathers.

1934   The McKees take their last trip to Europe, a 6-week Mediterranean cruise.

1936   BESSIE VAN WICKLE McKEE dies at Rhode Island Hospital after a fall on the staircase at Blithewold. Augustine divorces Quincy Shaw and spends a year at Blithewold with her children, Dee and Marjorie.

1937   AUGUSTINE marries ROBERT TOLAND and moves to Whitemarsh, Pennsylvania, with Dee and Marjorie.

1938   The devastating hurricane of 1938 causes great destruction at Blithewold. Hundreds of trees are destroyed, and the Water Garden is flooded with salt water for several days. The dock area is destroyed and the sandy beach is washed away.

1946   WILLIAM McKEE dies at Blithewold at the age of 83. MARJORIE buys her sister's share of Blithewold and thus becomes the sole owner of the estate.

1954   GEORGE LYON dies at the age of 75 in Providence.

1972   The Katsura tree, a gift to Marjorie from The Arnold Arboretum in thanks for her continued support, is planted in the Enclosed Garden.

1973   MARJORIE VAN WICKLE LYON's 90th birthday is celebrated at Blithewold.

1976   MARJORIE VAN WICKLE LYON dies at Blithewold at the age of 93. Ownership of Blithewold passes to the Heritage Foundation of Rhode Island. An endowment is left for upkeep of the estate.

1977   AUGUSTINE VAN WICKLE SHAW TOLAND dies at the
          age of 78 in Whitemarsh.

1978   Blithewold opens to the public on a limited basis. A grant
          from the Rhode Island Foundation supports the
          identification and marking of all the trees.

1991   A Visitors' Center is built between the parking lot and
          the Rose Garden at the southern end of the property.
          Hurricane Bob causes extensive damage at Blithewold;
          83 trees are lost, many of them significant specimens.
          Clean-up cost is $65,000.

1998   The Heritage Trust announces it can no longer maintain
          Blithewold.

1999   SAVE BLITHEWOLD INCORPORATED takes over the
          management of Blithewold to ensure that Marjorie Lyon's
          wishes that Blithewold remain open to the public are
          honored. Grants are secured to begin the monumental
          task of repairing and upgrading the property. In the
          Mansion, rooms are secured with railings and an alarm
          system to accommodate self-guided tours. Information
          sheets are written for each room and are placed in that
          room.

2000   Repair of the saltwater Pump House at the dock,
          restoration of the west-facing terrace and balustrade,
          and restoration of the Summerhouse are undertaken.
          Blithewold receives the first of many gifts of family
          archival material from Marjorie Lyon's niece, Marjorie
          Shaw Jeffries. It includes thousands of photographs,
          letters, journals, and documents. Interpretation and
          electronic transcription of all archival material begins.

2001   The first of 400 new trees and shrubs are planted on the
          property. Top dressing of all driveways and pathways
          with gravel begins, and continues as needed.

2002   A permanent tent site is constructed for weddings and
         events. More than 1000 feet of historic gravel paths
         connecting the gardens (all but hidden under layers of
         soil and grass) are located and restored. A new roof is
         put on the North Cottage and repairs to the roof and
         gutters of the Mansion are undertaken. A new Grounds
         Map is designed by David Macaulay for distribution to all
         visitors. The Carriage House is adapted for use as a
         Classroom and Plant Clinic. The "quiet phase" of the
         Capital Campaign begins.

2003   Interpretive signs are installed in all the key garden
         areas, a gift from a member. The Visitors' Center is
         expanded to accommodate the Gift Shop.

2004   Funds are raised for the rebuilding and restoration of the
         Greenhouse. A stone bench in the Water Garden is
         uncovered and restored, based on photographs from the
         Blithewold Archives. Archival study results in a
         comprehensive history of the Van Wickle and Pardee
         families, dating back to 1660. A new booklet on the
         history of Blithewold is published for sale in the Gift
         Shop. The "Dorrance Hamilton Visitors' Center" officially
         opens.

2005   The old Lord & Burnham greenhouse is completely
         rebuilt on its original footprint. Hundreds of trees are
         planted to replace old trees that had died.

2006   Blithewold's Board votes to change the organization's
         name to Blithewold, Inc., to reflect the belief that
         Blithewold has indeed been saved.

2008   Blithewold celebrates its Centennial with special events
         throughout the year. The Carriage House is stabilized
         and reshingled; it is now used as an education center.
         Restoration and conservation of paintings, textiles, and
         original wallpapers are undertaken in the Mansion. The

work of replacing the Mansion's one-hundred-year-old slate roof begins.

2009   A small group begins work on plans to implement a Master Plan for Blithewold.

2010   Replacement of the mansion's slate roof is completed. Blithewold hires Ann Beha Architects of Boston to formulate a Master Plan. A successful fund-raising campaign is launched to pay for the study; and a matching grant is received from IMLS for $145,000.

2011   Work begins on the reconstruction of the retaining wall in the North Garden. The North Star and other special stones will be replaced in their original positions.

Chapter I

THE PARDEES

Bessie Pardee Van Wickle McKee was born in 1860 in Hazleton, Pennsylvania, the twelfth child of coal-mining magnate Ario Pardee. She was brought up in a large city-block-square mansion in the center of Hazleton, with all the advantages of wealth and privilege. But her father, Ario Pardee, the provider of all these benefits, was not himself born to great wealth. With good reason he was known in the family as "Ario the Founder," the name serving to acknowledge his contribution to the well-being and success of generations of Pardees, and also to distinguish him from the many subsequent (and previous) Ario Pardees. (Indeed, for more than 200 years there was always at least one Ario Pardee.)

"ARIO THE FOUNDER"

Ariovistus Pardee,[1] known as Ario, was born in 1810 in Chatham, in the low hills of the Berkshires in Eastern New York State. His earliest recollections were of life on his father's humble farm in Stephentown, Rensselaer County. His formal education was limited to what he learned at the district school, but he was inspired to greater learning when an excellent teacher, the Reverend Moses Hunter, taught briefly at the school (to supplement his meager salary as a Presbyterian clergyman). Ario always credited the Reverend Hunter with inspiring in him a devotion to learning that lasted his whole life.[2] His formal education ended when he was 15, when he was obliged to leave school and work on the farm; but Ario remembered learning the classics from his father, sitting by the fireside in the modest family

---

[1] Father of Bessie Pardee Van Wickle McKee; grandfather of Marjorie Van Wickle Lyon and Augustine Van Wickle Shaw Toland.
[2] From William C. Cattell's Memorial Address delivered at Lafayette College on Founders Day, October 23, 1892. Blithewold Archives.

home and working at his books in his limited leisure time. His father, for whom he was named, was an insatiable reader, and, indeed, his paternal grandparents appear to have been Latin scholars for they named their sons Ariovistus, Paulus, and Flavius, and their daughters Lavinia and Palmyra. Ario always knew that he would not follow his father into farming.[1] He had examples of higher learning in the family — one Pardee had married into the Yale family who had founded Yale University in Saybrook, Connecticut, and another was associated with the Rensselaer Institute in Troy, New York. Ario would pursue his own education for the rest of his life,[2] and all his children were educated to the very best of their ability at the finest institutions of learning. He was known as a God-fearing man who became one of the richest men in America by his 50th year.[3] Although his first company was engaged in the extremely lucrative mining of anthracite, he soon diversified his business interests to include iron, lumber, and banking. Many of these businesses still exist today, enhanced and restructured by successive generations of Pardees to reflect changing times. In his own lifetime, Ario supported churches, hospitals, and schools in Hazleton. One of his most philanthropic gifts was a large donation to Lafayette College in 1864 to save the failing institution. He later gave a further half-million dollars (almost $12 million in today's values) to build, among other things, a science department there.

Ario's ancestors had come to America in the 1600s. The original immigrant, George Pardee, was born in Taunton, Somerset, England, in 1624, the son of a teacher and curate. By 1644, George was living in New Haven, Connecticut, where he was Rector of the Hopkins Grammar School. His son Joseph met and married Elizabeth Yale in

---

[1] C. Pardee Foulke and William G. Foulke. *Calvin Pardee.* Drake Press, Philadelphia, 1979, p. 27.

[2] *Pardee Genealogy*, edited by Donald Lines Jacobus, New Haven Colony Historical Society, 1927, p. 548.

[3] When Ario Pardee died in 1892 the *Philadelphia Press* (April 9, 1892) reported that Ario Pardee's property and personal estate were valued at $30 million. This would be more than $700 million in today's values.

1689. Joseph's son, John, born in 1697, moved to Sharon, Connecticut in 1738 and built a stone house there. The house is extant and is now owned by the Sharon Historical Society. It was John's grandson Calvin who moved to the farm in Stephentown where his son and grandson (both named Ariovistus) were born.

Ario Pardee[1]

In 1829, when young Ario was 19, he heard that a family acquaintance from Stephentown, Edwin A. Douglas, had been appointed to build the Delaware and Raritan Canal in New Jersey. He wrote to Mr. Douglas asking for a position under him. He was bitterly disappointed when Mr. Douglas, in his reply, told him that the Canal Company was hiring only men from New Jersey. Ario went back to his

---

[1] This photographic image and all subsequent images are from the Blithewold Photograph Collection, unless otherwise identified. Information on the Pardees from letters, journals, essays, and photographs are from the Blithewold Archival Collection; from the book *Calvin Pardee* by C. Pardee Foulke and William G. Foulke; and from the book *Dear Pa — And So It Goes* by Gertrude Keller Johnston.

work plowing, but a few days later his sister Rachael came racing across the field waving a letter that was to change the course of his life. Mr. Douglas had written to advise that if Ario could come to New Jersey immediately he could have the job of rodman[1] on the project. After Ario finished plowing the field that day, Saturday, he went home to gather his belongings. He rested on the Sabbath, and then left home before daylight on Monday morning, joining Mr. Douglas and his men a few miles north of Trenton, New Jersey.[2] When that part of the canal was finished, Ario moved west to Princeton to work on the middle division of the canal; after that it was on to Lambertville in the most western part of New Jersey. Ario Pardee's handwritten workbooks from that time show complicated mathematical calculations and diagrams showing how the canals were made to flow, the crucial gradients, and the workings of the locks.

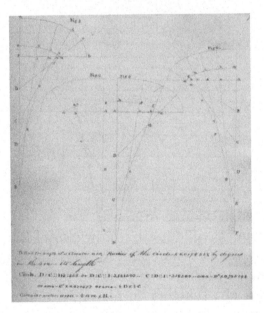

A page from Ario Pardee's workbook, 1832

---

[1] A rodman was a surveyor's assistant, so named because his job was to hold the rod used for surveying.
[2] In an April 6, 1876 letter, Ario Pardee told his friend Dr. William Cattell, *"You may well believe I lost no time, receiving the letter on Saturday and leaving home before daylight on Monday morning."*

At the same time, rich coal fields were being discovered in the hills of Pennsylvania. The coal was carried painstakingly by mules and wagons down the hills to the towns below, where it was loaded onto canal barges. The barges were pulled along the canals to the railways, which then delivered the coal to the cities where it was used for home heating and for industry. It was an inefficient system, and Edwin Douglas knew that if he could build a better means of transportation from the mines to the canals, the barges could take massive loads of coal to larger towns and cities, including Philadelphia. So he sent Ario to Beaver Meadow, Pennsylvania, to work on a survey for the Beaver Meadow Railroad Company. The railroad company, which owned coal mines near Hazleton, 100 miles north of Philadelphia, planned a simple gravity railroad to carry their coal to the Lehigh Canal at Maunch Chunk. Pulleys and cables lowered cars of coal down the hillside. Mules rode down in the cars with the coal; they then pulled the empty cars back up the hill for reloading.

The gravity railroad was completed in 1836, by which time Ario Pardee was beginning to see tremendous untapped opportunities in coal mining and railroads. He could see that the new gravity railroad was clumsy and that the canal system was already obsolete — not only was it very slow, but the canals froze over in the winter months rendering them useless when they were needed most. He foresaw that the canals would have to be replaced by railways. Ario went to visit his parents, who had moved to Ypsilanti, Michigan, to be close to their married daughters. He used this brief, unaccustomed leisure time to mull over his plan. When he returned to Hazleton (which at that time was scarcely more than a crossroad with ten houses and a small hotel for travelers), he signed on as superintendent of the Hazleton Railroad and Coal Company, determined to learn as much as he could and watch out for future opportunities. He boarded at the Hazleton House Hotel at the corner of Broad and Hazle Streets, built and run by Lewis Davenport whose relative, Elizabeth Jacobs, Ario married in 1838. In 1840, Ario was ready to make his big move. He suspected that there was much more coal in the Hazleton area than the current operators realized, so he started to buy land on speculation. At the age of 30 he became an independent coal operator and formed a company with his business partner, J. Gillingham Fell. Ario and Elizabeth lived very frugally, boarding with her parents and keeping careful notes of every cent earned and spent.[1] In 1843, when the young couple bought their own house, Ario wrote in his diary, *"Hazleton. Today I took dinner for the first time in 13 years at a table of my own."*[2]

Between 1839 and 1845, Elizabeth gave birth to four children, Ario Jr., Calvin, Alice, and Ellen. Two years later, Elizabeth died while giving birth to her fifth child, who also died. Ario was left a widower with four children under eight. His sister Juliet helped look after the children — Ario had given employment to Juliet's husband, Allen Stewart, and the Stewarts were willing to return the generosity Ario had shown them. They offered to help raise the children alongside their own three. But Ario instead decided to hire a governess, one Anna Maria Robison. Anna Maria came from a large, close family in Bloomsburg, Pennsylvania. Her parents, William and Betsey Barton Robison, were devoted to their 12 children, and were no doubt reluctant to see their daughter Anna Maria leave the quiet little town of Bloomsburg on the banks of the Susquehanna River to go up into the hills to the tiny mining community of Hazleton. But Anna Maria, who had trained as a teacher, took the job, willingly undertaking the task of caring for the four young, motherless children.

---

[1]As evidenced in Ario Pardee's diaries and ledgers in the Blithewold Archives.
[2] Ario Pardee's diary, Tuesday January 24, 1843. Blithewold Archives.

Anna Maria Robison Pardee

Within a few months Ario fell in love with Anna Maria. For the sake of propriety, Anna returned to her parents' home until a wedding could be arranged. During this time Ario sent her eloquent love letters.[1] *"I shall have no fears that we will get along...lovingly and cheerfully, helping each other over the rough and enjoying the smooth passages of our journey of life."*[2] He wrote her poems,[3] and quoted from Shakespeare. He gave her all the news of the town and its people, the details of his businesses, and accounts of his early philosophy on life. He was an avid reader, even studying Byron, and he was fascinated by the lives of the eminent men of the world. One of his sons later commented that his father seemed to know Sir Walter Scott's poetry by heart. Still only a modestly successful businessman,

[1] The letters quoted in this chapter, used with the kind permission of the descendants of Gertrude Keller Johnston, are from her book *Dear Pa ... And So it Goes* (henceforth shortened to *Dear Pa*). Private printing, 1971.
[2] Ario Pardee to Anna Maria Robison, July 21, 1848.
[3] Ario Pardee to Anna Maria Robison, August 24, 1848.

Ario anticipated a comfortable, middle-class life: *"I believe that the middle class are the happy class, and in that road, Dear Anna, we seem destined to travel, neither high enough for envy, nor low enough for contempt."*[1] Twenty years later, however, Ario Pardee was a very wealthy man.

Ario's speculation on the rich coal seams in the Hazleton area proved to be well-founded, and he projected that when his dream of replacing the canals with railroads was fulfilled, huge loads of coal could quickly get to the cities where it was needed to feed the new Industrial Revolution.[2] He quickly became the largest shipper of anthracite in Pennsylvania, and as his personal fortune grew so did Hazleton's. He built the Lehigh Valley Railroad, which eventually became an enormous transportation system that stretched from Beaver Meadows to Philadelphia, New York City, and Buffalo, N.Y.

Ario began to influence Hazleton's social, economic, and cultural institutions as well. As he built industries, he also founded banks, churches, schools, and libraries, ultimately being credited with "founding Hazleton," the highest city in Pennsylvania. He was described as a silent man, but one who possessed vision and organizational genius.[3] He was scrupulously honest in business, and it was said that his decisions were quick and indisputable.[4]

Misfortune, however, was to befall Ario over and over again. The mining industry was inherently plagued by floods, fires, explosions, and crippling accidents, but Ario Pardee always seemed to overcome adversity. Anna Maria learned very early in their relationship that Ario would apply his strict moral code to any situation, business or

---

[1] Ario Pardee to Anna Maria Robison, July 26, 1848.
[2] The Industrial Revolution in America lasted from approximately 1820 to 1870. During that time electricity was harnessed and industrial production was mechanized. Better means of transportation were needed to supply the new factories and to take the products to market.
[3] Donald L. Miller and Richard Sharpless in "The Kingdom of Coal." Wikipedia.
[4] From *Personal Reminiscences of Ario Pardee* by Frank Pardee. Blithewold Archives.

otherwise, sometimes at the expense of his family. In 1848, the house Ario was building for Anna Maria (which still stands at the corner of Broad and Poplar Streets and is now owned by the Knights of Columbus) was almost finished. Anna Maria was anxiously awaiting the move into her own home with her ready-made family of four young children when a devastating fire at one of Ario's companies — the Cranberry Works — completely destroyed the facility after a night watchman left a fire smoldering. The Cranberry workmen had families who depended on them, but they suddenly found themselves with no jobs and no means of support. Ario immediately stopped work on his own house and directed his resources and energies toward rebuilding the Cranberry Works. He wrote to Anna Maria: *"What is to be will be — it will be all one a hundred years hence, and there's an end to it. We shall both make the best of this...and be not a whit the less happy."*[1]

Ario and Anna Maria were married in Bloomsburg on August 29, 1848, and Anna's new house was completed soon after. She set up housekeeping and became pregnant within three months. But the couple's domestic life was complicated. Ario's children by his first wife, Elizabeth Jacobs, resented their new stepmother and began to behave badly. Anna Maria felt ill from her pregnancy and found it difficult to discipline the children, particularly the boys, Ario Jr. and Calvin, then aged nine and seven. The children were encouraged in their disobedience by the Davenports, relatives of their mother. They told the children that they did not have to obey Anna Maria — they reminded them that she was, after all, only their stepmother. Ario wrote to Anna from Philadelphia in January of 1849, *"I hope you will be able to give a good report of the behavior of the boys and girls. Tell Ario and Calvin that I hope you will be able to say they have been better boys since I was gone than when I was there."*[2] But Ario Jr. and Calvin became so troublesome that they were sent away to a boarding school in Wyoming, Pennsylvania, near Wilkes-Barre. A regular correspondence began between Ario and his sons. He urged them to settle down and take advantage of the opportunity to learn: *"Unless*

---

[1] Ario Pardee to Anna Maria Robison, August 1848.
[2] Ario Pardee to Anna Maria Pardee, January 24, 1849.

you lay a good foundation of learning and good behavior while you are boys you will not grow up to be good men."[1]

Ario and his son Calvin, ca. 1850

At Anna Maria's urging, Ario offered a job to her brother-in-law, George Markle, who was married to Anna Maria's favorite sister, Emily. Emily and George moved from Bloomsburg, where George had been a clerk in his father's harness and saddle store, and built a house next door to the Pardees. *"Mr. Markle is much pleased with Hazleton...He praises Em[ily] very much about having her house so nice and everything,"*[2] wrote Betsey Robison to Anna Maria. The sisters raised their children together, while George moved up rapidly in Ario's company, eventually becoming a coal operator in his own right. Ario's generosity was to come back to bite him, however. George Markle's son John later became Ario's adversary. He is probably the subject of comments made by Ario's son Frank many years later when Frank

---

[1] Ario Pardee to sons Ario and Calvin, July 30, 1850.
[2] Betsey Robison to her daughter Anna Maria Robison Pardee, June 6, 1849.

said of his father: "*It was hard for him to see the evil in others, and therefore his lieutenants in business were not always wisely chosen, and were often retained when it was patent to others that they were betraying his trust...he could not believe men he had raised from dire poverty to affluence should fail him.*"[1]

Anna Maria's first child, a son, was born in July 1849. Named William after Anna Maria's father, he was adored by his half-sisters Alice and Ellen. That same year Emily Markle gave birth to a daughter, Clora. (Clora would become a lifelong friend of the Pardees, despite her brother's alleged duplicity.)

Ario Jr. and Calvin became more wayward than ever at school. Ario scolded them for "*getting into the habit of smoking cigars,*" and said they must "*quit at once.*"[2] He urged them to:

> *...avoid all bad habits and bad language, be attentive to your studies, kind and polite and respectful to everyone, particularly to your teachers and the family where you board.*[3]

He also cautioned them about handling guns:

> *Be always careful whether you have the gun yourself or are with anyone who carries a gun. Never carry a gun cocked. Always carry it with the muzzle pointed up if you are in company with anyone...Never load a gun which is cocked...always think what you are about.*[4]

He tempered his admonishments with domestic news of the family, particularly news of their two younger sisters, Alice and Ellen. "*They*

---

[1] Report at Pardee Reunion, June 1913. Blithewold Archives.
[2] Ario Pardee to sons Ario Jr. and Calvin, February 21, 1850. Ario Jr. was by then 10 years old and Calvin was 8.
[3] Ario Pardee to sons Ario Jr. and Calvin, August 19, 1850.
[4] Ario Pardee to his sons Ario Jr. and Calvin, October 10, 1851.

amuse themselves with their Grace hoops considerably."[1] But the boys were unhappy away from home, and in November 1851 Ario Jr. wrote that he was *"getting tired of studying now. I have often wished I was home."* Both boys threatened to run away.

Grace Hoops

Alice and Ellen playing Grace Hoops[2]

Ario was spending a lot of his time away on business — most frequently in Philadelphia, where he stayed at the United States Hotel. His partner, J. Gillingham Fell, was in charge of marketing the coal and lived in Philadelphia. Ario very much missed Anna Maria and his home and wrote to his wife pleading for her to join him, offering social events in the City and shopping for the latest fashions. He reassured

---

[1] Ario Pardee to his sons Ario Jr. and Calvin, March 18, 1851. "Grace Hoops" was a game of tossing a ring into the air and catching it with sticks.
[2] Sketch by David O. Holmes, from *Dear Pa — And So It Goes*, by Gertrude K. Johnston, p. 43.

her of his deep love: *"Dearest, believe that though the stream may run beneath the surface, it is deep, and pure, and springs from the depths of the heart's innermost fountains."*[1] Anna Maria's letters to him were full of accounts of daily domestic life, and especially sickness in the town. She was terrified that the children would catch the life-threatening diseases of the time: cholera, dysentery, consumption, scarlet fever, yellow fever, typhoid, and smallpox.

Indeed, Anna Maria had good reason to be afraid. In May 1850, her sister Ellen and her young son Barton came to visit. Ellen's departure at the end of their visit was delayed because Barton was *"very sick, though he is better now — poor little fellow he has been so sick that he could not play with Willie* [baby William].*"*[2] In July baby William died, leaving Anna Maria desolate. She retreated to Bloomsburg, to the comfort of her family. In November, Ario wrote to her, urging her to return to Hazleton: *"I am getting rather lonesome...I think you had better turn your face homeward. Finish your visit, and when that is done you will be very welcome home."*[3]

Anna Maria did return home, and life went on. She tended her gardens, growing flowers and exchanging cuttings with her mother. Ario, too, was interested in horticulture. He wrote to Anna Maria:

Ruckman brought up for you a variety of creepers and woodbines and Honey suckles and Devils clubs and so on which Hal and I planted to the best of our knowledge...if everything lives and grows we should have a wilderness in a few years. The roses in the yard are now all in blossom and the pinks and sweet Williams and musk flowers and mock orange...the yard looks very pretty. Last week the locust was full of flowers, and a humming bird used to come about it every day.[4]

---

[1] Ario Pardee to his wife Anna Maria, January 19, 1851.
[2] Ario Pardee to his sons Ario Jr. and Calvin, May 21, 1850.
[3] Ario Pardee to his wife Anna Maria, November 4, 1850
[4] Ario Pardee to his wife Anna Maria, May 2, 1851.

Still distressed, Anna Maria turned to the church, becoming extremely devout. In May 1851, Ario pledged to pay $2,500 for a church to be built on land that he would donate. That church became the First Presbyterian Church on West Broad Street in Hazleton, where generations of Pardees subsequently worshiped. Ario supported the church all his life and brought up all his children to be committed Christians.

The Pardee business empire continued to grow as mines sprang up around Hazleton. In 1851, the town was incorporated as a borough. Ario employed many family members and financed others in their own ventures. His nephew, William Platt, son of his sister Caroline and her husband (and cousin) Edwin Platt, worked for Ario in Hazleton for a time. He then decided that he wanted to try his luck in the California gold rush. Ario paid his passage, and William Platt traveled overland via the Rocky Mountains and Nevada City, sending accounts of his adventures to Ario along the way, only to die of typhoid in California in 1856.

Anna Maria became pregnant again in 1852, with the baby due in mid-July. In May, though, she suffered food poisoning from *"Indian cakes"*[1] and went into premature labor. They were much surprised by the arrival of twin boys, two months early. One twin died two days later; the other was tiny and feeble, but stubbornly tenacious. He was named Israel Platt, but was called "Izzie" by the family. Izzie was always small and sickly as a child, but he grew to be a strong, feisty, robust man with a great sense of humor, one who lived a long productive life and was loved by everyone.[2]

In November of 1852, Calvin wrote from school to Ario, *"I want to come home. I will not come back here anymore."* When he came home for Christmas, the family enjoyed a Christmas dinner of turkey and oysters, and Ario began the family tradition of reading "The Night

---

[1] Quote from *Dear Pa* by Gertrude Keller Johnston, p. 57.
[2] C. Pardee Foulke and William F. Foulke. *Calvin Pardee.* Drake Press, Philadelphia, 1979, p. 38.

Before Christmas," by Clement Moore,[1] to his children every Christmas Eve. Although Calvin did go back to school after Christmas he later ran away. He was sent for a while to another school, in Easton, Pennsylvania, but he misbehaved there, too, and soon returned to his old school in Wyoming, Pennsylvania.

Anna Maria's family continued to grow, with a daughter, Anne, being born in February 1854. *"She is a pretty little thing; she came on Valentine's Day...Izzie can walk by chairs, and creep a little,"*[2] wrote Ellen to Calvin, referring to 20-month-old Israel. In May of 1854, when Izzie was 2 years old, Ario wrote *"We are...all well except Izzie. The poor little fellow seems to have a hard time of it in this world."* Anna Maria was always appreciative of her comfortable life, and she reached out to others less fortunate: *"How thankful we ought to be who have enough to eat and wear and if we have it to spare to give to those who are needy and not waste or spend foolishly."*[3]

Ario continued to bear the principal responsibility for his two older sons, Ario Jr. and Calvin. As always, his letters to them were full of advice and criticism, as well as domestic news:

> *In your letters you say "I want you to write," "I want you to do so and so..." That is all well enough but would it not sound better to put it in more polite phrase and say "We should be much pleased to have a letter from you soon"..."Please do so and so." I think it would, do not you?*[4]

A curious scolding was, *"You spoke of sending the pen wiper in a newspaper. But it is contrary to law to send anything or write in or on a newspaper. And aside from its always being best and honest to obey the Law, there is a fine of $5 attached to the offence."*[5]

---

[1] Clement Moore wrote "The Night Before Christmas" in 1822.
[2] Ellen Pardee to Calvin Pardee, February 17, 1854.
[3] Anna Maria Pardee to her stepson Calvin, January 19, 1854.
[4] Ario Pardee to his sons Ario Jr. and Calvin, March 17, 1853.
[5] Ario Pardee to his son Calvin, March 7, 1856.

Ario Jr. left the school in Wyoming later in 1854 to attend the West Jersey Collegiate School in Mt. Holly, New Jersey. From there he went to Rensselaer Polytechnic Institute in Troy, New York (the school Ario himself had dreamed of attending as a young man), where he studied civil engineering. (According to its founder, Stephen Van Rensselaer, the Institute's mission was *"to instruct people in the application of science to the common purposes of life."*[1]) Though Ario Jr. had now become a serious student, he found the work there very challenging. He wrote, *"I think that a person cannot fool away his time and [still] get through the Rensselaer Polytechnic Institute."*[2] Calvin, in turn, moved to the West Jersey Collegiate but his behavior continued to deteriorate. The headmaster wrote to Ario: *"Calvin's conduct has become seriously bad...he has been guilty of several very reprehensible acts of disorder, showing something worse than mere heedlessness, and seems disposed rather to resent punishment."*[3] Ario would have to wait quite some time for his second son to mature and find his purpose in life.

1855 was a year of travel for Ario. Apart from his regular visits to Philadelphia he went to Detroit; Washington, DC; Portland, Maine; and Albany, New York. He often traveled from early Monday morning to late Saturday, although he always returned to spend the Sabbath with his family.[4] His diaries consistently show strict attention to business six days a week, and only on Sunday did he allow himself any domestic reflection.

In May and June of 1855, Ario and Anna Maria took a long trip — first to Bloomsburg to pick up Anna Maria's mother, and from there to Ypsilanti, Michigan, to visit Ario's family. They then traveled to

---

[1] The History of Rensselaer Polytechnic Institute, by Palmer C. Rickettts 1914. RPI website. The Institute was founded in 1824 by Stephen Van Rensselaer.
[2] Ario Pardee Jr. to his father Ario, March 11, 1856.
[3] Samuel Miller, West Jersey Collegiate School, to Ario Pardee, December 17, 1855.
[4] C. Pardee Foulke and William F. Foulke. *Calvin Pardee.* Drake Press, Philadelphia, 1979, p. 79.

Niagara Falls and Chicago. Ario disliked Chicago, but predicted that it would become a great city:

> *Nothing would tempt me to live in Chicago. It must stink in hot weather for stagnant water stands in all the ditches and the houses can have no cellars for the water of the Lake is not more than two or three feet below the top of the ground. Still, Chicago is destined to be a large city, having the only tolerable port on the south end of Lake Michigan and some nine or ten Rail Roads radiating out from it.*[1]

This, almost 40 years before Chicago was cleaned up for the World's Fair!

In December of 1855, Anna Maria had another baby boy whom she named Barton, after her mother's family. 1856 turned out to be a year of respite for Anna Maria, with no new baby, but Ario contracted typhoid fever that year and contemplated his mortality: *"It brings solemn thoughts when we feel how suddenly we may be brought to the border of that shadowy land from which no man returneth."*[2] As soon as he recovered he continued with his heavy travel schedule, particularly to Philadelphia where his business partner, J. Gillingham Fell, was still in charge of marketing. On one particular trip, he and Mr. Fell took some time out and went to the Academy of Fine Arts in Philadelphia to see an exhibit of English watercolor paintings. The two men appeared to enjoy leisure time together — the following year they took a fishing trip to Lewis Island near Portland, Maine.

Even as Anna Maria became more and more occupied with her growing family, Ario became increasingly frustrated that she declined to join him on his travels. From Philadelphia he wrote: *"I hope you will be able to accompany me oftener in my journeys...I have no faculty for getting acquainted with the world, and am alone in the crowd. Everybody and his wife, except me and my wife, has been sleighing*

---

[1] Ario Pardee to his sons Ario Jr. and Calvin, June 8, 1855.
[2] Ario Pardee to his son Ario Jr., December 16, 1856.

today."¹ But in 1858 Anna Maria had just given birth to Frank, her fifth child in nine years. Alice (sixteen) and Ellen (fourteen) who were at boarding school in Ypsilanti wrote to Anna Maria, commenting on the name of the new baby. *"After 'Ariovistus,' 'Calvin,' and 'Israel' it seems as if he ought to have a fancy name!"* wrote Alice. When a smallpox scare that summer threatened the Hazleton community, Ario arranged to have a *"genuine"* smallpox vaccine scab sent from Philadelphia. He wrote to Anna Maria from Detroit, instructing her to have everyone in the house vaccinated.

In the same letter a little bit of family gossip lightened the mood. Ario reported that his nephew Sammy Post *"must have kicked a little over the traces before marriage, as they have a young son about 3 weeks old...by all accounts the sudden advent of the young stranger made quite a commotion."* But his generous nature mitigated the news somewhat, for he continued *"...the least fuss there is made about such accidents the better generally for all parties."²*

Anna Maria had a Daguerreotype photograph taken of herself with her two youngest children, Barton and Frank, for Ario to take with him on his lonely travels. *"It looks very life-like, I am yet foolish enough to like to look at your counterfeit resemblance when I cannot see the reality."³* Young Izzie, meanwhile, was gaining strength, if not stature, and he was described as *"acting like a little tiger."* He spent most of 1858 in Bloomsburg, Pennsylvania, with Anna Maria's mother. He thrived there with attention, strict discipline, good country food, and the company of many Robison cousins. Betsey Robison taught him to read and encouraged him to eat: *"He is getting to look quite healthy."⁴*

In 1857 Calvin joined his brother at Rensselaer Polytechnic Institute, and they boarded together for a year. After Ario Jr. graduated in 1858 as a Civil Engineer, he immediately took charge of

---

1 Ario Pardee to his wife Anna Maria, February 20, 1858.
2 Ario Pardee to his wife Anna Maria, July 9, 1858.
3 Ario Pardee to his wife Anna Maria, October 1858.
4 Betsey Robison to her daughter Anna Maria, October 1858.

the mines of his father's company, "A. Pardee and Company." One year later, on his twenty-first birthday, he married Mary F. Allison. Calvin, meanwhile, continued his carefree life at Rensselaer.

Bessie Pardee, 1862[1]

In January 1860, Anna Maria gave birth to the prettiest and gentlest of her children, and named her Bessie.[2] Bessie was the seventh of Anna's ten children,[3] born on her grandmother Robison's birthday, a good omen. Again Alice voiced her opinion on names, suggesting Lucy or Sarah, but eventually agreed that Bessie would be a good name.

In July, Ario traveled to Ypsilanti from Hazleton to collect Alice and Ellen from school and bring them home. Seven-year-old Izzie went with him, and they had good father-son times, traveling on the trains and stopping off to visit relatives along the way. Ario wrote *"Izzie*

---

[1] Photograph of Bessie taken from *Dear Pa*, p. 181.
[2] Bessie would later marry Augustus Van Wickle, and after his death William McKee, and would become the owner of Blithewold.
[3] Bessie was Ario's twelfth child.

stands it very well and eats all before him. So far he has enjoyed his trip very much and I keep him well by not giving him too much trash."[1]

While Ario was away, Anna Maria took over the planning for their grand new family home to be built on a large lot in the center of Hazleton, a whole square block bounded by Broad, Church, Green, and Laurel Streets. The house was a massive three-story stone mansion, with a porch on three sides, a tennis court, stables, greenhouses, spacious lawns, shaded porticos, and magnificent trees.

Pardee Mansion, Hazleton

Meanwhile, Calvin's career at Rensselaer was overshadowed by unruly behavior and inattention to academics, with tensions being brought to a head in early 1860. In Ario's letters, he expressed great disapproval of Calvin's extravagant ways and bad habits, as well as

---

[1] Ario Pardee to Anna Maria Pardee, July 11, 1860.

his mishandling of money. Several times he threatened to cut off Calvin's allowance. He admonished, *"Unless you make a radical change now you may rest satisfied that your life will be a failure, a miserable failure."*[1] Thankfully, and perhaps surprisingly, Calvin graduated from Rensselaer in 1860 with a degree in Civil Engineering. *"If he did graduate he must have applied himself more closely than usual,"* said his father. (One of Calvin's classmates was Alexander Cassatt,[2] who became president of the Pennsylvania Railroad and later built the tunnels under the Hudson River from New Jersey to New York so that his trains from Pennsylvania could run directly into Penn Station in Manhattan.) After graduation Calvin took a job at one of Ario's companies, the Glendon Iron Company in Easton, Pennsylvania.

In the fall of 1860, Alice and Ellen began school at Miss Green's (later The Graham School) at 1 Fifth Avenue in New York City, the school all the Pardee daughters, including Bessie, attended in their turn. The young sisters were very excited about the election campaign of Abraham Lincoln: *"A great many people here* [in New York] *are anticipating a very sorry time on account of Lincoln's election."*[3]

THE WAR YEARS

Early in 1861, it began to look as though war between the northern and southern states was inevitable. In February 1861 Ario was in Philadelphia on business and saw Abraham Lincoln, who had been elected President the year before. *"He is a much better looking man than* [the people] *supposed he was. He does not look as old, and*

---

[1] Letter from Ario Pardee to his son, Calvin, February 29, 1860. From Calvin Pardee Papers, Skillman Library, Lafayette College.
[2] C. Pardee Foulke and William F. Foulke. *Calvin Pardee.* Drake Press, Philadelphia, 1979, p. 47.
[3] Alice Pardee to her parents Ario and Anna Maria Pardee, November 28, 1860.

has not as coarse features as from his portraits you would suppose."[1]
Ario's sister Sarah wrote from Ypsilanti,

> *I rejoice in the belief that we now have a President who is*
> *both a patriot and statesman, worthy of all confidence,*
> *raised up for just this great emergency...God give our*
> *President the wisdom he seems to feel he needs, that he may*
> *rightly meet the great responsibilities resting upon him.*[2]

On April 12, 1861, in South Carolina, Confederate soldiers fired
on Fort Sumter, a Union garrison, marking the beginning of four long
years of hostilities. On April 15, President Lincoln called for 75,000
volunteers to serve for three months. Calvin immediately enlisted and
was one of 200 men sent to Harrisburg, Pennsylvania. Ario Sr. was so
emotionally invested in the justification for war that he raised a
company of men from Hazleton, most of whom were employees of A.
Pardee and Company. He fully equipped them at his own expense, not
only with flags, uniforms, and rifles, but with the cooking utensils and
food supplies that they would need. The flags and uniforms were made
by the women of Hazleton, and when these wore out the mothers,
wives, and sisters made more. At the age of 21, Ario Jr. was appointed
Captain of the "Pardee Rifles," the Hazleton company. The soldiers
could send money home to their families in Hazleton — *"all they had*
to do was to inform Captain Pardee, and relatives could draw on the
elder Pardee for the cash."[3] Calvin was anxious to join his brother once
his three months' service was completed. He wrote to his father,
"Please let me know as soon as Ario joins. I hear that you are raising a
regiment and it pleases me very much indeed."[4]

At school in New York, Alice and Ellen were swept up in the
excitement of war preparations, but at the same time terrified that
harm would come to their brothers. Alice was particularly afraid for
Calvin who was only nineteen years old: *"He is so young, still he has*

---

[1] Ario Pardee to his wife Anna Maria, February 21, 1861.
[2] Sarah Pardee to her brother Ario Pardee, April 3, 1861.
[3] "Pardee Reunion," Calvin Pardee. Blithewold Archives.
[4] Calvin Pardee to his father Ario, April 24, 1861.

Legacy of an American Family

been wishing for a more stirring life, and God grant he may return safely."[1] She reported that in New York everyone was wildly energized. All the buildings were decorated with flags, and she watched out her window as the 7th Regiment passed down Broadway — *"sons of the best families in the city...have been brought up in the greatest affluence. I wonder if they can bear the hardships."*[2] Alice was only seventeen years old herself but appears to have been wise beyond her years, with premonitions of things to come. *"Of course, we cannot realize yet the horror of a civil war...Oh! It is so terrible."*[3] She wrote frequently from New York, begging her parents for more war news, anxiously concerned for her brothers' safety, but at the same time very proud of them. She read the New York newspapers and then conveyed the news to Hazleton. In Bloomsburg, two of Anna Maria's younger brothers, Boyd and Isaiah Robison, enlisted, and two of her sisters, Jane and Belle Robison, went to Washington to work as nurses in the hospitals.

Baltimore welcomed the Union troops — Calvin wrote to Ario *"We have received nothing but the kindest treatment from the people of Maryland...The majority of the people are strong for the Union, and the Union cause is growing stronger daily. We were not molested in any way on our march through the city today; on the contrary we were cheered repeatedly."*[4] But Calvin was apprehensive about the crippling heat. He worried that as the summer progressed and they moved further south, the warm season would *"kill us off rapidly."*[5] His unit was *"anxious to meet the enemy"*[6] at Harpers Ferry before their term of enlistment expired. Calvin appeared to have at last found his passion, and he quickly showed signs of being a fearless, committed, and disciplined soldier. More importantly, he finally had his father's approval. He began to write home every few days, reporting on the war's progress. Ario posted the dispatches in his Company Store so

---

[1] Alice Pardee to her parents Ario and Anna Maria, April 19, 1861.
[2] Ibid.
[3] Ibid.
[4] Calvin Pardee to his father Ario, June 2, 1861.
[5] Ibid.
[6] Ibid.

that the people of Hazleton could keep up with the news and assure themselves of the whereabouts and circumstances of their fathers, sons, brothers, and husbands, despite the fact that the news was often alarming. The heat continued to be oppressive, and there was a smallpox epidemic, but Calvin was headed for Harpers Ferry, determined to *"crush this rebellion once and forever."*[1]

Calvin Pardee, ca. 1860

Anna Maria and her mother, Betsey Robison, exchanged news about their gardens. It must have helped to take their minds off the fate of their sons and daughters and given them comfort. Anna wrote: *"I took several turns in the garden, thinking all the time of war."*[2] Gertrude Keller Johnston wrote of her grandmother, Anna Maria: *"She had the anxiety for her boys fighting for their country, and getting her hands in the good earth was a true tonic."*[3] Betsey grew roses, Canterbury bells, whitlavia, and verbena, and exchanged cuttings with her friends and neighbors.

---

[1] Calvin Pardee to his father Ario, June 16, 1861.
[2] Anna Maria Pardee to her children, June 30, 1861.
[3] Gertrude Keller Johnston, in her book *Dear Pa*, p. 145.

Letters from the warfront from Ario Jr. and Calvin became more distressing as they described the appalling conditions. Ario outfitted a second Company, named Company A, 28th Regiment, and when Calvin was mustered out of the service at the end of his 3-month enlistment he reenlisted in this second company, along with Isaiah Robison. His father Ario frequently traveled to Washington and further south to visit his sons and Anna Maria's brothers and sisters, and to show support for his regiment, taking supplies and letters from home for the soldiers of Hazleton. At home, however, he tried to maintain a semblance of normalcy for his wife and children. Frank Pardee remembered being walked around the house standing on his father's feet, totally oblivious to the tension his father was feeling.

Ario Pardee and Little Frank

Ario Pardee and his young son Frank[1]

Frank wrote later, *"When the Civil War was raging, and his country was endangered at home, he walked up and down the hall*

---

[1] Sketch by David O. Holmes, from *Dear Pa — And So It Goes*, by Gertrude K. Johnston, p. 148.

with me standing on one foot, clasping his knee. Little did the three-year-old boy know his troubled thoughts."[1]

In October 1861, Alice and Ellen went to hear Abolitionist Henry Ward Beecher, the minister of Plymouth Church in New York, speak on the wrongs of slavery. (Beecher and his church were part of the Underground Railroad.) At Miss Green's school the young ladies knit stockings for the soldiers and called themselves the "Blue Stocking Society." Anna Maria's mother and sisters were also knitting *"for the boys,"* as well as raising money to purchase blankets for them.

Anna's sisters Jane and Belle were both working at one of the soldiers' hospitals in Washington,[2] where Jane was appointed Directress of Nurses. Winter came, and everyone seemed surprised that the war was lasting so long. In November 1861, Ario Jr. was made a Major;[3] and Calvin and Isaiah Robison developed typhoid fever.

April 1862 brought the spring and some pleasant distraction for Ario and Anna Maria as they coordinated the finishing touches on their new house in Hazleton. Plans for the grounds, for the "arrangement for trees," the grapery, and the greenhouse, were submitted by Henry Dreer of Dreer's Seed House and Nurseries of Philadelphia.[4]

In May, Ario Jr. and Calvin were on leave in Philadelphia; Calvin was still suffering from typhoid fever, however, and their return to duty was delayed. Ario went to Washington again and visited Anna Maria's sisters Jane and Belle. While there, he tried, unsuccessfully, to exert some influence to have Anna Maria's brother, Isaiah Robison, promoted to the safer rank of Sergeant. Boyd Robison, injured at the Battle of Richmond in August, was sent to Washington to be nursed

---

[1] Quote from *Personal Reminiscences of Ario Pardee* by Frank Pardee. Blithewold Archives.
[2] Many of the soldiers' hospitals in Washington were set up in various government buildings (Gertrude Keller Johnston, *Dear Pa*, p. 191).
[3] Wikipedia, biography of Ario Pardee, Jr. *Civil War in the East.*
[4] Dreer's Seed House and Nurseries later named a rose for Bessie, called the "Bessie Pardee."

by his sister Jane. He had been shot through the left hand between two of his knuckles. Calvin returned to his regiment in June, though still unwell; he consequently suffered a second attack of typhoid as his regiment approached Antietam. He was ordered back to the hospital the day before the great battle took place.

The Battle of Antietam

On September 17, 1862, Major Ario Pardee Jr. was in command of his regiment at the Battle of Antietam, the bloodiest single-day battle in American history, with about 23,000 casualties. The battle raged from dawn to dark. *"My horse killed but am unhurt...Will write again soon as I can, giving you all particulars,"* Ario Jr. reported to his father.[1] After the battle, he located all the wounded and missing men from his regiment and sent reports to his father so that the families in Hazleton could be kept informed.[2] And five days later,

> *You can have no idea, Pa, of the battle, and it is folly for me to attempt to describe it. The [Confederate] regiments suffered terribly under our fire. The ground was literally covered with their killed and wounded. We actually walked over and on them. It was a terrible day. A bloody battle, but* <u>*won*</u>*. The Hazleton Corps stood up to their words.*[3]

Ario Pardee hurried to Sharpsburg, Maryland, where he found Calvin, Isaiah Robison, and Ario Jr. suffering from battle injuries; Ario Jr. had been hospitalized with a serious back injury. Ario wrote home to Anna Maria *"I tried to get leave of absence for them, but could not."*[4] Ario Jr. gave his father his regiment's silk flag, which had been made by the women of Hazleton. He afterward realized that he had made a grave mistake, and he wrote to his father asking him to return the flag as soon as possible, before anyone noticed that it was missing. He

---

[1] Ario Pardee Jr. to his father Ario, September 18, 1862.
[2] Ibid.
[3] Ario Pardee Jr. to his father Ario, September 23, 1862.
[4] Ario Pardee to Anna Maria Pardee, September 30, 1862.

wrote, *"Please hurry up the flag. Nothing has been said concerning it, and I trust will not until I can produce it. I was most confounded foolish."[1]* The flag was returned in good order, but with one star missing, and Ario Jr. wondered if it had been removed in Hazleton.

Disillusioned and still suffering great pain, Ario Jr. tendered his resignation from the 28th Regiment on October 7, 1862. There was a long-standing personality clash, as well as serious tactical disagreements, between Ario Jr. and the regiment's leader, General John White Geary. Later in the month, Ario Jr. was placed in command of the 147th Pennsylvania Regiment.

At home in Hazleton, Anna Maria remained true to her "baby schedule," giving birth to her eighth child, a girl she named Edith. Ario's Aunt Sarah wrote *"I am glad the addition to your family is a girl, for it seems that our sons are born only to be slaughtered or maimed. Oh! This unnatural and cruel war! It...leaves its inexorable shadow on every hearth stone throughout the length and breadth of our country."[2]* Meanwhile, Anna Maria was sick with worry. To add to her misery, a false report reached her that Ario Jr. had died from his battle wounds. In fact, he had recovered somewhat from his injuries and had returned to the battlefront. Christmas came but it was impossible for Ario Jr. and Calvin to get home. On Christmas Eve Ario Jr. wrote, *"The prospects for a 'Merry Christmas' are very poor, but for a 'Happy New Year' we all hope."[3]* The people of Hazleton put together a Christmas dinner and sent it south to all their loved ones fighting with Ario Jr. and Calvin.

The New Year of 1863 found Ario Jr. suffering from typhoid fever, and a tremendous snowstorm in February made conditions close to intolerable. He succumbed temporarily to despair.[4] However, an article in the *Philadelphia Inquirer* describes Ario Jr. as *"an officer*

[1] Ario Pardee Jr. to his father Ario, September 30, 1862.
[2] Sarah Sackett to her nephew Ario Pardee, October 10, 1862.
[3] Ario Pardee Jr. to his father Ario, December 24, 1862.
[4] As evidenced in letters from Ario Jr. to his father, January and February 1863.

as brave as he is accomplished and able..."[1] In April, Ario Jr. wrote to his father asking him to take care of his wife Mary in the event that he should be killed in action. He also asked that, should he die in battle, his body be brought home and buried beside his mother, Elizabeth Jacobs, *"...in full uniform, provided I fall honorably."*

Back in Hazleton, threatened strikes by his mine workers added to Ario's concerns. Anna Maria again took solace in her garden: Her mother, Betsey, sent her plants for the gardens in Hazleton: *"I have sent for over 90 roses and 100 verbenas, 1 doz. Fuchsias, ½ doz. Lantanas...13 Dahlias...Lemon Verbena...Did those Chrysanthemums grow that I sent you? Mine look better now."*[2]

At the end of April, Ario Jr. and Isaiah Robison fought at the battle of Chancellorsville, a significant defeat for the Union army. General Robert E. Lee fought a brilliant strategic battle against the Union Army's Major General Joseph Hooker, but the death of General Stonewall Jackson was seen as something of a victory for the defeated Unionists. In May, Ario went again to Washington, hoping to get permission to go to Aquia Creek in Virginia where Ario Jr. and his regiment were camped. He reported the deaths of many Hazleton men at the Battle of Chancellorsville.[3]

The Battle of Gettysburg

In June of 1863, the North was greatly alarmed over the possibility of an invasion by the Confederacy. In spite of his wounded hand, Boyd Robison reenlisted for the emergency.[4] One month later, on Friday, July 3, Ario Jr. fought in the greatest battle of his career at Gettysburg. One part of the great battlefield of Gettysburg is commemorated as Pardee Field in honor of Ario Jr. In a lovely grassy spot at the foot of a little wooded hill lies a great boulder on which two

---

[1] *Philadelphia Inquirer*, February 11, 1863.
[2] Betsey Robison to her daughter Anna Maria Pardee, n.d. Spring 1863.
[3] Ario Jr. to his father, May 8, 1863, *"My loss is 94 killed, wounded and missing."*
[4] *Dear Pa* by Gertrude K. Johnston, p. 253.

bronze tablets tell of the brilliant charge that Ario Pardee Jr. and his men made across that field.[1] The stone marker reads:

> *At 5 A.M the one hundred and forty seventh Pennsylvania Volunteers (Lt. Co. Ario Pardee Jr.) was ordered to charge and carry the stone wall occupied by the enemy. This they did in handsome style, their firing causing heavy loss to the enemy who then abandoned the entire line of the stone wall.*

There were heavy losses on both sides: 6,655 killed, more than 29,000 wounded. A great number of the wounded would die of their injuries because of the lack of medical care, and of the 19,000 missing most would ultimately be declared dead.

Stone monument in "Pardee Field" at Gettysburg

---

[1] From Pardee Reunion address by Calvin Pardee.

Union Troops March South

By October 1863, Ario Jr.'s regiment was in Tennessee, and Isaiah reported that they were heading for Chattanooga. Ario Jr. was suffering with excruciating back pain, which would plague him for the rest of his life. The Union Army was running short of food rations: the men were put on two-thirds rations, and then half rations. They were running out of money and they had not been paid for four months. Ario Jr. asked his father to send him a map of Tennessee *"on muslin if it can be obtained."* In November Ario Jr. and Isaiah fought at the Battle of Lookout Mountain, which Isaiah described as *"another great victory."* But by the end of the year Ario Jr. was suffering from severe depression and intolerable back pain.[1] The conflict continued, however, and he was determined to *"see the war ended."*

In January 1864, Ario Jr. made his way further south, as the battle for Atlanta was foremost in the Unionists' plans. At home in Hazleton his father Ario took time out from his busy schedule to travel to Michigan to visit his parents. He dropped off Israel, then eleven years old, in Bloomsburg with his Robison grandparents, and continued on to Ypsilanti, Michigan. Israel accompanied his Aunt Belle Robison back to Washington, where she took him to a "President's Reception." Izzie (as he was always known by the family) met President Lincoln who reportedly asked him how old he was, and if he was a good boy.[2] Much later he remembered feeling humiliated when Aunt Belle answered on his behalf, *"Sometimes."* He divided his time in Washington between Aunt Belle and Aunt Jane, had his photograph taken, and on one occasion visited the Capitol Building.

---

[1] Ario Jr. to his father, Dec 30, 1863: *"My back ... produces much suffering. I feel so miserably and 'blue' that I have not sufficient energy to attend to my regiment."*
[2] Belle Robison to her sister Anna Maria Pardee, March 27, 1864.

Izzie Pardee, March 26, 1864. Washington, D.C.[1]

On the warfront, Ario Jr. and Isaiah got as far south as Bridgeport, Alabama, when an epidemic of scurvy broke out among the troops. Meanwhile, Belle Robison was sent to Fredericksburg, Virginia in May of 1864, where very heavy casualties were expected at the Battle of Spotsylvania. She was housed there in unspeakable conditions, and her days were occupied with nursing soldiers with the worst war wounds she had ever seen.[2] Spotsylvania saw the Civil War's most brutal battle. It lasted for thirteen days, the cannons fired continuously, and the stream of wounded soldiers was endless. Belle reported that 40,000 were killed and wounded. She had arrived at the camp without luggage (it was lost in transit). She had to sleep in a tent with the surgeons and was wet from the rain and the mud with no opportunity to dry out; food rations were sparse.

I worked so hard today and my feet are so sore I can scarcely stand on them Oh how much I've wished I had

---

[1] Photograph from *Dear Pa* by Gertrude Keller Johnston, p. 283.
[2] Belle Robison to her mother, Betsey Robison, May 1864: *"Dressed some terrible wounds, was afraid to undertake at first...I dressed one this morning that had maggots in it..."*

supplies to have given every soldier I see who asks for something to eat. They would give almost anything for some soft bread or decent crackers. We have been obliged to feed hard tack most of the time and it does go so hard for our severely wounded men. How often I'm reminded that you at home don't know anything of the realities of war.[1]

Knowing that victory in this battle would lead to an easy march on Richmond, the capital of the Confederacy,[2] her spirits were buoyed. In fact, Belle and Jane were offered work on a hospital steamer going to Richmond.

In June, Ario Jr. and Isaiah Robison were in Marietta, Georgia, preparing for the assault on Atlanta. Ario Jr. reported:

Tomorrow morning we march again in pursuit of the enemy — and I do not think we shall be obliged to go far to find them...if Sherman and Grant are successful we shall be able to see the end...I cannot tell you how much a private soldier suffers and sacrifices for his country.[3]

Tension continued to build up through June and into July. Then, on July 20, 1864 came the Battle of Peach Tree Creek, near Atlanta. Ario Jr. and Isaiah and their men fought a brave battle. Bates' *History of Pennsylvania Volunteers*, Volume IV, page 555, says,

The unwavering front presented by this regiment (Colonel Pardee Commanding), with the aid of the artillery posted in its line (two full batteries, twelve pieces), and the tenacity with which it held its ground, repelling with great slaughter the most desperate charges of the foe, undoubtedly saved the corps from disaster.

---

[1] Belle Robison to her sister Anna Maria Pardee, May 21, 1864.
[2] Belle Robison to her mother Betsey Robison, May 11, 1864: *"The news has been cheering since the commencement of this campaign. I do hope it will continue so and that the next official news will be we are in possession of Richmond."* From *Dear Pa* by Gertrude Keller Johnston, p. 292.
[3] Ario Pardee Jr. to his father Ario, June 8, 1864.

Isaiah Robison was killed in that battle, and by the end of September it became clear that his brother Boyd was missing. He had not appeared on lists of killed and wounded. What the family did not know, however, was that he had been captured and was in the infamous Libby Prison in Richmond. Betsey Robison desperately wanted to have Isaiah's body returned for burial in the family plot in Bloomsburg: *"Oh could he have been buried here what a consolation it would be to decorate his grave with flowers, he who fell in defense of his country, had endured so many perils, suffered so much, and now to be thrown in the ground uncared for."*[1] At the same time she prayed constantly for Boyd's safety and longed to have news of him.

> *Oh if he is alive and can outlive the cruelty of such Barbarians it will be a mercy. I can't give up the thought but we must see him again...if prayers will avail he has them in his behalf and may God in his mercy grant them. But I can't trust myself to think of my two dear boys — but one is at rest.* [2]

Her daughter Jane wrote letters of encouragement, *"It is time enough to take the worst when it comes..."*[3] But by Christmas 1864 there was still no news of Boyd.

On the home front Anna Maria had given birth to her ninth child in 1864 and named him Robert Johnson Pardee. In January of 1865, Ario Jr. was made a Brigadier General "for special gallantry and noble conduct at the battle of Peach Tree Creek." Two days later he successfully led his regiment into the Battle of Atlanta. Only Richmond remained in enemy hands. In March, Boyd was released from prison as part of a prisoner exchange program and made his way home to Bloomsburg. He was in poor health but determined to find work, either in the law (he had qualified as a lawyer in Mercer County, Pennsylvania) or in teaching.

---

[1] Betsey Robison to her daughter, Anna Maria Pardee, August 5, 1864.
[2] Betsey Robison to her daughter, Anna Maria Pardee, November 18, 1864.
[3] Jane Robison to her mother, Betsey Robison, December 4, 1864.

Brigadier General Ario Pardee, Jr. ca. 1864

The End of the War

April 1865 was a month that would change American history. On April 1, it became clear to the Confederate government in Richmond that they were totally outnumbered and would not be able to save Richmond from the advance of the Union Army now on its outskirts. General Robert E. Lee gave orders to the Confederate government to leave the city but to burn all papers, supplies, and liquor before their exodus. Fanned by strong winds, the deliberately set fires soon raged out of control, ultimately burning more than 54 blocks in the center of Richmond. As the Confederates fled, the Union Army, under General Godfrey Weitzel, entered the city and began to put out the fires and restore order. In celebration, Abraham Lincoln visited the city and urged his army to treat the citizens of Richmond compassionately. On April 9, General Lee surrendered at Appomattox, bringing the war at last to an end.

On Good Friday, April 15, 1865, just two weeks after the great Union victory at Richmond, Abraham Lincoln was assassinated in Washington. Lincoln, accompanied by his wife Mary, was attending a performance of *Our American Cousin* by Tom Taylor at Ford's Theatre when he was shot by actor and Confederate sympathizer, John Wilkes Booth. A contemporary sketch by Currier & Ives shows Booth entering the President's box and shooting Lincoln at point-blank range. Soon after, Jefferson Davis, President of the Confederate States of America, was captured and charged with treason for his part in the assassination plot. (Although Davis was not tried, he was stripped of eligibility to run for public office.)

THE ASSASSINATION OF PRESIDENT LINCOLN.
AT FORD'S THEATRE WASHINGTON, D.C. APRIL 14TH 1865.

"The Assassination of President Lincoln" by Currier & Ives[1]

At last the long war was over and the companies of soldiers began disbanding. Ario's Aunt Sarah Sackett wrote to Anna Maria, *"Ario will return in safety, after a four years war — it seems wonderful to me that one has escaped with life and limb."*[2] In her book *Dear Pa —*

---

[1] Image from Wikipedia.
[2] Sarah Sackett to Anna Maria Pardee. May 29, 1865.

And So It Goes, Gertrude Keller Johnston (Ario Pardee's granddaughter) asks,

> *What was it that gave courage and endurance both to those who tried new ways (the six who went to war, soldiers and nurses) and those who stayed at home? Loyalty, three-pronged; loyalty to their family, their country, and their God. The family was the most important unit in their society. The larger the family the greater the contribution to their country.*[1]

Ario Jr. returned from the war a broken man. He never recovered from his wartime back injuries, suffering chronic pain for the rest of his life. In 1868 he and his wife Mary took an extended, two-year trip to Europe, spending months at a time in England and in the south of France, hoping to restore Ario Jr.'s health and his optimism. According to family accounts, however, he became short-tempered and antisocial,[2] perhaps as a result of the constant pain. He died in 1901 at the age of 62. The memorial issued at his death by the Pennsylvania Commandery of the Military Order of the Loyal Legion testifies to his:

> *...consummate skill and unquestioned bravery...General Pardee was an American soldier and a patriot, one who loved his country with an intense love, and appreciated the fact that his country's destiny depended upon the success of the Union army, and that the great issue was personal freedom and human liberty.*[3]

FAMILY LIFE RESUMES

As peace descended once more on a united America, Ario Pardee Sr.'s business interests continued to grow and provide his

---

[1] *Dear Pa* by Gertrude Keller Johnston, p. 327.
[2] *Dear Pa* by Gertrude Keller Johnston, p. 328.
[3] C. Pardee Foulke and William F. Foulke. *Calvin Pardee.* Drake Press, Philadelphia, 1979.

large family with the best that money could buy. Anthracite was in greater demand than ever after the Civil War. New collieries were opened, and Ario built more railways to service them. Their good fortune did not protect them from one more tragedy, however — the baby Robert Johnson died within a year.

The last of Anna Maria and Ario's ten children was born in 1866. She was Gertrude, the much-loved baby of the family, and it was she who saved many of the Pardee letters. Ario had fathered fifteen children, all of them born in Hazleton. The ten who survived grew to be healthy, productive adults, and they gave Ario thirty-two grandchildren, most of them also born in Hazleton. As his businesses prospered, Ario bought additional holdings in Virginia, New Jersey, New York, and Idaho, as well as in Canada. (Ario Jr. and Calvin inherited their father's business acumen and worked tirelessly in the Pardee companies. When Calvin married Mary Byrne in 1867, they bought a house directly across Broad Street from the Pardee Mansion, where they raised their nine children, and later built a large home in Whitemarsh, Pennsylvania. As the years passed, Calvin amassed great wealth and became the patriarch of the family. He loved nothing more than to be surrounded by family and friends.)

ARIO SAVES LAFAYETTE COLLEGE

In 1864, Ario was approached with an urgent request from Dr. William Cattell, Dean of Lafayette College in Easton, Pennsylvania. Lafayette had been founded as a liberal arts college in 1826; named after the Marquis de Lafayette, it was strongly aligned with the Presbyterian Church. But by 1864 the future of the college hung by a thread after a prolonged struggle for financial survival. Dr. Cattell had inherited a severe deficit when he became Dean in 1864, and the Trustees were considering closing the school. Dr. Cattell immediately began a largely unsuccessful last-ditch fund-raising campaign; the future looked bleak. He knew nothing of Ario Pardee beyond the fact that he was a rich businessman from Hazleton, and that he was a member of the Presbyterian Church there. A lay-preacher, Dr. Cattell accepted an invitation to preach at the Pardees' Hazleton Church one Sunday, and he was invited to stay at the Pardee home.

As Dr. Cattell was walking through the gardens the next day with Ario Pardee, he found himself describing the struggles of the college and the urgency to find "generous donors" for its support. Ario listened patiently, and then Dr. Cattell made his move — *"and such a man I take you to be!"* Ario replied *"Yes, I see. I thought you had come to Hazleton to preach; but you came here to ask me for money to carry on a college. I would really like to know how much you expected to get from a plain business man like me."*[1] Dr. Cattell, bracing himself to ask for $500, or $1000 at most, could scarcely believe his own audacity on hearing himself asking for $20,000![2] Ario turned and walked into the house without saying a word, coming back with a promissory note for $20,000 and a check for $600. William Cattell said afterward, *"I stood in a sort of daze wondering if I had rightly understood, or whether indeed it was not all a delicious dream, but I had in my hand his note ... and his check. He bid me good morning."*[3] This was the beginning of a very close friendship.

Ario's initial gift saved the college, and he later gave a further half-million dollars[4] (almost $8 million in today's values) to build, among other things, a scientific building (Pardee Hall) patterned on Rensselaer Polytechnic Institute and the Sheffield Scientific School at Yale. He became very involved in college affairs, meeting regularly with Dr. Cattell throughout Dr. Cattell's twenty years as Dean to discuss principles of administration, internal policy, and executive details. Ario was later asked to become Chairman of the Board of Trustees. His generosity had brought scientific education within the reach of the

---

[1] David B. Skillman. *The Biography of a College.* The Scribner Press 1932, p. 266.
[2] Almost $300,000 in today's money.
[3] William C. Cattell, Memorial Address delivered at Lafayette College on Founders Day, October 23, 1892. Blithewold Archives.
[4] Pardee Genealogy, edited by Donald Lines Jacobus, New Haven Colony Historical Society, 1927, p. 372.

masses. When Pardee Hall was rededicated in 1880, Dr. Cattell said in his address that: *"Such wealth ought never to rouse the faintest sigh of envy. Every poor man in Pennsylvania has reason to be glad, and give thanks today, that Ario Pardee is rich."[1]*

Pardee Hall, Lafayette College, Easton, Pennsylvania

Ario had developed such faith in Dr. Cattell that he asked him to supervise the education of his minor children. In 1869 Dr. Cattell accompanied seventeen-year-old Israel and fifteen-year-old Anne on a one-year educational tour of Europe. They traveled as one large family — Dr. Cattell, his wife Elizabeth, their two children, James and Henry, and the two Pardees. Dr. Cattell was studying teaching methods in the polytechnic schools in Europe. They met up several times, in different capitals, with Ario Jr. and his wife, Mary, who were traveling with Ario Jr.'s twenty-three-year-old sister, Ellen. In July 1869, while the Cattell party was in England, they received an urgent message from Ario Jr. from Paris. Ellen had contracted typhoid fever and was desperately ill. Dr. Cattell immediately escorted Israel and Anne to Paris, but Ellen died on July 15, shortly after they arrived. She was buried in Paris, and Ario Jr. and Mary returned to America, heartbroken. The Cattell

---

[1] William C. Cattell, Memorial Address delivered at Lafayette College on Founders Day, October 23, 1892. Blithewold Archives.

party continued their tour, visiting Sweden, Norway, Finland, Russia, Poland, Prussia, Denmark, Saxony and Switzerland.[1]

In December of 1869, from Berlin, Anne wrote to Bessie describing the excitement leading up to Christmas in the German capital, ending her letter: *"Tell Pa when he reads 'The Night before Christmas'[2] on Christmas Eve, he must think of us, and so must you all. I have never spent Christmas away from home before ..."*[3] In the same envelope she sent a letter to her father on a rather more serious subject. She suffered from near-sightedness, and was having severe pain in her eyes. Dr. Cattell took her to eminent oculists in Paris and in Copenhagen. Both doctors had recommended surgery, and she was anxious to hear her father's opinion. Unfortunately, we do not know whether Anne had the surgery, but she suffered from poor eyesight all her life, becoming blind in her old age.[4]

When the group returned to the United States, Israel immediately enrolled in Lafayette College, so impressed was he with Dr. Cattell. He was the first Pardee to attend the college that his father had supported so generously. He graduated in 1874 with a degree in Chemistry, and then stayed for a further year to do postgraduate research. In 1875 he went to work for his father's iron company in Secaucus, New Jersey. Israel Pardee was a benefactor of Lafayette College for the rest of his life, serving on the Board of Trustees and helping to establish the college as a fine, progressive institution.

---

[1] Quote from the Israel Platt Pardee Diaries, 1869–1870. Skillman Library, Lafayette College.
[2] Referring to the Pardee tradition begun in 1852.
[3] Anne Pardee to Bessie Pardee, December, 1869. Blithewold Archives.
[4] Anne's older sister, Alice, also became totally blind. She learned to type and read Braille. Bessie, too, suffered from poor eyesight all her life.

THE GRAHAM SCHOOL

Anne Pardee's education continued after she returned to America. Her parents sent her to Miss Green's School in New York City, the same school that Alice and Ellen had attended. Her cousin, Ida Markle, went with her. Bessie, in turn, attended the school, though by the time she went in 1872 its name had changed to The Graham School. The school was situated at 1 Fifth Avenue, and the Pardee girls often referred to the school simply as "Number One." Bessie's letters home were more about clothing than academics — and her preoccupation with matters of dress lasted her whole life. Her letters were filled with long descriptions of clothing purchased or desired, and requests for money. Anne was charged with taking care of her younger sister: *"Bessie is fitting into school well...a good little girl...with classes arranged so as not to be 'too taxing'."* Bessie studied French, Geography, Arithmetic, and Music, and also took dancing and riding lessons. But it was her interest in fashion that predominated. When she was thirteen Bessie described a dress to her mother *"...a white dress decorated with a tea rose and a long smilax vine, one end of the vine caught up at the throat with the rose...I will wear the white dress no matter what Miss Graham thinks..."*[1]

By the time Bessie was seventeen her preoccupation had turned into a passion. In April 1877 she wrote to her mother,

> *I went to Arnolds...they showed me a perfect beauty which I immediately set my heart on. It is a Paris dress and one they had left over from last summer, marked down from $200 [almost $3000 in today's money] to $75. From the first figure you can imagine what a handsome dress it was. The material is raw silk. The color is something like a black and white stripe but giving the effect of a pretty light shade of grey, trimmed with black silk faced with a lovely shade of light blue. Besides wearing it this summer for best, I could wear it next winter for an evening dress. About the price. I do*

---

[1] Bessie Pardee to Anna Maria Pardee, October 6, 1874. Blithewold Archives.

not think it is very much. Certainly not more than I usually pay. If you think I had best not get it (I do hope you will let me) there are others that are cheaper but they are not to be compared to this other beauty. Please say yes![1]

Bessie got the dress.[2] Other references in Bessie's letters from school show her early love of flowers, as well as her predisposition to severe headaches. She had inherited the family trait of near-sightedness and wore glasses almost her whole life.

It was at The Graham School that Bessie met two young women who would remain among her very closest friends. They were Belle Grier from New York, and Alice Lee from Buffalo. Alice actually became Bessie's sister-in-law when she married Israel Pardee in 1889. Both Alice and Belle were bridesmaids at Bessie's wedding to Augustus Van Wickle in 1882, and both became regular visitors at Blithewold. Bessie's younger sisters, Edith and Gertrude, would follow Bessie to The Graham School in 1879 and 1883. Taking care of them all was Estelle Clements, a young woman with Hazleton connections. Estelle paid particular attention to the Pardee girls, took responsibility for them on holidays and weekends, and took them often to her family apartment in New York City to visit her mother.[3]

---

[1] Bessie Pardee to Anna Maria Pardee, April 7, 1877. Blithewold Archives.
[2] From a study of Bessie Pardee by Mary C. Philbrick.
[3] Estelle Clements enjoyed a very close lifelong friendship with all the Pardees, and also with the Markle family. All the Pardee and Markle children called her "Aunt." When Estelle's father (a New York City doctor) died, his widow and daughter went to live in Hazleton. Estelle's mother may have been from Hazleton; a true familial relationship has yet to be determined, however.

MISSES GRAHAM,

SUCCESSORS TO THE

MISSES GREEN,

SCHOOL FOR YOUNG LADIES

FIFTH AVENUE,

FIRST HOUSE FROM WASHINGTON SQUARE,

NEW-YORK.

The Course of Instruction includes the French, English, and Latin Languages; Geography, Astronomy, Chemistry, and the other Natural Sciences; Arithmetic, Algebra, and Geometry; History, Belles-Lettres, Moral Science, Elocution, and Writing.

TERMS FOR THE COURSE.

Senior Department,		including Fuel and Stationery,	$225	per Annum.
Junior Department,		" " "	150	" "
Primary Do. First Division,		" " "	100	" "
Do. Do. Second Do.		" " "	80	" "
Day Boarders,			200	"
Use of Piano for Day Scholars,			12	" "
Instruction in French only,			125	" "

Terms for the Italian, Spanish, and German Languages, Music, Drawing, and other extra branches, regulated by those of the masters employed.

Terms for the Family, $800 per annum, including the regular course of tuition, board, fuel, and stationery.

Each young lady to be provided with bed-linen, towels, napkins, silver fork and spoons, marked in full.

Use of Piano, $15; Laundress, $50, semi-annually.

School in session from the 26th of September to the 15th of June. Pupils will be received at any intermediate period, the proportion only of the year from the time of engagement to enter being charged.

In case of the removal of a pupil before the expiration of the school year, payment for the full year will be required. No deduction made for absence.

Bills payable in advance, on the 26th of September and the 1st of February.

Brochure for The Graham School, 1872

Chapter II

THE VAN WICKLES

Sometime toward the end of the 1860s, another coal-mining company began to show huge growth and enormous profits in the Hazleton area — Van Wickle, Stout & Company, based in New Jersey. The company, in which Simon Van Wickle and his brother-in-law Augustus Stout were business partners, had large holdings in Hazleton. Simon, who was president of the company, ran it from New Brunswick, New Jersey, and New York City at 1 Broadway.

Simon Van Wickle, ca. 1860[1]

The Van Wickles were from a long line of Dutch immigrants. Simon's ancestor, Evert Van Wickle, came to America from Friesland in Holland in 1664 and bought 800 acres of land on the Raritan River in New Jersey. In 1722, Evert's son Symen built a house on his father's land in Somerset, New Jersey. (Somerset, a small town near New Brunswick, was favored by Dutch immigrants.) The house that

---

[1] Photograph of Simon Van Wickle, a gift of Robert Stout, 2000.

Symen built is still standing, known today as the Symen Van Wickle House. In 1725 Symen married Gerardina Couvenhoven, a member of the De Sille family originally from Arnheim, Holland. It was at this time that the De Sille family crest came to be part of the Van Wickle legacy.[1]

Symen Van Wickle House, Somerset, New Jersey, built in 1722
(Image courtesy of the Meadows Foundation, Somerset, New Jersey)

One hundred years later, in 1821, Simon Van Wickle, Symen's direct descendant, was born not far from Somerset, in New Brunswick, New Jersey. In 1852 he married Anna Randolph Stout, from a prominent New Jersey family. Anna was descended from Nathaniel Fitz Randolph,[2] who in 1753 gave a plot of land and money to Princeton University. (This generous gift was to play a part in the lives of Bessie Van Wickle McKee and Marjorie Van Wickle many years later.)

Princeton University, chartered in 1746, was originally called the College of New Jersey and located in Newark, New Jersey. When the college needed to expand in the early 1750s, four towns vied for

---

[1] For image, see Chapter III

[2] Note that Augustus Van Wickle's middle name was "Stout," and his daughter Marjorie's middle name was "Randolph," both named for the Fitz Randolph Stout side of the family.

the privilege of being its home. In 1753 Nathaniel Fitz Randolph put together a package of funds and 4½ acres of his own land in Princeton. The offer was accepted, and Nassau Hall (now the center of Princeton University) was built on the land. At that time, Nassau Hall was the entire college — classrooms, dormitories, library, chapel, dining room, and kitchen. Nathaniel Fitz Randolph was later buried in the family ground, where Holder Hall now stands.[1]

When Augustus Van Wickle, son of Simon and Anna Van Wickle, and first husband of Bessie Pardee Van Wickle McKee, died in 1898 his estate provided for the total restoration of Nassau Hall, and for the building of the gates known as the Fitz Randolph Gates, designed by Charles McKim of McKim, Mead & White. The Gates were dedicated and officially opened in 1905 by Bessie and Augustus's daughter Marjorie. Princeton president Woodrow Wilson and former United States President Grover Cleveland attended the dedication. (Grover Cleveland's son Francis later married Calvin Pardee's granddaughter, Alice Erdman, in Princeton.)

But before the Gates were even thought of, Simon and Anna Van Wickle were raising their two sons in New Brunswick, New Jersey. Simon and Anna's sons, George and Augustus, were both born in New Brunswick in the family home at 74 Carral Place (now the site of Rutgers University). George, the older son, born in 1854, was the less talented as well as the less ambitious of the two boys. He was a disappointment to his parents, leaving school at 15 and joining the military before working in the family's company store in New Brunswick. His parents fretted over him, dismayed by his lack of interest in education, his questionable choice of friends, and his total

---

[1] In 1909 the president of Princeton, Woodrow Wilson, directed that a memorial tablet be installed under the eastern arch of Holder Hall, expressing Princeton's gratitude to Nathaniel Fitz Randolph. It reads:

Near this spot
Lie the remains of Nathaniel Fitz Randolph
The generous giver of the land upon which
The Original Buildings of this University were erected.

want of religious discipline. Anna Van Wickle wrote to Augustus: *"It tries me to know he reads his bible so little, does not care to study...you must pray for him that God would keep him in the path of duty and make him a useful member of society."*[1] The Van Wickles appeared to put all their hopes in their younger son, Augustus, who was born in 1856.[2]

Augustus Stout Van Wickle, ca. 1893

Augustus's parents sent him to the New Jersey Classical and Scientific Institute (now The Peddie School) in 1871; in 1873 he entered Brown University in Providence, Rhode Island, where he

---

[1] Anna Van Wickle to Augustus Van Wickle, February 22, 1875. Blithewold Archives.

[2] It is interesting to note that, in naming their sons George and Augustus, Anna and Simon Van Wickle broke with the strong Van Wickle family tradition of naming all their children after their Van Wickle ancestors. Both sons were named after Anna's side of the family — George Stout was Anna's father and Augustus Stout was her older brother.

eventually earned a degree in Liberal Arts. Augustus had been accepted into an advanced program at Brown as a sophomore, an academic honor. On January 4, 1875, his proud father wrote to Augustus on his 19th birthday,

> *Happy New Year. How is my 19 year old boy...Only two years now and you will be a man in the eyes of the land, and will then have to account for yourself. And I trust and hope that by education and the grace of God you will be prepared to take a prominent position before the world, and [be] the instrument in the plan of the Lord of doing great good in the world.*[1]

This expensive education prompted Anna Van Wickle to write to Augustus, *"You must keep on learning to keep up with the age. I do hope we shall not be disappointed in you, for we do expect great things of you after all these advantages given you."*[2]

Anna Randolph Stout Van Wickle, ca. 1860[3]

---

[1] Simon Van Wickle to his son Augustus Van Wickle, January 4, 1875. Blithewold Archives.
[2] Anna Van Wickle to Augustus Van Wickle, n.d. circa 1876. Blithewold Archives.
[3] Photograph of Anna Randolph Stout Van Wickle, gift of Robert Stout, 2000.

On graduating from Brown in 1876, twenty-year-old Augustus joined his father's coal-mining company, Van Wickle & Stout. Simon sent his son to the mines in Ebervale, Pennsylvania, near Hazleton, to be trained in every aspect of the business. Augustus's first job there was in the Shipping Department. In November Simon wrote to his son,

> *You now have a chance to show what you can do in respect to the shipping...The money handed to you by Mr. Harris was for your second month's wages...I hope, my son, you will learn to know the worth of money in your youth, and not spend it for unnecessary articles. Now is the time to start right in all things.[1]*

Anna Van Wickle, much gentler with her son, encouraged his spiritual growth all her life. The Van Wickles were committed Baptists and Anna often urged Augustus to pray for his irreverent brother George: "*...that George might see the error of his ways.*" On January 4, 1877, Augustus Van Wickle's twenty-first birthday, Anna sent him a pocket watch and wrote to him,

> *My Dear Son, As this is your twenty first Birth-day I feel like addressing a few lines this lovely morning. I can scarcely realize the fact, and I feel as if I ought to bless and praise the Lord for preserving you in health and strength through all these years. He has enabled you thus far to hold out, amid so many temptations you have passed through, both at school and in college...I hope you will keep the beautiful watch as a memento of our best love, and wish for your future prosperity of soul and body. "May the Lord ever guide you by his Holy Spirit is the prayer of your mother."[2]*

Anna seemed aware of her comfortable position in life; she sympathized with those less fortunate and commented on current

---

[1] Simon Van Wickle to his son Augustus Van Wickle, November, 1876. Blithewold Archives.
[2] Anna Wickle to her son Augustus Van Wickle, January 4, 1877. Blithewold Archives.

events in her letters to Augustus. *"Business is dull music just now. I suppose it will pick up after the election of President is over, I hope so. There are so many men out of employment in our place, never have known such destitution among families."*[1]

Anna had the reputation of being an excellent cook. She spent her summers "putting up" jars and cans of fruits and vegetables from her garden, and sending baskets of tomatoes, peaches, and blueberries to her children. Augustus frequently asked her to send more of her "jellies" to share with his friends.

In Pennsylvania, young Augustus Van Wickle welcomed the challenge of learning his father's business. He was determined to progress quickly and to expand the company. He made an early success of the shipping in Ebervale, and within two years was made Superintendent of the company. Even as his star rose, Augustus took time to play the sports he loved so much, and to meet other young people in the Hazleton area. Anna Van Wickle wrote to Augustus saying that she was very glad to hear that Augustus was *"...making the acquaintance of young ladies."* It was at this time that he met and fell in love with Ario Pardee's daughter Bessie. The coal industry around Hazleton was by then dominated by three families — the Pardees, the Markles, and the Van Wickles. Augustus was thus considered a suitable match for Bessie Pardee, and he now felt in a position to ask Bessie to marry him. She accepted his proposal on her twentieth birthday on January 30, 1880. Augustus's mother, Anna, wrote to her son of her pleasure with his choice of *"...one you love so dearly out of so many young ladies you have met since you were a lad."*[2]

Augustus was anxious to carve out a rewarding career for himself in order to be able to offer Bessie the kind of life to which she had become accustomed as the daughter of Hazleton's richest citizen.

[1] Anna Van Wickle to her son Augustus Van Wickle, February 1, 1877. Blithewold Archives.
[2] Anna Van Wickle to Augustus Van Wickle, January 20, 1880. Blithewold Archives.

He was very enthusiastic about a new mining company that his father Simon had inspected in Ohio. In 1880 Augustus wrote to Simon, *"I have become possessed of the idea that this 'Ohio Scheme' should not be abandoned,"* and *"I am anxious to get into something where I can make my own efforts count for you, and for myself at the same time. While the tide is running in I want to get my boat launched."*[1] He begged his father to buy the Ohio company and give him total authority and a share in ownership. (Around this time Simon sold a property to his brother-in-law Lewis Stout, perhaps to raise money for the proposed project.) Simon did buy the Ohio company and named it The New York & Ohio Coal Company and situated it at 170 Superior Street, Cleveland. Company officers were Augustus, his father, his uncles Augustus and Lee Stout (brothers of Anna Van Wickle), and Augustus Stout's son-in-law Ezekiel Wade.[2] Simon Van Wickle had at first been reluctant to trust his son with sole authority, but Augustus persisted. He wrote:

> *I ask for and want, at present, no increase of salary, but I simply have a pride in having the entire management of my end of the business...I ask for the charge of the Company's business. If this can be arranged, I shall have the greatest interest and pride in the success of the move.*[3]

Simon was persuaded, and Augustus was appointed General Manager. Augustus moved to Cleveland and the company became enormously successful. He was 25 years old, and his spectacular career and meteoric rise in the world had begun.

Meanwhile, Bessie was making plans for her wedding. She wrote to her younger sister, Edith, *"I have been very busy working on the suspenders I am making for Mr. Van. I finished them today, and*

---

[1] Augustus Van Wickle to Simon Van Wickle, December 28, 1880. Blithewold Archives.
[2] Augustus and Jane Stout's daughter, Annie, had married Ezekiel Wade of Cleveland, Ohio.
[3] Augustus Van Wickle to Simon Van Wickle, February 18, 1881. Blithewold Archives.

tomorrow I will take them to be made up — they are light blue satin with daisies scattered over them."[1] Daisies were Bessie's favorite flowers, and as she planned her wedding outfit and trousseau she had daisies embroidered on everything, from petticoats and nightgowns to stockings and handkerchiefs. Bessie's wedding dress, made by Worth of Paris, was of ivory silk with hand-embroidered daisies covering the whole gown.[2] Augustus wore the blue satin suspenders on their wedding day, and they are now preserved in the archives at Blithewold.

Bessie Pardee, ca. 1885

[1] Bessie Pardee to Edith Pardee, December 14, 1881. Blithewold Archives.
[2] Bessie's wedding gown and all the accessories are presently housed with the Colonial Dames of Boston, and are periodically brought to Blithewold for exhibit.

Bessie was romantic and sentimental, writing to Augustus shortly before her wedding,

> *I am so anxious to see you, my darling. Won't you come on the noon train? We can dine out and hunt for daisies. It will be nice to find wild ones for me to carry.*[1] A few days later she wrote: *My own precious Augustus, This will be the last letter I will write to you from my home.*[2]

Bessie Pardee and Augustus Van Wickle were married before 800 wedding guests at the Presbyterian Church in Hazleton on September 20, 1882. Dr. William Cattell, at the family's request, officiated. *The Hazleton Sentinel* of September 21 wrote effusively of the event:

> *The most important society event in years has taken place in our town with the marriage of Miss Bessie, daughter of our wealthy and esteemed citizen, Ario Pardee, Esq. to Augustus Van Wickle...everything had been arranged in a style to correspond with the social standing of the families of the bride and groom. The Presbyterian service was performed by the President of Lafayette College, assisted by the minister of the church...The reception was at the Pardee House and the grounds were illuminated...ferns, flowers, and rare plants, hundreds of Chinese lanterns, gas lights inside...[There were] gifts of silver, gold, and precious stones...as if the stock rooms at Tiffany's had been taken up bodily. The entertainment provided by the liberal father of the bride was perfect in its detail. [Food was provided by] a city caterer [from Philadelphia] with trained servants amidst decorations of ferns and natural flowers.*

---

[1] Bessie Pardee to Augustus Van Wickle, September 12, 1882. Blithewold Archives.
[2] Bessie Pardee to Augustus Van Wickle, September 16, 1882. Blithewold Archives.

Chapter III

AUGUSTUS AND BESSIE VAN WICKLE

After their honeymoon in Niagara, Augustus and Bessie Van Wickle set up housekeeping at 940 Wilson Avenue[1] in Cleveland, Ohio.

Augustus and Bessie's first home, in Cleveland, Ohio, ca. 1883

Bessie embraced her new family and wrote warm letters to her mother-in-law, Anna Van Wickle. Anna, in her correspondence, shared recipes with her new daughter-in-law, including two favorites, Van Wickle Rice Pudding ("The Best There Is") and Whortleberry Pudding, the latter one of Augustus's favorites.[2]

The Van Wickle family had its own family crest that had come into the family when Symen Van Wickle married Gerardina

---

[1] A few months later, the street numbers were changed, and the Van Wickles' house number changed to 1129 Wilson Avenue.
[2] Both recipes are in Bessie's handwritten recipe book in the Blithewold Archives.

Couvenhoven[1] in 1725. The crest, of green velvet embroidered with metallic threads, showed the family motto "Silence and Hope" in Latin. Bessie proudly had her writing paper dye-stamped with the image of her new family crest.

The Van Wickle family crest, dating from ca. 1725

Augustus travelled often on business, and the new couple exchanged many loving letters during this time. Bessie became

---

[1] Gerardina Couvenhoven was a member of the De Sille family, an important family from Arnheim, Holland, descended from Nicosius De Sille. De Sille came to America in 1653 as first councilor to Director General Peter Stuyvesant. (Taken from Genealogical studies in the Blithewold Archives, compiled by Bessie.) The crest hung for many years in Marjorie Van Wickle's bedroom at Blithewold. It has recently been stabilized and conserved, and is displayed periodically in the Billiard Room.

pregnant within a few months, and in April 1883 Augustus wrote to her, *"I feel that we are growing to fit and suit each other, and I do rejoice. My love for you has grown more and more tender."* In her letters, Bessie had suggested that their baby might be called Donald; Augustus replied, *"Donald Van Wickle is very vigorous and quite pretty. Would it be egotistical to say that August Van Wickle looks and sounds swell, also?"*[1] In April 1883, Bessie went to stay in New York with her sister, Alice Pardee Earle, and they went on a shopping expedition together. They bought "bonnets" for themselves, a maternity wardrobe for Bessie, and a layette for the baby. They laughed together, remembering that only one year previously they had gone to New York together to shop for Bessie's wedding trousseau. Bessie was shocked at the cost of outfitting a new baby, and was glad to have Alice's advice and experience: *"My dear,"* wrote Bessie to Augustus,

> *I have only bought the necessaries and you have no idea how expensive babies are. One hundred and fifty dollars will about cover the outfits — there are still other things that are "must haves." I was so glad to have Alice, because she knew so well about everything, and she is so sensible.*[2]

WELCOMING MARJORIE

On September 12, 1883, Bessie gave birth to a baby girl in Cleveland. If Augustus had been hoping for a boy, it was soon forgotten. He was totally smitten with his new daughter, and they would develop an extremely close, loving relationship. Augustus sent telegrams both to his father's office in New York and to his parents' home in New Brunswick. Simon Van Wickle, who had hoped they would have a boy and name him Simon, sent his congratulations for the *"gift of God"* and asked for further details: *"...who does it look like and what is the*

---

[1] Augustus Van Wickle to Bessie Van Wickle, April 19, 1883. Blithewold Archives.
[2] Bessie Pardee Van Wickle to Augustus Van Wickle, April 19, 1883. Blithewold Archives.

color of its hair and eyes, and what is to be its name?"[1] Suggestions for names flowed in from the Pardee family. Anna Maria sent a list of 70 names, including Verbena, Lucinda, Dorcas, Georgiana, Adela, Amarilla, and Flora, but ended by saying *"Nora is lovely, and so is Marjorie."* She suggested that Bessie *"...look up the meaning of a name before adopting it."* Ario Pardee, who was much blunter, told his family *"Never you mind — let them name their own baby!"* They finally named her Marjorie Randolph Van Wickle, in honor of Augustus's mother's Fitz Randolph heritage. Bessie's brother Israel teasingly nicknamed the new baby "Miss RanDickles," a name that stuck throughout her childhood. Anna Maria and Bessie's sister Anne went to Cleveland to help Bessie with the new baby.

Augustus was very comfortable with his wife's family. Shortly after Marjorie's birth, Bessie's younger sister Gertrude began her studies at The Graham School. She had boarded previously at Miss Dana's School in Morristown, New Jersey, but she was very homesick in New York and Augustus wrote to reassure her:

> *I particularly remember my first night at school. I had no roommate and it turned out that you had to furnish your own lamps to light your room. Well, I did not find it out in time, so I had no light, and had to sit in my room in the dark, and oh, how homesick I was. I went to bed about eight o'clock and the next day I became acquainted and soon liked it immensely. I hope you soon will find friends, and if you feel a little lonely you can sit down and write to your brother Augustus.*[2]

Augustus and Bessie traveled to Hazleton with baby Marjorie in December 1883 to spend Christmas with the Pardee family. Augustus returned to Cleveland in January, leaving Bessie and Marjorie in Hazleton for a few days longer. A cold spell in Cleveland

---

[1] Simon Van Wickle to Augustus Van Wickle, September 14, 1882. Blithewold Archives.
[2] Augustus Van Wickle to Gertrude Pardee, December 15, 1883. Blithewold Archives.

delayed Bessie's return. Augustus had written to Bessie, urging her not to travel with the baby in such cold weather, and with so much snow in Cleveland.

> *The view from our Sitting Room is the prettiest winter landscape I have ever seen…I can hardly keep warm these bitter nights and I would like very much to have Marjorie's mother in the near neighborhood. Yes, my darling Betsy,[1] I would love to have you back.[2]*

Marjorie Randolph Van Wickle, 1884

---

[1] Augustus often called Bessie "Betsy."
[2] Augustus Van Wickle to Bessie Van Wickle, January 9, 1884. Blithewold Archives.

The next two years saw a flurry of letter-writing between the Pardee siblings. Bessie wrote regularly to Edith and Gertrude, her two younger sisters who were at The Graham School in New York. She exchanged baby news and child-care advice with her older sisters, Alice and Anne, still in Hazleton, as the next generation began to flourish there. Bessie missed her family desperately and frequently returned to Hazleton for extended stays at her parents' house. These visits were a whirlwind of excitement — the whole family gathered together and organized teas, dinners, parties, and picnics. In the summer months the sisters and the aunts would sit on rocking chairs on the Pardee mansion's wide, shady porch, knitting and talking and drinking tea.

Shady porch of Pardee Mansion, Hazleton, ca. 1890

In Cleveland, Bessie missed her church as well as her family. Shortly after the wedding, Simon Van Wickle, Augustus's father, had advised the young couple to choose one religious denomination: *"Decide promptly with what church you will cast in your lot. It will be better for each of you."*[1] So Bessie left her own strong Presbyterian affiliation and joined the Baptist Church in Cleveland, sponsored by Augustus's uncle and aunt, Augustus and Jane Stout. Bessie wrote proudly to Anna Van Wickle *"I am very happy about it and, as one of the ladies in church told me this morning, I feel that Augustus and I will go more truly hand in hand now."*[2]

As Augustus's travels took him away from home more often, Bessie began to spend more and more time in Hazleton. It was on one such visit to her parents in February 1887 that Bessie first met William McKee.[3] The Presbyterian Church that Ario Pardee had built was looking for a new Pastor, and it had invited Dr. William Stitt to spend a weekend with them and preach the Sunday sermon. Dr. Stitt arrived with his wife and younger stepson, William McKee. They stayed with the Pardees and charmed everyone. The Church was delighted with Dr. Stitt and offered him the position as leader of their congregation. In the meantime, Bessie wrote to Augustus telling him about the new Pastor and his family. She thought that Augustus and the Pastor's son, William McKee, might become friends, which indeed they did. Their shared interests included business, hunting, fishing, riding, golf, and sailing, and both were devout Christians. Bessie wrote to Augustus's mother:

> *I was so glad to be here for this Sunday as it was the new Pastor's first Sunday here. We are all delighted with him and the part of his family who came with him — his wife and youngest son. They were our guests until this morning, and it*

---

[1] Letter from Simon Van Wickle to Augustus Van Wickle November 27, 1882. Blithewold Archives.
[2] Letter from Bessie Van Wickle to Anna Van Wickle, March 28, 1886. Blithewold Archives.
[3] William McKee would marry Bessie in 1901, three years after Augustus's death.

was with great regret that we let them go. I think the Church will be greatly blessed in their Pastor and his wife.[1]

MORRISTOWN, NEW JERSEY

In 1887, Augustus decided to move the family to Morristown, New Jersey. He was spending more and more time at the head office in New York City, although he still had commitments in Cleveland and Hazleton. He chose Morristown as a base because of its location as a hub between the other cities. An added advantage was that it was near his own parents, who still lived in New Brunswick, New Jersey. Augustus and Bessie bought a large house at 150 Madison Avenue, Morristown, about a mile from the center of town. Augustus divided his time between New York, Hazleton, and Cleveland, and began to diversify his business interests, investing in iron and lumber, and in banking. He traveled constantly by train, looking after his companies.

The young couple was introduced to the Stout[2] side of the family in New Jersey. Bessie quickly made friends and began to enjoy life in Morristown. She planted strawberries and peas in her new garden (*"the finest you ever saw"*), and three-year-old Marjorie began to show an early love of nature. Bessie wrote,

> *We have enjoyed our new house very much...Marjorie is profoundly happy and seems entirely well. She does so enjoy the woods and never tires of picking the wild flowers. We drove into the country the other day and found everything in full bloom — how lovely the country is at the season. People tell us that we will find lovely drives in every direction about Morristown.*[3]

---

[1] Bessie Van Wickle to Anna Van Wickle, February 15, 1887. Blithewold Archives.
[2] Augustus's mother's family.
[3] Bessie Van Wickle to Anna Van Wickle, May 17, 1887. Blithewold Archives.

Early on, apparently, there were servant problems, although they were eventually sorted out. It was probably at this time that Katrina Gluck first came to live with the Van Wickles as Bessie's maid. She would stay with Bessie for almost 50 years.

In the summer of 1887 the Van Wickles rented a house on the New Jersey shore, in a small town called Sea Bright. The name of the house was "Blithewold," — a name that was to loom large in their future. Bessie wrote to her sister Gertrude, "*Sea Bright is not an extensive place, you know. We have our boat here, and find amusement, besides diving there has been rowing on the little lake. I think the rowing will be good exercise for me.*"[1] This house was Marjorie's first memory. In her ninetieth year, Marjorie said,

> *The first place I remember was Sea Bright, New Jersey. The place was named "Blithewold." I was three that summer. I do remember distinctly going through the wood and suddenly, through the trees, I saw the sea. I have never forgotten that first sight of it, so bright through the dark shadows of the woods.*[2]

Marjorie's next clear memory was the Blizzard of 1888, which hit Morristown with unusual ferocity.

> *One of the things I really remember well in Morristown was the Great Blizzard of 1888. I woke up in the morning to find eight to ten feet of snow. Well, it seemed like that to me then! My father, who went every day to his office in New York City, got into the carriage to go to the train station, but the horses couldn't make any progress at all. So he unhitched them, and saddled up, and rode to the station instead. There he caught the last train that ran during the three days of the storm. When Mother realized that we were going to be*

[1] Bessie to her sister, Anne. The letter, written on the "Blithewold, Sea Bright" printed letterhead, is in the Blithewold Archives.
[2] *Reminiscences of Marjorie Van Wickle Lyon in her 90th Year,* recounted to her niece, Marjorie Shaw Jeffries. Blithewold Archives.

isolated in the house for an indefinite time (the nearest store was a mile away and nobody could go anywhere while the storm lasted), she decided to ration the food. She explained to the maids and me what rationing meant. I understood perfectly well what she said. The first day I didn't suffer too much. The second day, though, I just about starved. Finally, I couldn't stand it. I knew where the sugar bowl was kept. I climbed up on a chair and I ate a lump of sugar. Nobody saw me. Nobody caught me. I never told, but I have had a guilt complex ever since.[1]

Later in the year, on May 15, 1888, Augustus's father, Simon Van Wickle, died at the age of 67. The following year Augustus purchased the Coleraine Coal Company near Hazleton, which was to become his most lucrative company. He also became sole owner of the mines that had been operated by the Stout Company of Milnesville. Around the same time, he founded the Hazleton National Bank, with himself as President, Bessie's brother Frank Pardee as Vice President, and Ario Pardee, then 79 years old, as a Director. All these companies required even more travel, but he managed the various businesses with a touch of genius.

Augustus and Bessie both wanted another baby, and were beginning to worry that Marjorie might be their only child. Augustus confided in his mother, *"Give my love to Ida* [his cousin] *and to her baby boy a kiss. I want to see that boy. I wish I had one myself, with all my heart."[2] He* wrote home often as he traveled, complaining of homesickness and missing his little daughter Marjorie: *"Tell Marjorie I miss her 'goodbyes' at the window!"[3]* And, *"I hate to go away from you*

---

[1] *Reminiscences of Marjorie Van Wickle Lyon in her 90th Year,* recounted to her niece, Marjorie Shaw Jeffries. Blithewold Archives.

[2] Augustus Van Wickle to Anna Van Wickle, August 17, 1889. Blithewold Archives.

[3] Augustus Van Wickle to Bessie Van Wickle, November 2, 1889. Blithewold Archives.

and our pretty home and my lovely little girl. I love you both too much to be happy away."[1]

Marjorie, age 5

Traditionally, the young Van Wickle family spent the Christmas holidays in Hazleton with Bessie's family. The Pardees were by then a very large family, most of them living in the Hazleton area. They would gather together at the Old Homestead for Christmas and Ario Pardee would continue his tradition of reading "The Night Before Christmas" on Christmas Eve. Christmas Day was a deluge of gift-giving. The children would start making their "lists" early, but most of their gifts to the adults were home-made — embroidered dusters, carefully worked handkerchiefs, pen-wipers, notebooks, and doilies. The most

---

[1] Augustus Van Wickle to Bessie Van Wickle, June 10, 1890. Blithewold Archives.

exciting party was New Year's Day, when the whole family gathered for the "New Year Bag." Augustus wrote to his mother on January 3, 1890, describing this wildly popular Pardee tradition.

> *In the evening we had the New Year bag for the children and grown up folks, and as usual it was lots of fun and a hilarious time. How Marjorie did enjoy it. The bag is tied up and each one is blindfolded in turn and given a stick and given three chances to hit and break the bag, the bag being suspended from the ceiling. Sometimes it goes twice through the whole family, big and little, before the bag is hurt much, and when it is burst open the children have a wild scramble for the contents on the floor...Most of the blows fall on simply air.[1]*

This tradition was always the highlight of the holiday, with the adults secretly gathering small gifts for the bag over several weeks. The children's anticipation and excitement built to a frenzy over those weeks.

In the summer of 1890, Augustus returned to Brown for the first time since his graduation 14 years previously. He stayed in Newport at the Ocean Hotel with Bessie and Marjorie, visited Narragansett Pier (by boat from Newport), and went to see the tennis championship tournament. They next traveled to Providence to see the old (and new) university buildings, and then took the overnight boat from there back to New York. Augustus began to think that he would like to spend more time in Rhode Island.

A TRIP TO FLORIDA ENDS BADLY

In March 1892, Augustus and Bessie and nine-year-old Marjorie set off on a vacation to Florida with Bessie's parents, Ario and

---

[1]Augustus Van Wickle to his mother Anna Van Wickle: January 3, 1890. Blithewold Archives.

Anna Maria Pardee, and other family members, including Bessie's sisters Gertrude and Anne and Augustus's cousin Annie Wade.[1] William McKee and his mother were also with the party. They took the train[2] to Florida, stopping off at various resorts along the way. They spent several days in St. Augustine at the Ponce de Leon Hotel,[3] which Bessie described as:

> *a perfect dream of beauty...The place seemed like a fairyland...I have never seen a more beautiful place than this hotel and its surroundings. Words are inadequate to express the charm of all its beauties. The grounds are beautiful in their tropical luxuriousness of plants and flowers and fountains.*[4]

She went on to say that while Marjorie was in good health and very happy, she, Bessie, was very anxious about her mother, who seemed especially tired and had *"several little set-backs."* Five days later Augustus wrote to his mother that *"Mrs. Pardee does not seem very well."* Their next stop was the Hotel Indian River in Rock Ledge, Florida,[5] where they hoped Anna Maria could rest and recover. The hotel letterhead shows a beautiful, modern hotel building large enough to accommodate 400 guests, surrounded by palm trees and situated on the banks of the Indian River. A long dock stretches out into the water where a pleasure steamer waits to take visitors down the river. Sailing boats enjoy a stiff breeze, watched by elegant couples strolling along the rocky footpaths. An orange grove is heavy with fruit and underplanted with pineapples. The hotel advertised itself as "The Tropical Health and Pleasure Resort of America, open Jan. 1 to April 10."

---

[1] Augustus and Jane Stout's older daughter, Annie Stout, married Ezekiel Wade of Cleveland, who died of consumption in 1889.

[2] This would have been the Henry Flagler railway.

[3] The hotel was built by Henry Flagler to accommodate the wealthy passengers of his new railway.

[4] Letter from Bessie Van Wickle to Anna Van Wickle, March 14, 1892. Blithewold Archives.

[5] Another of Henry Flagler's luxurious hotels.

Letterhead from the Hotel Indian River, 1892

Everyone enjoyed their stay here at first. Bessie was enchanted with the flora — pineapples, orange groves, mangoes, guavas, air plants, banana blossom, and many lovely wildflowers.[1] Everyone except Mr. and Mrs. Pardee went fishing and together caught seventeen fish, bass and pickerel. Augustus shot a couple of ducks, and William McKee shot a water moccasin snake. They sent a shipment of oranges to Augustus's mother in New Jersey. But their vacation was about to be cut short.

Within a few days of their arrival many members of the party began to feel ill with "the fever," probably typhoid. Bessie, Annie Wade, Gertrude, Ario, and Anna Maria were stricken. Ario was the sickest; his condition deteriorated rapidly and he died suddenly at the hotel. The traumatized family group immediately left for home to plan the funeral. On the day of Ario Pardee's funeral in Hazleton, Anna Maria's condition worsened and Marjorie became ill. Anna Maria died a few weeks later. Marjorie and Bessie slowly recovered, as did Annie Wade and Gertrude Pardee. Augustus wrote to his mother that he thought

---

[1] Bessie to Anna Van Wickle, March 25, 1892. Blithewold Archives.

they had all eaten too many oranges during their stay, and ended his letter, *"No more Florida for me."*[1]

BACK TO HAZLETON, PENNSYLVANIA

In April 1892, Augustus made the difficult decision to return to Hazleton to live. Bessie was sinking into depression over losing her father and her mother so suddenly and wanted to be near her family. It meant that Augustus would be further from his own mother, though. He wrote to Anna Van Wickle, justifying his decision to move from Morristown back to Hazleton:

> *Owing to the changes occasioned by the recent "coal deal" etc. I find it is going to be absolutely necessary for me to be at Hazleton so much that I have concluded to live here, and to travel from here to New York every week or two to attend to my business at the New York office. We will continue the office business in N.Y. the same as usual, but my interests here now are so important that if I lived at Morristown I should have to be away from home about half the time, or more, and that would not do.*

He sweetened the news to his mother by assuring her that he would still see her frequently:

> *When I go down to New York I can come out and spend the night with you, and in that way you will see as much and probably more of me than you have before. I will have a long-distance telephone right in my house that I will have here, and can thereby talk direct to New York, New Brunswick, or*

---

[1] Augustus Van Wickle to Anna Van Wickle, March 1892. Blithewold Archives.

anywhere else. Morristown was getting very inconvenient for me. My business is very good.[1]

In 1892 the young Van Wickle family moved into a handsome house in Hazleton at 175 North Church Street. Augustus described the new house to his mother:

The Van Wickles' house at 175 North Church Street, Hazleton, ca. 1892

They are getting along today with the Library mantel and hearth. I wish you could come and see our house. It is really quite pretty and comfortable and you would enjoy it. We have all new carpets and rugs downstairs and some upstairs, and our parlor furniture is all new and some of our dining room. The library is a great big lovely room full of

---

[1] Augustus Van Wickle to his mother Anna Van Wickle, April 15, 1892. Blithewold Archives.

comfort and a home-like air. We have a window in there in which the glass above measures nearly six feet long and about five feet high. We have plenty of guest rooms and we will be pleased indeed to see you here. We have electric lights, steam heat, long-distance telephone, and every convenience.[1]

Marjorie reading in the library at 175 North Church Street, Hazleton, by the window "six feet long and five feet high."[2] Ca. 1892

---

[1] Augustus Van Wickle to Anna Van Wickle, September 12, 1892. Blithewold Archives.

[2] Note the Library table in the right-hand side of the photograph; it is currently in the entrance hall at Blithewold. The bronze sculpture is now on the mantle in Marjorie's Bedroom, and the Tiffany lamp is in Collections Storage at Blithewold. The Delft plaque above Marjorie's head is in the Dining Room at Blithewold.

Augustus built and maintained a small park in Hazleton; he also built a sporting facility near his home for entertaining his friends that he named The Casino[1]. Augustus was an excellent sportsman with a wiry, athletic build, and he used the casino in the winter to play tennis, to bowl, and to *"enjoy athletic apparatus."*[2] There was also a reading room with current newspapers and periodicals. Three evenings a week he opened up the casino for the use of the young men of Hazleton who were living in boardinghouses and hotels and had few recreational opportunities.

The Casino, Hazleton, ca. 1895

Augustus began to take hunting, hiking, and fishing trips with his brothers-in-law, Frank Pardee, Israel Pardee, and Sandidge Allison, and his friend William McKee who would visit from his home in Rome, Georgia. The men visited Loon Lake and Saranac Lake in New York State and camps in Chattanooga, Tennessee, and the

---

[1] The name describes a location for relaxation and sporting activities and does not imply gambling.

[2] Quote from the obituary of Augustus Van Wickle in the *Hazleton Sentinel*, June 11, 1898. Blithewold Archives.

Georgia mountains. The trips were productive as well as relaxing, and the men were able to send home catches of birds and fish.

WORLD'S COLUMBIAN EXPOSITION, 1893

The year after their move back to Hazleton in 1892, Augustus helped plan a trip to the World's Columbian Exposition in Chicago. There were twelve in the party, including some of Bessie's brothers and sisters, Reverend and Mrs. Stitt, and William McKee. They took the Lehigh Valley Rail Road, arriving in Chicago on June 2, 1893. The party stayed at the Vendôme Club on Oglesby Avenue, close to the Exposition site.

The Fair was a masterpiece of American ingenuity. Business leaders, including George Pullman, J. P. Morgan, and Stuyvesant Fish, had raised $10 million to bring the Fair to Chicago. Architect Daniel H. Burnham and landscape architect Frederick Law Olmsted took an unremarkable 633-acre site and turned it into a dazzling spectacle in less than three years. The 14 main buildings were built in Beaux Arts style and covered with white stucco, and all were accessible by elevated railway lines and boats. Frederick Law Olmsted built a system of lagoons and waterways fed by Lake Michigan, so visitors could move easily from one building to another on motorized launches. President Grover Cleveland officially opened the Exposition by pressing a lever that turned on the electricity.[1] It was the first time that most of the fair's 27 million visitors had seen electric lights and electric machines.

---

[1] Nikola Tesla and George Westinghouse won the contract to light the Fair, after a fierce competitive battle with Thomas Edison.

World's Columbian Exposition, 1893[1]

Manufacturers from around the world built impressive displays, combining goods for sale with exhibits of historical and artistic interest. Americans were introduced to carbonated soda, cotton candy, Juicy Fruit gum, and hamburgers. A young engineer, George Washington Gale Ferris, introduced the Ferris wheel, an engineering marvel that both terrified and exhilarated almost one and a half million intrepid riders between June and October. Each of the huge wheel's 36 cars held 60 people; a ride was one 20-minute revolution that offered spectacular views of the entire exhibition grounds — the whole scene lit by Nikola Tesla's new electric lights.

---

[1] Image of the World's Columbian Exposition from Wikipedia.

George Ferris's Great Wheel, 1893[1]

For two weeks the Van Wickles and Pardees and their friends went from one astonishing exhibit to another. Augustus wrote to his mother,

> *Here we are at the World's Fair and we are enjoying a spectacle such as I never expect to see again. Words fail utterly to express in any degree the beauty and magnificence of this Exposition. The buildings themselves, in the grouping and arrangement, and the grand architectural effects attained, together with the superb landscape and gardening effects make the exposition as seen from the lagoons a wonderful dream of beauty. Two nights ago we went to see the grounds and buildings illuminated by electricity, and this was the most wonderful thing I ever expect to see.*[2]

---

[1] Image of the Ferris Wheel from Wikipedia.
[2] Augustus Van Wickle to Anna Van Wickle, June 8, 1893. Blithewold Archives.

BESSIE GOES TO DANSVILLE SANITARIUM

A few months later, exhausted from her trip and still grieving the loss of her parents, Bessie succumbed to severe headaches and neuralgia and to depression over her inability to conceive another child.[1] Augustus later wrote confidentially to his mother, *"Mrs. Allison is daily expecting a new arrival...she hopes for a little girl. Bessie wishes she was the one, and so do I. However, please say nothing to Bessie about it."*[2]

On November 1, 1893, Augustus reluctantly arranged for Bessie to go to the Dansville Sanitarium in New York State. The facility advertised: *"Health, Rest, Comfort. A magnificent Health Institution established in 1858. Open all the year. On the Delaware, Lackawana & Western Railroad, a night's ride from New York City and two hours from Buffalo. Fire Proof Main Building. All modern improvements; service highest grade. If seeking health or rest...write for illustrated literature."*[3]

Dansville Sanitarium, Dansville, New York.

---

[1] As evidenced in letters from Augustus Van Wickle to his mother. Blithewold Archives.
[2] Augustus Van Wickle to his mother, January 21, 1895. Blithewold Archives.
[3] Advertising copy in Blithewold Archives.

Bessie's sister Anne accompanied her to Dansville and stayed with her there. Ten-year-old Marjorie stayed home in Hazleton with her father, looked after for several months by the Pardees. Augustus wrote to Bessie, *"It was pretty tough on me to see you go away on that train this morning. I felt my spirits go down to zero."* But he tried to reassure her that Marjorie would be fine, *"Marjorie and I had a lovely walk and a long sing tonight, and she went to bed happy and bright...God bless you, and bring you health and strength."*[1]

Two weeks later Bessie wrote to Marjorie that although she weighed only 115 pounds,[2] she was to be weighed again — *"I hope I have gained."*[3] Augustus went to Dansville to visit Bessie and reported to Marjorie that *"Mama is gaining in health and strength."*[4]

Ten-year-old Marjorie missed her mother desperately, but this time of Bessie's absence encouraged a special and long-lasting bond between father and daughter. They began a routine of having tea together every afternoon that they both enjoyed. Augustus wrote frequently to Bessie about their activities:

> *Marjorie sat in your chair and has been quite matronly. She poured out two cups of tea for me tonight as we had our tea together, and there were no grounds so she was very proud.*[5]

Seven weeks later Bessie was still recovering, although she had been released from the Sanitarium and was convalescing in New York at The Waldorf Hotel with Augustus, while he carried on business in his New York office.

Back in Hazleton, Marjorie spent Thanksgiving with her aunts Edith and Gertrude at the Pardee Mansion. She spent most of her free time with Frank Pardee's family — his wife Kate and their five children. Kate Schuyler Pardee, a warm, generous young woman, took

---

[1] Augustus Van Wickle to Bessie Van Wickle, November 1, 1893. Blithewold Archives.
[2] Bessie was around 5'9" tall.
[3] Bessie to Marjorie, November 13, 1893. Blithewold Archives.
[4] Augustus to Marjorie, November 25, 1893. Blithewold Archives.
[5] Augustus Van Wickle to Bessie Van Wickle, November 1, 1893. Blithewold Archives.

77

on the extra responsibility of another child with grace.[1] Marjorie missed her father greatly, though, when he went to Dansville or New York to see Bessie. She wrote in November,

> *Dear Papa, I am so glad that you are having such a nice time — I shall be glad to pour your tea when you come back. I miss our Sunday walk very much. I counted up and found there are only 3 weeks and 4 days till Christmas.*[2]

Augustus and Bessie arrived home just in time for Christmas.

---

[1] As evidenced in letters between Augustus and Bessie Van Wickle. Blithewold Archives.
[2] Marjorie Van Wickle to Augustus Van Wickle, November 1893. Blithewold Archives.

Chapter IV

BRISTOL, RHODE ISLAND

Bessie gradually recovered from what now appears to have been a nervous collapse in 1893. The following year was a significant one for the Van Wickles. Augustus was by then a very wealthy man, and that summer he took Marjorie on an extended trip around New England, looking for the perfect place to build a summer home. He had happy memories of Rhode Island from his years at Brown University and wanted to renew his acquaintances there. While he and Marjorie were staying in Narragansett, they received an invitation from an old family friend from Philadelphia who was summering in Bristol. Dr. Herbert Howe had a summer home on Ferry Hill, and a magnificent 85-foot Herreshoff steam yacht named *Polyanthus*. The Howes sailed down to Narragansett, picked up Augustus and Marjorie, and took them for a sail on Narragansett Bay, ending up in Bristol. Many years later Marjorie remembered that momentous day:

> *We spent the day in the old Howe homestead on Ferry Hill.*
> *There were only three or four houses in the area at that time,*
> *the Lowe bungalow, the Mills house (now the Livingstons),*
> *the Thurbers near the lighthouse, and the Dexter Thurbers.*

Dr. Howe took Augustus to meet John B. Herreshoff, famed boat builder of Bristol, known for building the very successful America's Cup–winning yachts.[1] Marjorie continued:

> *During the day, Mr. John Herreshoff took us in his carriage to*
> *see the new yacht he had just designed and built. My*

---

[1] America's Cup defenders *Vigilant, Defender, Columbia,* and *Reliance* were all designed by John B.'s younger brother, Nathanael G. Herreshoff, who had attended MIT and was known as a mathematical and mechanical genius. The yachts were all built in Bristol at the Herreshoff Manufacturing Company.

recollection was that he drove the carriage himself, although he was blind at the time![1]

John Herreshoff showed Augustus the new 78-foot steam yacht *Eugenia* that he had built for his wife. *"My father fell in love with the yacht and bought it right then and there. He renamed her* Marjorie. *We could not sail away in her, as the embroidered names on the linen had to be changed!"[2]*

Marjorie I *ca. 1896*

That same day, Mr. Howe took Augustus to see a 70-acre estate on Narragansett Bay that had once belonged to John Rogers Gardner. Marjorie remembered:

My father loved the place. But he restrained himself from buying it to at least consult his wife! A week or two later, we went to Narragansett again. This time my mother was with us. Mr. Herreshoff came to meet us in the new yacht to bring us to Bristol for the day. My father brought out some Sauterne to drink to the owner of the yacht. My mother,

---

[1] John B. Herreshoff became blind at the age of 15.
[2] *Reminiscences of Marjorie Van Wickle Lyon in her 90th Year,* recounted to her niece, Marjorie Shaw Jeffries. Blithewold Archives.

naturally, drank to Mrs. Herreshoff, who as far as she knew was the owner. But Mrs. Herreshoff, who was in on the secret, drank to my mother! There was great fun over that. Then my father brought mother to see the Gardners' place. She fell in love with it also, and so the family became the owners of Blithewold.[1]

The Gardner estate was a spectacular property, with seventy acres of fertile land sweeping down to Narragansett Bay. It offered a protected deep-water harbor for boats, with superb sailing on the Bay and easy access to the Atlantic Ocean. In his time, Mr. Gardner,[2] an amateur horticulturist, made many improvements to the property. He planted rare specimens of trees,[3] established rose gardens, laid out the Enclosed Garden, and built greenhouses filled with exotic plants: *"Pineapples, peaches, nectarines, figs, grapes, and strawberries,"* as well as *"the first orchids in that part of the country."*[4] The house itself, however, was not large enough for the Van Wickles, and it was too near to Ferry Road for them (it was close to where the well-head is now). Augustus and Bessie decided to move the old house to the southern part of the property and build a new house further back from Ferry Road. In order not to damage the stately trees, the old house was cut in half and moved *"by donkey engine"* all the way down the slope of the Great Lawn, around the trees, and to the water. It was then floated south, brought back up on land, and re-erected near the road.

---

[1] *Reminiscences of Marjorie Van Wickle Lyon in her 90th Year,* recounted to her niece, Marjorie Shaw Jeffries. Blithewold Archives.
[2] In 1871 John R. Gardner presented, as a gift to Bristol, the St. Michael's church clock. He hoped that the sound of the striking clock would reach a radius of two miles *"so that the rich and the poor may know the hour of the day as well as of the night, and that it would be a great comfort to the sick and the sorrowful who are frequently deprived of the means of knowing the passing moments."* St. Michael's Centennial Brochure. Blithewold Archives.
[3] From "The History of Blithewold, Bristol, Rhode Island," an essay by John DeWolf, ca. 1905. Blithewold Archives.
[4] Ibid.

The Gardner house was a gracious shingled dwelling that dated back to pre-Revolutionary times, with beautiful windows and a large wrap-around porch. It had, in its time, played host to United States presidents and ambassadors, and had been for a short time the summer home of the Sackville-Wests, grandparents of Vita Sackville-West. For the next thirty-seven years it would be used first by the Van Wickles — and then by the McKees — as a guest house.

Planning for the Van Wickles' new, larger house began immediately. The elegant Queen Anne–style shingled mansion designed by Francis Hoppin[1] of Newport was built far back from the road. Augustus also had Francis Hoppin design a large stable complex for his horses and carriages and a barn for cows; a summerhouse in the Enclosed Garden; and a well-head on the front lawn near Ferry Road. Augustus and Bessie named the estate "Blithewold."[2] Augustus made frequent trips to Bristol to check on the progress of construction and took an active role in the development of the property. In December 1895, as he set out for Bristol, he wrote to 12-year-old

---

[1] Francis L. V. Hoppin, 1867–1941. He was educated at Brown University and MIT Architectural School, and then trained in his brother Howard's architectural firm, Hoppin & Ely, in Providence, Rhode Island. Later he apprenticed with the architectural firm of McKim, Mead & White in New York City, where he met Terence Koen. Hoppin and Koen started up their own architectural practice, Hoppin & Koen, in New York City in 1894. Blithewold was one of their first commissions. Their reputation grew rapidly five years later when they were chosen to design The Mount, Edith Wharton's house in Lenox, Massachusetts. Edith Wharton later wrote in *A Backward Glance*, *"The Mount was my first real home...its blessed influence still lives in me."* (D. Appleton-Century Company, Inc., 1934, p. 125.) Hoppin & Koen went on to design many important houses in Newport, New York, and Palm Beach, including Southways, Henry Flagler's magnificent mansion in Palm Beach, Florida.
[2] Blithewold may have been named after a house the Van Wickles had rented for the summer in 1887 in Sea Bright, New Jersey. That house and its proximity to the sea was Marjorie's first memory.

Marjorie *"I am anxious to get the first glimpse of our new country home that we will all love so much."*[1]

JOHN DEWOLF, LANDSCAPE GARDENER

Bessie, who had inherited her mother Anna Maria's talent for horticulture, set about executing her visionary master plan for the property. She engaged Bristol landscape gardener John DeWolf to help her design the gardens, which included plans to create an arboretum, a rose garden, rock garden, water garden, cutting gardens, new greenhouses, a palm house, and a great ten-acre lawn for outdoor activities. Bessie's intention was *"...to create a park with distinctive features, using the house as a centre...to create an estate in which new beauties are constantly revealed, and the perfect accord between architecture and grounds is ever apparent."*[2]

Landscape Gardener, John DeWolf, ca. 1890

---

[1] Letter to Marjorie Van Wickle from her father, Augustus, December 16, 1895. Blithewold Archives.
[2] Quote from a wood-bound album describing Blithewold, with text and photographs, hand-written by Samuel Dean, in Bessie's voice. Ca. 1915. Blithewold Archives.

John DeWolf was intimately connected with the Blithewold property from childhood, his DeWolf ancestors having owned the land that in the 18th century ran from Mount Hope Bay to Bristol Harbor. He wrote[1] that the land was owned and cultivated[2] by the Wampanoag Indians until the death of the Indian leader Metacom at the hands of the Colonials in 1676. In 1680, the land in Bristol was granted to four British settlers[3] by King Charles II, and a house was built on the property on Ferry Road[4] that is now Blithewold. During the Revolutionary War, the British marched through Bristol, setting fire to as many houses as they could, including the house on Ferry Road. The fire was extinguished and the house saved, but the four English settlers were evicted from the land when the infant country gained its independence from Britain. The property was then bought by the DeWolf family, who owned it for more than 60 years. They, in turn, sold it in 1841 to John Rogers Gardner. When Mr. Gardner died in 1888, his widow sold the estate to Samuel P. Colt, and it was bought six years later by Augustus Van Wickle.

From 1898 until 1906 John DeWolf was connected with the New York City Parks Department and with Prospect and Carroll Parks in Brooklyn. He wrote prolifically for respected horticultural publications,[5] and he was involved as a publisher of at least one of these publications. He advertised himself as *"John DeWolf, Landscape Architect and Gardener. Consultations and visits to Country Places at reasonable rates. 5A Lafayette Place, New York."*[6] At the same time, he was working on designing the grounds of Blithewold, first for the Van

---

[1] From "The History of Blithewold, Bristol, Rhode Island," an essay by John DeWolf, ca. 1905. Blithewold Archives.
[2] The Indians are said to have grown corn on the land.
[3] Messrs. Hayman, Sandford, Ellery, and Usher.
[4] This house became known as the Gardner house, although it was not built by John Gardner. It was built sometime between 1680 and 1760, and John Gardner later altered it considerably.
[5] *Garden and Forest,* and *American Garden.* He also published many articles in *The Brooklyn Daily Eagle* and *The Bristol Phoenix.*
[6] *Garden and Forest,* May 1891. From a study of articles by and references to John DeWolf by Karen L. Jessup, Ph.D.

Wickles and then the McKees, from 1895 until his death in 1913. He and Bessie sought to create an informal landscape with gently sloping lawns and wide borders of flowers, shrubs, and trees. John DeWolf laid out the Bosquet (where more than 50,000 daffodils now bloom each spring), a nut grove, a rose garden, and an extensive shrub walk from the Bosquet to the Bay. In 1910 he helped lay out the Sunken Garden,[1] with its formal pathways and parterres. He was responsible, too, for planting the "big tree" at Blithewold. He had grown the Giant Sequoia in a greenhouse at Prospect Park in Brooklyn. In 1903, when the tree outgrew its location there, DeWolf shipped it by train to Bristol and planted it at Blithewold near the greenhouse. In 1911, he moved it to its permanent location in the Enclosed Garden and surrounded it with smaller trees to protect it. It has survived the northern climate and several hurricanes and is now, at almost 100 feet, the largest of its species in New England. (Marjorie Lyon studied propagation techniques to ensure its continued existence, and there are now twelve more Sequoias on the property; and several others were given by Marjorie to the town of Bristol as gifts.)

Much of what is evident horticulturally on the property today is testament to John DeWolf's knowledge and imagination, including the Water Garden, the Moon Gate, the statuary, and the gravel paths that meander through the grounds. Mr. DeWolf followed up on Bessie's request for exotic trees as well as native ones by planting species from Europe, China, and Japan. He included weeping forms of plants when he could, and it was thanks to him that the family planted a border of evergreens on the northern edge of the Great Lawn and deciduous trees and shrubs on the southern border.[2] During the summer of 1913, he was paying particular attention to the Water Garden and the Rock Garden. He was engaged in preparing the gardens of Blithewold for Marjorie's wedding which was to take place the following year. He died a few months later, in November, at his sister's house in Bristol.

---

[1] Now known as the North Garden.
[2] From *Blithewold Mansion, Gardens & Arboretum,* by Julie L. Morris and Margaret Whitehead. 2004.

ESTELLE CLEMENTS

Estelle Clements had been a little-known part of Blithewold's history until a study of her diaries and letters helped clarify her role in the family history.[1] This unassuming, cultured woman played an influential role in the life and well-being of Bessie Van Wickle (later McKee) and her family for more than 50 years. Through her writings — letters, diaries, and journals — she left behind not only an interesting self-portrait, but also valuable information about people and places connected with Blithewold.

Estelle was born in 1849 in New York to James William Clements, M.D., and Caroline Ward Clements. She had two brothers, William and Henry, who both became engineers and worked on the levee system in Greenville, Mississippi. (Estelle would later live with her brothers in Mississippi two months of the year,[2] the only times she was not with Bessie and her family.[3])

Estelle Clements, 1908

---

[1] Study of the life of Estelle Clements by Mary C. Philbrick. Blithewold Archives.

[2] As evidenced in Estelle's letters and diaries between 1904 and 1928. Blithewold Archives.

[3] On her journeys to and from Mississippi Estelle would visit members of the Pardee and Markle families in Hazleton, New York, and Connecticut before arriving in Boston to spend the rest of the year with Bessie.

Estelle was teaching at The Graham School in New York and living with her parents in Manhattan when Bessie arrived at the school as a 12-year-old student in 1872. Twenty years later, the Clements family fell on hard times, probably due to the death of Estelle's father in 1892, and mother and daughter returned to Hazleton. (Caroline Clements may have been from Hazleton, and was perhaps even a distant relative of the Pardees on the Robison side.) Although all the Clements were well educated and well connected (Estelle, like Bessie, was a member of the prestigious Colonial Dames of America), they lived with little financial security.

Estelle was also close friends with several of Bessie's sisters, particularly Anne Pardee Allison, and Bessie's cousins Clora and Ida Markle. (All the Pardee grandchildren called her Aunt Dellie and later supported her in her old age.) Now back in Hazleton, Estelle began teaching elementary education to a small group of Pardee children, including Marjorie Van Wickle. Augustus wrote to Bessie in 1893:

I can hear the children in the school room below my office, and they seem to be spelling. They enjoy this school with Miss Clements as teacher. There are four of them in this school. Dorothy, Gladys, Katharine [Frank and Kate Pardee's daughters] *and Marjorie, and they are a happy quartet.*[1]

Estelle was thus a natural choice to step in to look after Marjorie and Augustus when Bessie became ill.[2] She came to live with them at the house on North Church Street, where she was to take care of the household and also oversee Marjorie's education. (Her mother and brother William also took up residence with the Van Wickles periodically to lend their support and to help out.)

---

[1] Augustus Van Wickle to Bessie Van Wickle, November 1893. Blithewold Archives.
[2] From a study of the life of Estelle Clements by Mary C. Philbrick, Blithewold Archives.

Estelle's Role at Blithewold

Estelle was a trusted companion to Bessie, reading to her every evening, tending to her correspondence, and playing Mah Jongg[1] with her (in the living room and, in good weather, on the North Porch). As the years passed she became a dear friend to Marjorie and, later, a beloved "second mother" to Bessie's second daughter, Augustine, born in 1898. The girls adored Estelle, calling her Aunt Dellie with great affection. A particularly tender relationship developed between the childless Aunt Dellie and the young Augustine. It was Estelle who taught Augustine to garden and to identify birds and leaves, as well as giving the young girl advice on clothing and room decoration. She generally spoiled and praised Bessie's beautiful younger daughter, and it was to Estelle's room that Augustine came late one night to whisper of Mr. McKee's consent to her engagement to Quincy Shaw in June 1918.

Estelle was accepted as a member of the family, traveling with them, dining with them, and entertaining alongside them. Because Bessie's health remained frail, Estelle helped run the household, dealing with the servants, hiring and firing staff and paying their wages, writing invitations, and paying bills. She loved Blithewold, where she was respected by everyone, upstairs and down,[2] and she had many friends in Bristol as well. Eleanor Rae, the daughter of long-time chauffeur Arthur Rae, who was brought up at Blithewold, has fond memories of Estelle. She remembers her as warm, compassionate, and friendly, and as the one who acted as a buffer between the staff and the McKees.[3] She taught the maids to play "Bristol Solitaire," a card game, and kept a watchful eye on the many young people who visited Blithewold.

---

[1] Estelle's Mah Jongg set was a Christmas gift from Bessie's daughters Marjorie and Augustine. It is in the Blithewold Collection.
[2] Interview with Eleanor Rae Gladding, October 12, 2007. Mrs. Gladding's father, Arthur Rae, worked for the family for more than 50 years and lived in the south garage apartment.
[3] Ibid.

Estelle's life at Blithewold is well documented through letters to and from the family, and from her own detailed diaries. Her first journal was a gift from Bessie at Christmas in 1903. From that time, until her death in 1928, she wrote in her diary every day.[1] In the journals she recorded the comings and goings of the family in great detail, local and world historical events, and the attitudes and manners of the day.

In 1900 she accompanied Bessie, Marjorie, and baby Augustine on the yacht *Marjorie II* to the Caribbean, and in 1908 she traveled as Marjorie's companion to Europe. Estelle loved books and reading aloud and "singing in the parlor."

Estelle the Gardener

Estelle shared Bessie's love of gardens and, like Bessie, was a hands-on gardener. In 1904 she began her meticulous daily accounts of activities in the gardens at Blithewold — she began every entry in her diary with the weather and the temperature of the day. These garden references are a valuable record of the development of the property over almost three decades. She worked alongside John DeWolf, the landscape gardener, and the two became close friends. Not only did she record her planting, pruning, staking, and weeding, but she made garden lists and harvested fruits and vegetables. The water garden was her favorite spot, and she walked down to it every day to check on its progress. In her later years, when she found it too difficult to walk as far as the water garden, she would have someone push her in a wheelchair.

The diaries are of great value to present-day Blithewold horticulturists. Study of those records tells them not only what the original plantings were, but often where they came from and how they were cultivated and cared for. They are used even today in the ongoing efforts to identify and restore Blithewold's historic gardens.

---

[1] Estelle's diaries from 1904 to 1928 are kept in the Blithewold Archives.

A Self-Sacrificing Life

By today's standards Estelle Clements' life appears sadly limited, but there are no signs of regret or envy in her prolific writings. She seemed fulfilled in her role as nurturer to Bessie and her family. In 1928, Estelle was in Greenville, Mississippi, visiting her brother William when she died suddenly at the age of seventy-nine. Will Clements made the last entry in his sister's diary, which seems a perfect summation: *"Thus ends a most wonderfully self-sacrificing life."*

1895 — PLANS FOR THE FUTURE

Sometime during 1895, Augustus and Marjorie went to have their photographs taken. Augustus had several taken of himself, and then a lovely portrait of the two of them, father and daughter. Marjorie wore a pretty pink pleated silk dress with lace and ribbons. The photograph is displayed in Marjorie's bedroom, and the dress is carefully preserved in the textile storage area at Blithewold.

Augustus Van Wickle and his daughter Marjorie, 1895

Also in 1895, amid the excitement over the new estate's construction, Augustus's mother Anna Van Wickle died. She never got to see Blithewold.

Near the end of the year, Bessie was once again suffering from nervous exhaustion, and she left for the Dansville sanitarium sometime in October 1895. By the end of November she was recuperating at the Waldorf Hotel in New York City. Augustus wrote to Marjorie, *"Mother is feeling very comfortable again today. She has to be very careful with her diet but this is all she needs now to become well and, my hope, strong."*[1] Marjorie, then twelve years old, was thrust back into a life without her mother, and this time without her father, too, since Augustus stayed most of the time with Bessie. Once again Marjorie was left in Hazleton in the care of Frank and Kate Pardee.

Marjorie began to exhibit concern for her mother's health,[2] and this preoccupation would stay with her for the rest of Bessie's life. Marjorie's frequent letters to her mother (every two or three days) suggest symptoms of separation anxiety. On December 9 she wrote, *"I dreamt last night that you were home..."* and three days later, *"Dearest Mother, You do not know how much I enjoyed your letter, because it is the first you have written. I am so glad you are well enough to sit up and write."* On December 14, *"I hope you can come home soon."* And on the 16th, *"It is only seven more days now..."* But she was to be disappointed yet again. On December 23, just two days before Christmas, Marjorie wrote *"I hope you and Papa are coming home soon and are well and are having a nice time."* Her attempts to be brave and generous became ever more transparent.

Augustus and Bessie did return to Hazleton in time for Christmas, but in January of 1896 Bessie was back at the Waldorf in New York, still recuperating. On February 26 Augustus wrote, *"We are coming home Monday, Tuesday, or possibly Saturday."* But another letter the following day said *"I fear you will be disappointed that we are*

---

[1] Augustus Van Wickle to Marjorie, December 2, 1895. Blithewold Archives.
[2] Concluded from a study of letters written by Marjorie during this period.

not coming home on Saturday. We cannot leave until Monday." But they did not return on the Monday either, and ten days later they announced their decision to take a trip to the Jekyll Island Club in Georgia, *"...with Miss Mabel and Mr. Harry Lee. I wish that you were one of the party also. However, it probably is best for you to stick to school now."*[1] They hoped to be home in two weeks.

From Jekyll Island Augustus wrote, *"Our impressions so far of the Club are exceedingly pleasant and we all think we shall like it very much."*[2]

Letter from Augustus Van Wickle to Marjorie,
written on his first visit to Jekyll Island, March 9, 1896

---

[1] Augustus Van Wickle to Marjorie, March 7, 1896. Blithewold Archives.
[2] Augustus Van Wickle to Marjorie, March 9, 1896. Blithewold Archives.

BLITHEWOLD I — THE GOLDEN INTERLUDE

The new mansion was ready for occupancy in the summer of 1896, its rooms furnished with beautiful antiques and fine reproduction furniture.[1] The name "Blithewold" was carved into a large granite stone over the living room fireplace. Servants and gardeners were hired to take care of the family and guests, and to tend Bessie's new gardens.

Blithewold I, 1896

Guests began to flow into Blithewold immediately, filling the guest books with poems, tributes, watercolors, and messages of delight.[2] William McKee's signature is the first entry, followed by Blithewold's architect, Francis Hoppin. Augustus, Bessie, and Marjorie quickly became immersed in the social life of Bristol's privileged

---

[1] Most of the furniture in the present Blithewold dates from this time.

[2] The guest books, preserved in the Archives at Blithewold, provide detailed information about guests and their activities at Blithewold over a period of 80 years.

classes.[1] Friends and neighbors came to call, and visits were returned. The Van Wickles took parties out on their fine new yacht *Marjorie*, serving elegant luncheons on board as they cruised to Newport to watch the National Tennis Championships on Bellevue Avenue.[2]

Onboard the Marjorie, *1896. Seated, Bessie and Augustus Van Wickle: standing, William McKee in white hat, with three Pardee cousins*

A tennis court and a golf course were laid out on the southern part of the property, complete with a clubhouse[3] for entertaining (fondly named "The Rendezvous" by the family). Augustus was named President of the golf club and the *Bristol Phoenix* reported that he was *"an expert golfer, making some remarkable scores in his golf playing*

[1] The first guest book records dates, names, and addresses of callers, and when the calls were returned. Blithewold Archives.
[2] As recorded in the *Marjorie's* log book. Blithewold Archives.
[3] Designed by Francis Hoppin.

both in Bristol and at Newport which he visited nearly every day in his steam yacht."[1] Bathhouses, a dock, and a swimming platform were built on the waterfront, and fine sand was brought in from Edgartown, Martha's Vineyard, to create a sandy beach.

The Blithewold stone set into the Living Room fireplace of Blithewold I [2]

Bessie and Augustus were very hospitable, and the house was constantly full of guests — some stayed in the mansion, others in the Gardner House south of Blithewold. Still others spent the entire

---

[1] A newspaper clipping from the *Bristol Phoenix.* (Summer 1896 or 1897).
[2] Most of the furniture seen in this photograph ca. 1896, can be seen in Blithewold II today. The table and the two upholstered chairs are in the Living Room; the carved Dutch chest (seen behind the lamp) is also in the Living Room; and the Paul de Longpré watercolor of flowers in a vase hangs in Augustine's Room. The rug is in Marjorie's Room. The clock and the desk and desk chair are in Collections Storage, as are parts of the lamp.

summer at Valmer, the large Victorian house next door to Blithewold on the north side.[1]

The gardens were an ongoing project into which Bessie seemingly poured her physical and emotional energies. She was a hands-on gardener, and encouraged her guests to help out whenever they could. She was known to leave garden tools out in the entrance hall as a gentle hint. When not occupied in the gardens, the five Pardee sisters delighted in being together with time to catch up on news, and they sat for hours on the wide porches facing the Bay or the North Garden, drinking tea, knitting, reading, and napping. The men played pool and golf, sailed, and organized tennis and baseball games. In the evenings, family and guests would gather in the living room to play parlor games and to sing around the piano. Marjorie started to take painting lessons from Bristol artist Louise Pratt. Two charming paintings survive from this era, *Lighthouse at Bristol Ferry* and *Path through the Enclosed Garden, Looking North.*[2]

Marjorie's earliest known painting: Lighthouse at Bristol Ferry, *1899*[3]

---

[1] The house is extant and remains largely unchanged. The architect was James Renwick, who built it for his own family in 1860. Renwick designed St. Patrick's Cathedral in New York City in 1879.

[2] These paintings are preserved in the Archives at Blithewold and are displayed periodically.

[3] Marjorie was 15 years old at the time she did this painting.

Augustus, who had been elected Commodore of the Bristol Yacht Club, purchased two Herreshoff sailing boats, the *Esperanza* and the *Wild Swan,* for racing. During the summer of 1897, even when Augustus was not in Bristol, his boats would be raced by his boat captain (for many years Captain Slocum[1]).[2]

Wild Swan

---

[1] Captain Slocum lived in a small cottage near Blithewold's dock, and was still living there as late as 1932.
[2] As shown by clippings from the "News Service." This was a service offered to wealthy patrons whereby a 'clipper' would, for a fee, collect articles or notices related to the family from any newspaper. Hundreds of these clippings relating to their social activities were saved by the Van Wickles and the McKees.

THE LATTIMER MASSACRE

It may have been while Augustus was enjoying the summer of 1897 with his family in Bristol that the calamitous mine-workers' strikes began in Hazleton. In August, men from the newly formed United Mine Workers Union walked out of the Van Wickle mine at Coleraine, striking for fairer wages. Augustus tried to replace the striking workers with nonunion Slavic immigrants, but when they joined the strike as well, he quickly backed down and agreed to the workers' demands. The general unrest was spreading, however, and in September several hundred strikers headed toward Calvin Pardee's still-working Lattimer mines. Encouraged by the Union, strikers began marching from one mine to another to persuade *all* mine workers to join them in their demand for fair wages and safer conditions. The unarmed miners marched peacefully behind a large American flag. The Luzerne County Sheriff, James Martin, gathered together 80 deputies armed with Winchester rifles and formed a roadblock to stop the marchers from entering colliery premises. A scuffle ensued and the Sheriff gave the order to shoot. Nineteen miners were killed. At a subsequent enquiry, Sheriff Martin testified that he ordered his men to shoot because the crowd had turned on them. However, since almost all the victims had supposedly been shot in the back, his story would appear to be false. He was nevertheless acquitted.

It was the worst incident of labor violence in the nation, and a turning point in the history of the United Mine Workers. Public opinion had been provoked, and on September 19 the *New York Herald* published a full-page article addressing the miners' grievances, citing, among others, the Pardees and the Van Wickles. As a result, mining companies offered substantial wage increases to their workers, and significant new mine safety standards were put in place.[1]

With the worst of the labor unrest behind him, Augustus now planned to move forward and take his companies to new heights.

---

[1] From *Lattimer: A Time to Remember,* by John Radzilowski, and from Wikipedia.

Despite the reprobation of newspapers of the day, he had personally earned the reputation of being fair, of helping families in need, and of being an honest, compassionate employer.[1]

"DEAR MR. LEWIS"

In Bristol, Marjorie struck up a friendship with Lewis Herreshoff, brother of Nathanael G. and John B. Herreshoff. Lewis was legally blind and lived with his mother in a house overlooking the Bay, (and next to the Herreshoff boatbuilding workshops). He was sociable and outgoing and took it upon himself to correspond regularly with all the summer people to let them know what was going on in Bristol while they were away.[2] He typed long letters to them, the missives serving almost as a village newspaper. He was connected with all the influential people in town, and he loved music and literature — the young ladies of Bristol would take it in turns to read to him. In 1898 he was very concerned about the Spanish Civil War and possible American involvement.[3] In February 1898 he wrote to Marjorie about the first torpedo boats being built at the Herreshoff workshops. His cousin, Bertie Chesebrough,[4] was the designer of the torpedo boats.

Bert has amused me greatly by wanting me to move away from this house. He says we are soon to have war with Spain, and the first thing is a Spanish ship will come up the Bay to burn the shops where they are now building torpedo

---

[1] From Augustus's obituary in the *Hazleton Sentinel*, June 9, 1898.
[2] Lewis Herreshoff's letters to Augustus, Marjorie, and Augustine are in the Blithewold Archives.
[3] Letter to Marjorie from Lewis Herreshoff, February 27, 1898. Blithewold Archives.
[4] Bertie Chesebrough was married to Emma Bullock, Judge Jonathan Bullock's daughter. Judge Bullock, born in and a lifelong resident of Bristol, was a federal judge on the United States District Court for Rhode Island, nominated by President Abraham Lincoln. According to letters from Lewis Herreshoff to Marjorie, Emma's father disapproved of the marriage and the couple eloped.

boats, and of course this house will be burned also, as well as his Mother's. He is really earnest about it; I suspect we shall have plenty of time to get away if the ship comes up here, which I don't believe. But really, Marjorie, it does seem almost as if we should have war, is it not dreadful, but the horrible war in Cuba and the loss of the Maine[1] *seem reasons why our country should put an end to the wicked cruelty that the Spanish are inflicting on the poor Cubans. I do wish this country would say to Spain — Just stop it and let Cuba be free, they have earned freedom. The worst thing about the* Maine *is that I doubt that it can ever be told if the cause of the explosions was an accident or if it was done by some hand outside, but is it not a dreadful thing? The 2 small torpedo boats that they are building here are now finished and one of them has been flying about the Bay getting ready for trials. I dare say you have seen accounts of her in the papers, she has done 21¾ knots and as she must do by the contract but 20 knots there is no doubt about the results. I fancy she will go at once to the Harbor of New York to help defend it in case of war. She is too small to go South. There are two just alike, 100 feet long and a third is being built that is 140 feet long, which will be finished in July so you will see her making her trials in that month. It is amusing to watch them; they do go like a streak.*[2]

The Spanish Navy did not, of course, cruise into Bristol Harbor, and for two glorious summers the Van Wickles enjoyed their beautiful new home. They filled it with friends and relatives, making memories and traditions that they no doubt thought would last forever.

---

[1] The sinking of the *Maine*, a U.S. Navy battleship that sank in Havana harbor on February 15, 1898, was one of the events that led to the Spanish-American War. The cause of the explosion that sank the ship remained a mystery until recently, when investigators concluded that the explosion was caused by the accidental ignition of gunpowder stored too close to the coal furnace on the ship.

[2] Letter from Lewis Herreshoff to Marjorie Van Wickle, February 27, 1898. Blithewold Archives.

JEKYLL ISLAND, GEORGIA

In 1898, Augustus commissioned the building of a new 174-foot yacht to replace the *Marjorie.* He had recently been invited to join the exclusive Jekyll Island Club on Jekyll Island off the coast of Georgia. It had been founded in 1886 as a winter retreat for wealthy American businessmen, most of them from New York and Philadelphia. The Queen Anne–style clubhouse was completed in 1887 and families began constructing their own "cottages" soon after. The resort offered miles of white sandy beaches for bathing, cycle paths, fishing, polo, and tennis. But the chief entertainment for the men was hunting.[1]

Jekyll Island Club, circa 1890

J. P. Morgan and Jay Gould were both members of the club; Augustus had been sponsored for membership by Jay Stickney, owner of the Mount Washington Hotel in New Hampshire.[2] It was fashionable

---

[1] From an article in *The New York Times,* April 23, 1886.
[2] Information from the Jekyll Island Club Museum Archives.

for club members to sail their large yachts down through the Inland Waterway to Jekyll Island, and this may be why Augustus decided he needed a much larger vessel. He had already purchased two prime-location sites at the club, planning to build another vacation home there, as well as buying space in the club stables for his horses. He and Bessie spent two wonderful vacations at Jekyll in 1896 and 1897, one with William McKee, Mabel Schuyler, and Harry Lee as their guests, and another with Marjorie.[1] Many years later, Marjorie and George Lyon became members of the club, and George won the Jekyll Island tennis championship in 1938.

Jekyll Island Beach, *watercolor by Marjorie Lyon*

---

[1] From the Club's Guest Register at the Jekyll Island Club Museum.

Chapter V

TRAGEDY AND JOY

DEATH OF AUGUSTUS VAN WICKLE

In the spring of 1898 Bessie and Augustus were overjoyed to find that, after fourteen agonizing years of worrying and waiting, Bessie was pregnant. Their second child was due in November. The joy, however, was short-lived; on June 8, 1898, while Bessie was packing trunks to move to Bristol for the summer, Augustus went out skeet-shooting with his brother-in-law and close friend, Sandidge Allison. "Sandy" Allison was married to Bessie's older sister Anne (and was also the younger brother of Ario Pardee Jr.'s wife, Mary Allison Pardee). Augustus left the house on North Church Street shortly after 4 o'clock in the afternoon and headed for an empty lot between Church and Laurel Streets. The men were accompanied by two servants, Augustus's coachman, William Walton, and his gardener, William Woodring. After about an hour of shooting, Augustus stood aside to let Sandy Allison take his turn.[1] What happened next has been the subject of much speculation. The official version, as related by both the servants present, states that Augustus put his gun down on the ground *"The stock resting on the earth and the barrel against his left side, just below his heart."*[2] He then leaned over his gun to scratch his score in the sand when the gun accidentally fired, discharging the full load, a shell that contained an ounce and a quarter of No. 8 shot, into his chest. He threw up his hands and fell backward, mortally wounded. The three men lifted him into the carriage and raced toward his home. His last words were reported to be *"Don't tell Bessie."* Within the hour he was dead. Bessie's brother Frank immediately took charge of all the funeral arrangements, and became Bessie's constant advisor.

---

[1] Account by William Woodring, *Hazleton Sentinel,* June 9, 1898.
[2] *Hazleton Sentinel,* June 9, 1898.

The account begs the question: Why would an experienced marksman and superb athlete act in such an ill-advised and dangerous way? Frank Pardee's daughter-in-law, Alice DeWolf Pardee, who was something of a family historian, wrote a slightly different version of the tragedy. She reported in her book *Blithewold* that Augustus had been climbing over a stone wall when the accident happened.[1] Present-day descendants Marjorie Shaw Jeffries (Augustus's granddaughter) and Nancy Pardee Abercrombie (Frank Pardee's granddaughter) both remember elderly relatives whispering alternative theories — one premise being that Augustus was accidentally nudged, or bumped, perhaps by Sandidge Allison. Marjorie Shaw Jeffries reports that she always thought that her grandfather had been accidentally shot by Sandidge Allison as Allison followed the arc of the clay disc with his gun.[2]

Augustus's funeral on Friday, June 10, was a sad affair. The *Hazleton Sentinel* reported:

> *The funeral was held...from the late home of the deceased on North Church Street, Hazleton. Never has the funeral of a private citizen in Hazleton attracted such throngs...All classes of the community were represented in the quiet and sorrowing crowd. Men prominent in coal business, politics, literature and higher walks of human activity, mingled with the many hundreds, if not thousands, who had known Mr. Van Wickle as a kind employer or a true friend in need. Mrs. Van Wickle was prostrated and unable to attend the funeral. Many of the stores and other branches of business closed during the hours of the funeral. The Y.M.C.A., of which Mr. Van Wickle was director, remained closed until six o'clock. Hazleton Iron Works of which he was president shut down for the day and the employees attended in a body. The Roberts colliery remained idle, and many of the workmen were noticed in the procession...The features of the deceased*

---

[1] Alice DeWolf Pardee. *Blithewold*. Private printing, 1978, p. 60.
[2] Interview with Marjorie Shaw Jeffries, February 20, 2009.

were remarkably preserved and very natural, and looked as though he just laid down to a quiet sleep. It would require several rooms in the house to hold the floral offerings. There were scores of designs of rare beauty, among them a wreath three feet in diameter. It contained white roses, interspersed with lilies and palms. Across it on a ribbon were the words "Our Friend." This was sent by the employees in Milnesville and Coleraine...It was an exquisite collection, showing the profound sympathy and containing expressions of esteem of all the friends of Mr. Van Wickle. At the Church a vast congregation assembled, and when the body was taken to Hazle cemetery another large crowd had gathered there, the largest ever known in its history.[1]

Augustus Van Wickle's gravestone, Hazleton[2]

The *New York Times* described Augustus as a true philanthropist — *"He was many times a millionaire, and although much of his time was spent on his private yacht or at his Summer*

---

[1] From *The Hazleton Sentinel*, June 11, 1898.
[2] This gravestone is almost identical to the one erected at the Juniper Hill Cemetery in Bristol 38 years later for Bessie.

residence in Bristol, R.I., his attention to the less fortunate people of the mining regions was never overlooked."[1]

The list of Augustus's achievements and connections in society was lengthy. Besides owning some eight companies, he was a member of the boards of trustees of the Peddie Institute, the Metropolitan Museum of Art in New York, and the Museum of Natural History, New York. He was a member of the New York Yacht Club, the Jekyll Island Club, President of the Bristol Golf Club, and Commodore of the Bristol Yacht Club.[2]

Bessie was thirty-eight years old, four months pregnant, and in a vulnerable state of health. Predictably, the Pardee family gathered around to protect and support her. Two weeks after the funeral, a large contingent of Pardees departed for Blithewold where Bessie spent the rest of the summer surrounded and protected by the people she loved most. Blithewold itself was full to capacity; the Allison family took up residence at the Gardner House, and the Frank Pardee family rented Valmer, the house next door. All arrived with their own servants and governesses. Bessie and Marjorie spent what must have been a very sad but healthy summer, enjoying the fresh air and sea breezes of Bristol.

A NEW LIFE

The Van Wickles returned to Hazleton in September, as Marjorie turned fifteen, and on November 10, 1898, Bessie gave birth to her second daughter. It was at this time that Estelle Clements came to live with Bessie on a more or less permanent basis, to help her raise her two daughters. Marjorie grew up very quickly and became even more protective of her mother. Several weeks after the birth, Marjorie wrote to her Aunt Molly:

---

[1] *The New York Times,* June 8, 1898.
[2] Obituary of Augustus Van Wickle, *Bristol Phoenix,* June 1898.

Mother is getting on very nicely, and sat up for twenty minutes yesterday, which I think was doing very well, as it was the first time she has been out of bed. The baby is also doing very well, and is just as sweet as she can possibly be. I think that she will probably be dark like Papa, for her eyes, although blue, are very dark, and her hair is almost black. She measures twenty-one inches exactly, or at least did when she was two weeks old, and weighs about eight pounds...We have not yet decided on the baby's name, but will write you when we do.[1]

The baby girl was eventually named Augustine after her father Augustus. Augustine was an exceptionally beautiful child, charming and enchanting, and she captivated the whole family.[2]

Bessie adored her baby, and as Augustine grew into a toddler her every word and antic was recorded and commented on.[3] Her baby words became part of the family vocabulary — all her life her sister Marjorie was known as "Isch"[4] and anything costly was referred to as "spensy." She was Bessie's constant companion and comfort. Marjorie, meanwhile, continued to hover over her mother, urging her to rest and take care of herself, sympathizing constantly over Bessie's headaches and neuralgia, and taking on the role of care-taker. In letters, she addressed Bessie as *"Dearest Little Mother"* and signed herself *"Your BIG daughter, Marjorie."* It is easy to imagine that Marjorie must have felt defenseless and vulnerable; her future must have seemed out of her control. She now knew that terrible things could happen without warning.

---

[1] Marjorie Van Wickle to her Aunt Molly December 4, 1898. Blithewold Archives.
[2] As evidenced by photographs, and in letters and diaries over the next several years between Bessie, Marjorie, and Estelle Clements.
[3] As evidenced by Bessie's letters to her family during this period.
[4] The baby's pronunciation of "Sister."

Augustine Van Wickle, 1899

Marjorie and Augustine, 1899

To add to the family's pain, another family tragedy occurred in January of 1899. Sandidge Allison, Augustus's close friend and brother-in-law, who was with him the day he died, died himself in a mine accident. He was inspecting an iron mine in Minnesota when the cable of the cage in which he was descending broke, and the cage plunged to the bottom of the shaft.[1] His wife Anne, Bessie's older sister, left with three small children (Douglas, Winifred, and Lois),

---

[1] C. Pardee Foulke and William F. Foulke. *Calvin Pardee.* Drake Press, Philadelphia, 1979, p. 112.

moved into the Pardee mansion in Hazleton to live with her unmarried sister, Edith. The two sisters lived there together until 1923 when the mansion was sold[1], at which time they moved to Harwichport on Cape Cod.

AMERICA'S CUP TRIALS

Bessie and Marjorie and baby Augustine spent the summer of 1899 quietly at Blithewold. But in August there was a flurry of excitement on Narragansett Bay, all played out in the waters off Blithewold. The Herreshoff boat-building company in Bristol had built a yacht that they intended to sail in the America's Cup Race, a 40-meter yacht named *Columbia*, designed by the brilliant Nathanael G. Herreshoff. It had an 1189-square-meter sail area, and in an effort to build a lighter, faster, more maneuverable racing yacht, the Herreshoff designer had created a telescoping aluminum mainmast. *"She is faster than we expected,"* wrote the Cup defense team. In August they were engaged in trials on the Bay when suddenly the mainmast collapsed, sending the mainsail toppling into the water. The enormous canvas sail was soon waterlogged and became too heavy to bring back onboard.

The Captain and promoter of the yacht, Sir Oliver Iselin, considered his options and quickly identified Blithewold's Great Lawn as the only space in the area large enough to spread the sail out to dry. He sent a message to Bessie,[2] asking for her permission to use the lawn, which she granted. It took 80 men that day to haul the sail onto the land to dry, and many more a few days later to steady it as it was taken slowly along Ferry Road back to the Herreshoff workshop.

---

[1] The Pardee Mansion was demolished to make way for the Hotel Altamont, and in the 1960s the hotel became a Lutheran Retirement Home.
[2] Oliver Iselin's letter of request and a letter of thanks, both handwritten on "On board Columbia" writing paper, are in the Blithewold Archives. Letters to Bessie Van Wickle, August 3 and August 6, 1899.

Columbia sailing past the Blithewold dock

Columbia *with collapsed mainmast, off Blithewold, 1899*
Photograph courtesy of the Herreshoff Marine Museum

Columbia's *sail being taken back to the boatyard, 1899*
Photograph courtesy of the Herreshoff Marine Museum

    Columbia later won the America's Cup Race of 1899,[1] beating
its stiffest competition, Sir Thomas Lipton's *Shamrock II.* The *Columbia*
was the third winning Cup defender built by the famed boat builders,
Herreshoff Manufacturing Company, and a fourth would follow.

---

[1] By then, the aluminum mast had been replaced with a wooden mast made
of Oregon pine.

Chapter VI

A NEW CENTURY

WILLIAM LEANDER MCKEE

By 1899, William McKee's business had moved from Rome, Georgia, to Boston, and Will was spending a lot of time with Bessie. From the time in Hazleton in 1887 when he had first met and become friends with the Van Wickles, William McKee had been included in many of the Van Wickles' social activities, including trips to Jekyll Island, the fateful trip to Florida in 1892, the visit to the World's Columbian Exposition in Chicago in 1893, weekends at Blithewold, and cruises on the *Marjorie*.

William Leander McKee, ca. 1890

Emmons & McKee, Rome, Georgia, 1887,
men's outfitters and dry goods store

After William McKee graduated from Phillips Exeter Academy, he opened a men's clothing and dry goods store, Emmons & McKee, with a partner, in Rome, Georgia. The store was bought out in 1890 by Arthur White Tedcastle.[1] When Tedcastle returned to the North (his wife was from Somerville, Massachusetts) in 1898, with William McKee

---

[1] Arthur Tedcastle was born in London of a Scottish family, grew up in New Jersey, and worked on Wall Street in a New York private bank. When his employer bought a bank in Rome, Georgia, in 1875 and moved there, 20-year-old Tedcastle went with him, taking a job as bookkeeper in William McKee's small wholesale shoe and dry goods business. By 1890 Tedcastle owned the company, by then much expanded and renamed A. W. Tedcastle, Manufacturers and Jobbers of Boots and Shoes. From Nash K. Burger, *The Road to West 43rd Street.* University Press of Mississippi, 1995, p. 51.

as his partner in the new company, he opened a large facility on the corner of Lincoln and Beach Streets in Boston.[1]

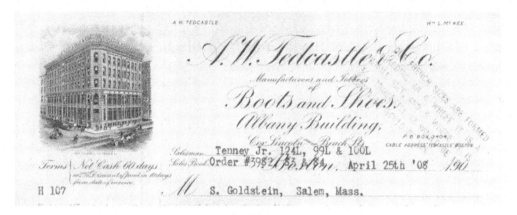

Letterhead from A.W. Tedcastle & Co.,
showing its headquarters in Boston, 1908

No letters or diaries in the Blithewold Archives exist that suggest how or when a romantic relationship began between the widowed Bessie Van Wickle and her husband's friend William McKee, but Bessie and Augustine remained at Blithewold after the summer season of 1899 (presumably to be nearer to Will). Marjorie returned to Hazleton, while Bessie was chaperoned at Blithewold by Estelle Clements. All was not well, however, and Bessie had to return to the Dansville Sanitarium for another rest cure.

MAIDEN CRUISE OF THE *MARJORIE II*

In the spring of 1900, Bessie took possession of the new 174-foot yacht that Augustus had commissioned two years earlier. It was built by the Delaware River Iron Shipbuilding and Engine Works in Chester, Pennsylvania, and was a beautiful vessel, capable of

---

[1] From Nash K. Burger, *The Road to West 43rd St.* University Press of Mississippi, 1995, p. 51.

extended ocean journeys. The Herreshoff *Marjorie* was sold,[1] and its two carved wooden nameplates transferred to the new yacht. *Marjorie II* was ready to sail! Bessie, with her usual attention to detail, ordered Minton china and Baccarat crystal for the yacht, each piece engraved with the crossed flags of the *Marjorie* and the New York Yacht Club.[2] An exciting maiden voyage was planned.

Marjorie II *being loaded with supplies in Cuba, 1900.*
Marjorie can be seen on deck holding baby Augustine,
next to her cousin Dorothy Pardee

---

[1] *Marjorie I* was sold to Joseph A. Vandergrist of Philadelphia. In 1905 she was sold again, to Henry W. Savage of New York. There is no record of the yacht *Marjorie* after 1911.
[2] The collection of china and crystal from the *Marjorie* is displayed at Blithewold in the Butler's Pantry.

In March 1900 *Marjorie II* left New York carrying Bessie and Marjorie and baby Augustine and accompanied by a full crew of 18, a nursemaid for Augustine, a physician for Bessie (who was still under doctors' care), William McKee, Estelle Clements, and Marjorie's cousin Dorothy Pardee. During the two-months-long cruise they visited Cuba, Puerto Rico, and Jamaica. At the end of the cruise, Bessie Van Wickle and William McKee announced that they planned to be married.

In May 1900, right after the *Marjorie II* returned from Jamaica, Bessie became ill again. She was taken to Roosevelt Hospital in New York where she had surgery, although the reason for the surgery is unknown. Seventeen-year-old Marjorie was again sent away, this time to stay with Bessie's cousin Helen Riddell in Shippensburg, Pennsylvania, for a month. Augustine was looked after at Blithewold by Estelle Clements, who wrote regularly to Marjorie to report on Bessie's progress and give her family news.

Later in 1900 Bessie sold the *Marjorie II* to Isaac Emerson of Baltimore who had made an immense fortune as the inventor of Bromo-Seltzer. Emerson renamed the yacht *Margaret* after his youngest daughter who cruised to Europe on her honeymoon on the vessel in 1902. In August 1917 the *Margaret* was requisitioned by the U.S. Navy for overseas service in World War I. Following the conversion the ship was placed in commission. In November 1917 she began a voyage to the European war zone, towing a French submarine chaser and accompanied by several other converted yachts. The trip, plagued by mechanical troubles, ended in the Azores where the *Margaret* remained for several months. She returned to the United States in November 1918 following the Armistice, and was decommissioned. She was sold again at the end of September 1921,[1] after which no further records of her were found.

---

[1] From *eNotes.com Reference*

MISS VINTON'S SCHOOL

In the fall of 1900, Marjorie was sent to Miss Vinton's School, a boarding school in Ridgefield, Connecticut, while Bessie stayed on at Blithewold with her sister Anne and Estelle Clements. At Miss Vinton's, Marjorie found stability and discipline and made lifelong friends. The school had only 18 young women, most from the Boston area. Marjorie's first roommate was Louise Smith from Boston and York Harbor, Maine, daughter of Arthur Cosslett Smith, the author. They remained the very closest of friends for the rest of their lives, even traveling together in Europe in 1908. Other enduring friendships were with Gay Dexter[1] from Topsfield, Massachusetts, Zaidee Goff from Osterville, Massachusetts, and Priscilla Harding,[2] from Beacon Hill in Boston, and Woods Hole, Massachusetts.

Marjorie's regular letters home, both to her mother and to Estelle Clements, form a comprehensive account of life at a girls' boarding school at the turn of the century. She wrote letters of ten to twelve pages every two or three days, in which she described her studies, the teachers, her accommodations and food, the other students and their clothing, free-time activities, travel to and from school, and all the emotional highs and lows of adolescent girls everywhere.

A favorite activity of the girls at Miss Vinton's school was baseball. Marjorie wrote to her mother, *"Baseball has started up again and is just as much fun as ever. I wish you could see us playing — skirts, sweaters, and tams covered with mud, and our rubbers tied on with string — Oh we are lovely sights!"[3]*

---

[1] Gay Dexter was the younger sister of Julian Dexter, the pilot who would bring the airplane to Blithewold on July Fourth, 1926. Gay later married Tom Pierce.

[2] Priscilla Harding married Jim Sherrard, an Englishman, and lived in England for the rest of her life. Priscilla's daughter Mary was Marjorie's goddaughter.

[3] Marjorie to Bessie, March 16, 1902. Blithewold Archives.

Miss Vinton's School, 1900.
Marjorie is seated in the middle row, center.

Distance from her mother seemed to make Marjorie more concerned than ever about Bessie's health. She constantly urged Bessie not to tax herself, even to refrain from writing her such long letters in case she should get a headache, though it is clear that Marjorie craved news from home. Bessie's letters to Marjorie, on the other hand, were full of accounts of her exciting new social life, trips to New York to her favorite gown shop, Fox & Co., detailed descriptions of her purchases and her visits to the theaters, and, of course, endless tales of Augustine. Marjorie, generous by nature, responded to the reports on Augustine with enthusiasm, showing no sign of sibling rivalry,

The pictures of the baby are simply great!! I don't think I ever enjoyed anything so much in all my life. Isn't she just the

119

dearest thing...And that one of her and Sara Ito[1] on the steps is one of the prettiest pictures I have ever seen! I have shown them to Miss Vinton and to most of the girls. They are all crazy over them![2]

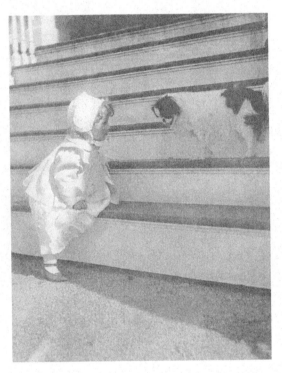

Augustine with Sara Ito on the steps of Blithewold I, 1900

But time and again Marjorie would be disappointed when Bessie failed to attend important events at the school:

Prize Day...most all the mothers and fathers are coming up, and I do want you dreadfully [and] Do you think you could possibly come to Prize Day, dear little Mother. [And again,] Have you decided about Prize Day yet?[3]

---

[1] Sara Ito was a Japanese Spaniel that had belonged to Augustus Van Wickle.
[2] Marjorie Van Wickle to Bessie Van Wickle, November 18, 1900. Blithewold Archives.
[3] Marjorie to Bessie, April 24, 1902 and May 18, 1902. Blithewold Archives.

April 1901 saw Blithewold in the throes of feverish excitement as Bessie finalized her plans to marry William McKee at the estate. She asked Marjorie not to tell anyone at school about the forthcoming event but to try to get permission to leave school early, at the end of May, in order to attend the wedding. Miss Vinton was most reluctant to release Marjorie early without a good reason, so Marjorie finally shared the news. Miss Vinton was *"very surprised...I thought Miss Vinton would fall over backward!"[1]*

William McKee was himself congratulated. Just before the wedding he received a letter from Thomas Caldwell, an old friend of Augustus's from Morristown. *"It would not be other than pleasing to dear Augustus that you, his best friend, should marry Mrs. Van Wickle. I feel sure of this."[2]* Bessie's husband-to-be, Will McKee, was an outgoing man, energetic and charming, interested in a variety of outdoor sports, and an enthusiastic sailor and traveler. Marjorie and Augustine always referred to him as "Father Dear," and from all accounts their relationship with their stepfather was one of affection and loyalty.[3]

MR. AND MRS. WILLIAM MCKEE

Bessie and Will McKee's wedding took place at Blithewold on May 29, 1901, the service conducted by Will's stepfather, Reverend William Stitt. Marjorie wrote to her mother the next day:

> *My Dearest Darling Mother, We all feel like the day after the ball today. And, oh how we miss you! Didn't everything go off perfectly yesterday? It couldn't have been better or prettier in any way. And everyone seemed to be having such a lovely time. I can tell you I heard and overheard such a lot*

---

[1] Marjorie to Bessie, May 6, 1901. Blithewold Archives.
[2] Letter from Thomas W. Caldwell to William L. McKee, March 21, 1901. Blithewold Archives.
[3] As evidenced by a study of the McKee files by Mary C. Philbrick. Blithewold Archives.

of nice things said about you...You deserve them, every one, you dear, pretty, sweet mother! I slept with the wedding cake under my pillow...Please give my love to that dear new relative of mine, and tell him I would have never forgiven him for taking you off if he hadn't been so perfectly dear himself.[1]

Indeed, William McKee was accepted immediately into the family, and Bessie was happily married to him for the rest of her life.[2] After the wedding, Bessie and Will left for a honeymoon in England, and Marjorie and Augustine were looked after at Blithewold by Estelle Clements. Marjorie's friends from Miss Vinton's School, Priscilla Harding, Louise Smith, and Zaidee Goff, all kept Marjorie company for the month of June at Blithewold, where the four young friends had *"the time of our lives."* They sailed, played tennis, swam, and partied with friends in Bristol.

THE VAN WICKLE GATES AT BROWN UNIVERSITY

While Bessie and Will were away on their honeymoon in London, Marjorie represented her mother as the guest of honor at a very important ceremony. When Augustus Van Wickle died, his will revealed a generous bequest to Brown University — funds to pay for a new administration building, as well as iron gates to be designed by Francis and Howard Hoppin.[3] The inscription on the gates, cast in bronze, reads: "In memory of Augustus Stout Van Wickle of the class of 1876. By achievement he honored, by gift he remembered, his Alma Mater." The Brown administration wanted to dedicate the Van Wickle Gates at the June 1901 commencement ceremony and had asked Bessie to officially "open" them. Marjorie took Bessie's place at the

---

[1] Marjorie to Bessie May 30, 1901. Blithewold Archives.

[2] As evidenced in letters between Marjorie and Augustine in the early 1930s: *"I never can forget the 31 years of happiness and cheerful kindness he [McKee] has brought into our lives. Also his unfailing love and courtesy to Mother."* Marjorie to Augustine, June 15, 1932. Blithewold Archives.

[3] The Hoppin brothers were both trained in architecture at the Massachusetts Institute of Technology.

ceremony. She was accompanied by Estelle Clements, Priscilla Harding, Francis Hoppin, and two friends from Newport who had been at Miss Vinton's School with her, Violet Cruger and Cynthia Roche. She wrote to Bessie, describing the events of the day:

> *About three o'clock we walked over to the college grounds and took our seats right near the corner stone. Then the keys of the gates were presented to Dr. Faunce and he made a speech and then opened the gates, and all the whole procession of officers, alumni and students walked through — all taking off their hats to salute as they passed under the gateway. It was all so solemn and grand — and I can't tell you how proud of dear Papa I felt! But especially afterward when the students cheered his name! It was just splendid. Next came my part of the program — the laying of the corner stone. Dr. Horr, a class mate of Papa's made a splendid speech and said lots of nice things about dear Papa...I forgot to say that Dr. Horr referred to me as the "chief guest of honor," which made me feel very proud. Altogether it was a most happy day for me.[1]*

This was the beginning of a tradition at Brown that continues to this day: the opening of the Van Wickle Gates twice a year, once in the fall to let in the new students, and again in the spring to let out the new graduates. President of the University W.H.P. Faunce wrote to Bessie afterward, congratulating her on Marjorie's fine performance as honored guest:

> *I send you...a copy of our "Alumni Monthly," showing your daughter in the act of laying the cornerstone...She bore herself with admirable grace and dignity and we were delighted to have her represent your family on the occasion. The gates evoke universal approval and admiration.[2]*

---

[1] Marjorie to Bessie, June 20, 1901. Blithewold Archives.
[2] W.H.P. Faunce to Bessie McKee, August 3, 1901. Blithewold Archives.

(Other bequests had been left by Augustus to Princeton University and Lafayette College. At Lafayette the funds were used to build a new library with a stained-glass window. At Princeton, Augustus's gift provided for the total restoration of Nassau Hall [the building that had originally encompassed the whole college], and the construction of the Fitz Randolph Gates, all in recognition of Augustus's ancestor Nathaniel Fitz Randolph, who had been so instrumental in building the college in Princeton. The Princeton Gates were designed by Charles McKim of McKim, Mead & White.)

Marjorie (center) at the opening of the Van Wickle Gates at Brown University, June 1901

THE MCKEES MOVE TO BOSTON

After Bessie's marriage to William McKee, the couple moved to Boston, where William McKee's business was now thriving. (It was probably shortly after their marriage that Bessie lent money to William McKee from her trust fund to give him a more equitable standing in the company of A. W. Tedcastle, Manufacturing, and for many years that investment served them well.) Initially they lived at 316 Beacon

Street, but then bought a house at 1 Gloucester Street, on the corner of Beacon Street. They lived there for 2 years while their "dream" townhouse one block away at 284 Commonwealth Avenue was being totally gutted and renovated. The work was supervised by a young architectural company, Kilham & Hopkins of Boston. In the spring of 1906 they moved into the new family home on Commonwealth Avenue that would be their primary residence for almost thirty years.

284 Commonwealth Avenue, Boston, ca. 1906

With Bristol now only an hour or two away by car, the family began to spend more time at Blithewold, which allowed Bessie to continue her work on the gardens. The sad days were over, and the McKees began to entertain in great style, both in Boston and at Blithewold. They attended the opera in Boston, took out a subscription to the symphony, and went to the theater several times a week.[1] Bessie slowly familiarized herself with the fashion of New

---

[1] The McKees kept all their programs from the opera, symphony, and theater. Their collection is preserved at Blithewold.

England, which was somewhat different from what she was used to. She wrote to her sisters:

> *I am beginning to get a little accustomed to the Boston shops and find them very satisfactory. I think we shall be able to do most of Marjorie's dressmaking here. Of course, I am not ready to leave Fox yet. I am wondering whether you people in Hazleton are still using your plumes, because, much to my disgust, I find that here in Boston they are not considered the thing at all.[1]*

In the same letter, Bessie commented on a wedding she had attended, showing more interest in the fashion displayed than in the ceremony: *"The bride was not very pretty, but beautifully dressed...I was looking more than listening."*

Marjorie faced another emotional challenge when she moved with her mother and stepfather to Boston in 1901. Wrenched away from the love and support of her Pardee family in Hazleton, she was lonely in Boston. She felt she had few friends in the city, and when it came time to be introduced into society as a debutante she protested and wanted nothing to do with it. She agonized over the prospect, finally writing to her mother from school:

> *Louise and I were talking about the future yesterday, and discovered we were both in the same fix about coming out and what to do next year. Isn't it dreadful? She has decided not to go to school next year, but doesn't want to "come out"...And I sort of hate to think of going to school with so much younger girls, but I <u>don't want to come out next year</u> and don't believe I ever will. I wish you, Augustine, Father*

---

[1] Letter from Bessie McKee to her family, February 1902. Blithewold Archives.

and I could go abroad for five years, until I am too old to "come out"![1]

Bessie gave in to her daughter's plea and agreed to let Marjorie absent herself from Boston society and go to Europe for a year when she was nineteen years old and finished with school. In the meantime, Marjorie had one more year of school to complete.

MISS HASKELL'S SCHOOL FOR GIRLS

In May 1902, Marjorie got the good news that she had been accepted to Miss Haskell's School for Girls in Boston for her final school year; her friend Priscilla Harding had already been at the school since January of that year, and Marjorie was anxious to join her there. Places were very difficult to secure at this small, progressive, and very popular school.[2] Headmistress Mary Elizabeth Haskell was a close friend of, and mentor to, the Lebanese artist and poet Kahlil Gibran, whom she had met at Gibran's first art exhibit in Boston at Wellesley College.[3] It may have been Miss Haskell's commitment to the arts that influenced Marjorie Van Wickle's artistic and intellectual development, thus shaping her future. (Miss Haskell went on to become headmistress of the renowned Cambridge School in Cambridge, Massachusetts.)

In June of 1903, Marjorie was ready for her "Grand Tour" of Europe. Bessie engaged the services of Miss Helen Macartnay, a professional chaperone who specialized in extended tours of the

---

[1] Marjorie Van Wickle to Bessie Van Wickle McKee, April 24, 1902. Blithewold Archives.

[2] Letter from Marjorie to Bessie, November 17, 1901. Marjorie was very worried that she wouldn't be offered a place, even though she had high marks in school. Blithewold Archives.

[3] Kahlil Gibran was born in Lebanon and moved to Boston as a young child with his mother. Miss Haskell taught him English and tutored him for many years, ultimately providing the funds for Gibran to study painting and drawing for two years in Paris.

capitals of Europe for young women, with a focus on the study of art and history. It was agreed that Dorothy Pardee, Frank and Kate's daughter and Marjorie's closest friend, should go too. Miss Helen pointed out that for travel and accommodation purposes four people would be better than three. She asked if another client might join the party, and Bessie agreed to the new arrangement. Gertrude Vaughn from Wilkes Barre was the same age as Marjorie, and the three young women got along exceedingly well. Gertrude subsequently became a regular visitor to Blithewold and was a bridesmaid at Marjorie's wedding 11 years later.

Chapter VII

EUROPEAN TOUR, 1903

On June 6, 1903, the three young women and their chaperone boarded the *Deutschland*, a luxury ocean liner of the Hamburg Amerika Line, and holder of the "Blue Riband of the Atlantic" award for speed and luxury.

Hamburg Amerika Line's Deutschland[1]

Bessie and William McKee were at the dockside in New York to wave goodbye as Marjorie set off on her eleven-month adventure. Every comfort was thought of and provided for on board, and there was constant entertainment, including parties and dances every night. The famous opera singer, Ernestine Schumann Heinke, gave a concert one evening. Marjorie, who had been invited to dine at the Captain's table, described the Captain's Dinner, the highlight of the voyage:

---

[1] Postcard in the Blithewold Archives.

The room was decorated with the flags of the nations, and on every table were fascinating flags and all manner of festive "set pieces" — statues of Liberty, etc. As dessert time drew near, all the lights were extinguished and an illuminated model of the Deutschland *was let down in the middle of the room and all the waiters came in (80 of them) single file, and each wearing cocked hat and the German colors and carrying a lighted torch and a big platter of ice cream with illuminated Swiss cottages as a garnish. They marched round and round the lovely tables making a most picturesque scene...Then we had "crackers" and wee flags passed round as souvenirs. Learned Doctors appeared in paper caps, and everyone went back to their childish days and had a jolly time.[1]*

EUROPE

The first stop on the tour was Paris, where the group stayed at the Normandie Hotel near the Opera House. Marjorie visited the Louvre several times and began to develop a new appreciation for European art. From Paris they went to London, following a popular tourist route from there to Oxford, Stratford, Warwick, Chester, North Wales, Loch Katrin in the Highlands of Scotland, Edinburgh, Roslyn, and Melrose. Marjorie wrote letters and postcards home every week — dozens of pages in each letter, full of descriptions of her travel experiences, the hotels, the people she met, the architecture and the gardens, and her own observations on the culture and traditions of the different European countries. Everywhere they went they were armed with their trusty *Baedeker* guides (popular travel books of the time), letters of introduction, and addresses for the nearest Thomas Cook's travel office where they could pick up their mail from home and draw cash on their letters of credit.

---

[1] Marjorie Van Wickle to Bessie Pardee McKee, June 11, 1903. Blithewold Archives.

In London they attended a gala performance in Covent Garden in honor of Emile Loubet, the first French president to visit London after Edward VII introduced the Entente Cordiale. The young American women were afraid their dresses would be unsuitable since the tickets said "Evening Dress Required," so they took a pair of scissors with them in case they needed to cut their bodices low in front to make them look like evening gowns! They need not have worried, however: their dresses were fine, and from their excellent front-row balcony seats they were able to look out over the distinguished audience and admire the gowns and jewels and the dashing uniforms.

From England they traveled across the North Sea to Norway, Sweden, and Denmark, then south to Germany and Austria, visiting museums and attending concerts and operas in all the major cities. When they arrived in Venice in September, Marjorie began a love affair with Italy that was to last the rest of her life.

Her first impressions of Venice were poetic. As she walked out of the train station she gasped as she caught her first glimpse of the Grand Canal:

We could hardly believe our eyes. All the picturesque old Venetian palaces were there spread out before us, such as we had dreamt of all our lives, and at our feet lay a gondola ready to take us and our trunks to the Hotel. A more fairy-like ride I never had — the soft cushioned gondola with its graceful rowers and gorgeous blue of the canal. It was perfect weather, warm like mid-summer, and as we wound in and out of the labyrinth of piccolo canali and under the quaint stone bridges and looked up at the soft tinted houses with their vine covered balconies, I thought it must be very like Heaven... [The next day] *we breakfasted looking out over the Grand Canal and watched gondolas gliding up and down with their slender black hulls and white-suited gondoliers.[1]*

They stayed at the Grand Hotel across the Grand Canal from the Santa Margarita Church. They dined at Florian's, bought embroidered linens at Jesurum's, and took afternoon tea at Caffe Quadri's[2] — all in St. Mark's Square with its magnificent views of the cathedral of San Marco.

Their next stop was Florence, where they stayed for 6 weeks, soaking up the art, studying the Medicis, and taking great pleasure in the people and the architecture. Based at the Hotel de la Ville on the Arno River, they took trips into the surrounding hills, to Fiesole, Siena, Pisa, Perugia, Assisi, and Orvieto, visiting churches, gardens, and museums, as well as studying the history of the country with Miss Macartnay.

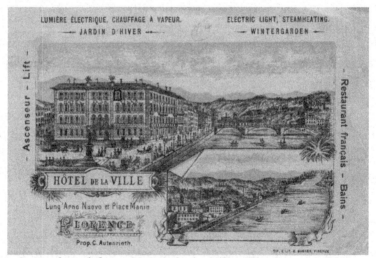

Letterhead from Hotel de la Ville, Florence, 1903[3]

---

[1] Marjorie Van Wickle to Bessie Van Wickle McKee, September 1903. Blithewold Archives.

[2] All of these establishments are still doing business in St. Mark's Square today.

[3] Careful scrutiny of the letterhead shows the window that Marjorie marked as her room at the hotel on the top floor where it faces the Place Manin.

Europe expanded Marjorie's understanding of art and music, and she began to see art in a completely different way. She wrote *"Do you remember that I used to say I didn't like Art Galleries? Well, I've changed my mind for good and all!"*[1]

After Florence, they traveled to Rome, and from there they journeyed south to Sorrento, Naples, Pompeii, Taormina, and Amalfi. Bessie saved all the *"postales"* that Marjorie sent to her from Europe and put them into albums, creating a pictorial souvenir of the trip. The albums are preserved in the Archives at Blithewold.

At the end of 1903, first Dorothy and then Gertrude left the party to return to America. Marjorie and Miss Macartnay returned to Rome and spent Christmas 1903 at the Hotel Russie — Marjorie's first Christmas away from home. They bought flowers for their rooms from flower sellers on the Spanish Steps, and enjoyed the Italian festivities. On their last day they threw coins into the Trevi Fountain to ensure their return to Rome. Marjorie had asked for and received permission from her parents to stay on in Europe and to add on a 3-month trip to Egypt.

EGYPT

On January 11, 1904, Marjorie and Helen Macartnay traveled south by train to Brindisi, Italy, and from there they set sail for Alexandria, Egypt. From Alexandria they took another train on a 3-hour journey to Cairo. The intrepid travelers spent a week at the historic Shepheard's Hotel in Cairo, where it was said that if you sat long enough on the terrace there, you would see the world go by. Marjorie wrote, *"I never sat long enough!"* Hiring a dragoman[2] to take care of them, they visited mosques and bazaars, silk shops and carpet weavers. Marjorie was fascinated to see how large silk carpets were

---

[1] Marjorie Van Wickle to Bessie Van Wickle McKee, June 22, 1903. Blithewold Archives.
[2] Egyptian guide and interpreter.

woven, the loom stretched right out into the street, the weavers walking up and down weaving with huge shuttles. With great excitement they boarded the famous paddle steamer *Rameses the Great* for their journey up the River Nile to Luxor and Aswan. *"We have got our single rooms on the <u>upper</u> deck of the Rameses Great,"* wrote Marjorie. *"The very ones we wanted — they are on the sunny side and the best cabins on the boat."*[1]

They stopped off to see almost every palace on the river, in each place hiring donkey-boys to guide them. In the Valley of the Kings, Marjorie was given a donkey named "George Washington," and her donkey-boy taught her a poem in Arabic, which pleased her immensely. She later proudly repeated it to their head dragoman, who was horrified. *"Oh Miss,"* he said, *"You must never say that again!"*[2]

Marjorie on board the Nile steamer, Rameses the Great, *1904*

---

[1] Marjorie Van Wickle to Bessie Van Wickle McKee, January 17, 1904. Blithewold Archives.
[2] *Reminiscences by Marjorie Van Wickle Lyon in her 90th Year,* as told to her niece Marjorie Shaw Jeffries. Blithewold Archives.

The highlight of the steamer trip was a visit to the great temple of Abu Simbel, which they saw first at sunset and then later by moonrise. On February 11, Marjorie got up at 4:30 a.m. to see the temple and its huge regal carvings at daybreak. As the sun came up she saw:

> *...beam after beam slowly creeping down the mountainside until the crowns, and then the faces, and finally the whole of the great figures were lit to a blaze of glory. Was it imagination, or did they really smile when the sun's rays first kissed them?[1]*

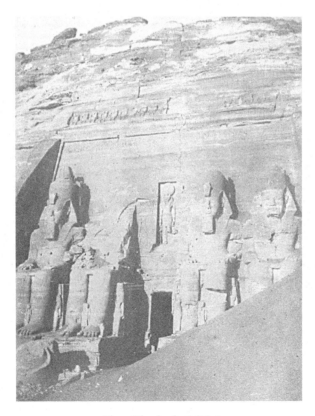

Abu Simbel, 1904

---

[1] Letter from Marjorie to Bessie, February 21, 1904. Blithewold Archives.

The next stop was the Island of Philae, near the first Cataract in Upper Egypt, where Marjorie found one of the loveliest temples in the country. The temple had withstood two thousand years of visitors and wars, but when the Aswan Dam was built in 1898 the temple had been flooded and was now threatened with total destruction. Marjorie and Miss Macartnay floated through the temple and its courts in small boats, between the columns, admiring the grace and beauty of the buildings reflected in the water.[1] (Many years later, the temple was stabilized and moved to higher ground.)

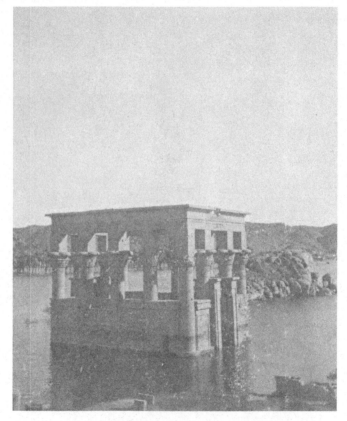

Philae – Jewel of the Nile, 1904

---

[1] Marjorie to Bessie, February 21, 1904: *"...going in boats through courts and pylons ...the reflections in the water were truly lovely."* Blithewold Archives.

At the hotel in Aswan, Marjorie and Miss Helen were asked to sit at the same dining table as an English gentleman and his two daughters (*"Luckily they were very nice!"*). He was Sir William Preece,[1] a famous British scientist. In February 1904, Marjorie wrote:

In the evening we sat with the Preeces and had the greatest of treats for Sir William took us up to his room, and in the dark showed us his precious atom of "radium." It was under a microscope — so tiny that you couldn't see it at all by the naked eye. As we looked though we could see a substance like silver fire, shining and seething. It was very still for an instant, but kept rippling like the surface of the water, and sending out curious little seaweed-like fingers in all directions. It was most interesting. It's the nearest thing to perpetual motion they have ever found, Sir William Preece says; he told us lots about it, if I could only remember it. But I couldn't even understand but half. I know that it's made from a mineral substance called Pitch Blend that is found in Germany and that a ton of it, after being reduced and reduced and all the unusable part thrown away, makes a very small fraction of an ounce of Radium.[2]

Marjorie had unknowingly witnessed a tangible illustration of an important scientific discovery.

Back in Cairo, they took land carts to see the great pyramids and the Sphinx. Marjorie was so moved by the Sphinx that she went

---

[1] Sir William Preece was one of the few scientists to support Guglielmo Marconi in his quest for wireless communication. Sir William supported him financially, and encouraged him in the face of fierce opposition and efforts to discredit him. In 1903 Marconi had made the first transatlantic telephone call, from Cape Cod, 3,000 miles across the ocean, to King Edward VII in London. From Erik Larson, *Thunderstruck,* Crown Publishers, 2006, p. 240.
[2] Letter from Marjorie to her mother Bessie, February 1904. Blithewold Archives. Radium had been discovered by Marie Curie in1898.

back later to see it by moonlight: *"I sat down on the sand beneath her feeling awed at the great presence."*[1]

Rameses II, Luxor

When Marjorie arrived back in New York on May 5, 1904, after having been away for eleven months, her family was at the dock to greet her. She was returning a wiser young woman, with a lifelong devotion to travel, music, and art. And she was already planning her next trip to Europe.[2] In the meantime, though, she was only too happy to spend the summer of 1904 at her beloved Blithewold, entertaining her friends and cousins, playing tennis, and sailing.

---

[1] *Reminiscences by Marjorie Van Wickle Lyon in her 90th Year*, as told to her niece, Marjorie Shaw Jeffries. Blithewold Archives.
[2] In many of the letters written to Bessie during the trip of 1903–1904, Marjorie suggests that the whole family might do the trip together so that they could share her experiences.

Chapter VIII

HOME AGAIN

THE FITZ RANDOLPH GATES AT PRINCETON

In August 1904 Bessie had a letter from Woodrow Wilson who was then the president of Princeton University, assuring her that plans for the Gates at Princeton were progressing well. They were being designed by Charles McKim of McKim, Mead & White. Woodrow Wilson wrote:

I think Professor Hibben showed you the beautiful English gates we were thinking of copying. Mr. McKim modified them for our use, and the result is a most beautiful design which will give extraordinary dignity to the front of the campus...we are hoping that the stone work may be completed as we wished before frost comes. We are all extremely glad to have got this important matter underway. We have for a long time been looking forward very eagerly to the erection of these gates, as the only thing needed to complete the beauty of the older part of the Princeton grounds.[1]

The installation and dedication were planned for the following summer. The decision was made to name the gates "The Fitz Randolph Gates," in honor of Augustus's ancestor. The wording on the gates themselves reads "1905 Gift of Augustus Van Wickle to Commemorate Nathaniel Fitz Randolph of Princeton, Donor of the Original Campus." The gates were officially opened in June 1905, by Marjorie. Bessie and William McKee were in attendance, along with the college's president, Woodrow Wilson, and former President of the United States, Grover Cleveland.

---

[1] Woodrow Wilson to Bessie Van Wickle McKee, August 23, 1904. Blithewold Archives.

The Fitz Randolph Gates at Princeton University

Later that summer, Bessie and Marjorie began to plan a grand party to celebrate Marjorie's twenty-first birthday on September 12, 1904, at Blithewold. Guest lists were made and invitations sent. George Lyon's name appears on a preliminary list of invitees but it was crossed out, perhaps because he was not able to attend. (This is the first time that George's name is mentioned in the Blithewold Archives.) The two hundred invited guests came from New York, Hazleton, Boston, and New Jersey. Bessie's friend, Belle Grier, wrote afterward:

> *None of us shall ever be able to forget all the beautiful things crowded into the days, and the 12th September, and I'm glad to have those beautiful memories...I do hope you are getting rested and that you will not collapse now that it is all over — but I'm sure you must feel that it was all the greatest success possible.*[1]

---

[1] Belle Grier to Bessie Van Wickle McKee, September 14, 1904. Blithewold Archives.

And Marjorie's friend from Boston, George Clarke, wrote to Bessie,

> *...a delightful visit replete with pleasure from start to finish. I shall long remember your daughter's birthday and the charming hospitality of Blithewold. It seems a happy augur that you and Mr. McKee have...made her coming of age a day of happiness not only for her but for all her, and your, friends.[1]*

The McKees spent New Year 1905 in Hazleton with Marjorie and Augustine. But instead of staying at the Pardee Mansion as they usually did, they returned to the house at 175 North Church Street that had been the Van Wickle family home. Bessie wrote to Estelle Clements on January 6, 1905:

> *We have had a beautiful time — the being in this dear house has been lovely. You would be amazed, as we all were, to see how sweet and homelike it has been. It did not seem possible that we had been away for so long. But now that the time has come for our leaving it, it makes another heartache — I am sad at leaving.[2]*

Two years later, after Bessie purchased the house on Commonwealth Avenue in Boston, she decided to sell the Hazleton house. She wrote to Estelle,

> *I am glad to have sold the house to the Bullocks, for while we did not get what I would like for the house, still it is worth a good deal to have nice people in the house. I will enjoy thinking of them there for I know they have a lovely home life.[3]*

---

[1] George L. Clarke to Bessie Van Wickle McKee, September 14, 1904. Blithewold Archives.
[2] Bessie to Estelle Clements, January 6, 1905. Blithewold Archives.
[3] Bessie to Estelle Clements, February 8, 1907. Blithewold Archives.

EUROPE 1906

Marjorie's extended trip to Europe in 1903 and 1904 had inspired in her a life-long desire to travel. In the spring of 1906, Marjorie and Bessie went to Paris, where they rented an apartment near the Arc de Triomphe for three months. Marjorie's favorite cousin, Dorothy Pardee, went with them, and Priscilla Harding (Marjorie's close friend from Miss Vinton's School) joined them for a time. Marjorie was anxious to show her mother all the wonderful things she had seen in 1903. At some point during their stay in Paris, Bessie met and befriended a Mlle. Minot. Mlle. Minot became very fond of Bessie and Marjorie and organized a dinner party to introduce them to some of her friends. Marjorie said later, *"I particularly remember that dinner because each person had a little menu on a silver stand."*[1] Included in the party were Monsieur and Madame Nayral de Puybusque, who became close friends of Bessie and Marjorie. They brought their daughter Irma, who was the same age as Marjorie and was training to become an opera singer. On the day before their return to America, Bessie invited Irma to go back with them and spend the summer at Blithewold. Irma, who spoke not a word of English, was ecstatic and sailed with them to New York on what was to be the first of many visits to Blithewold. Irma and Marjorie became dear friends, sharing many adventures and travels over the years. (When Marjorie married George Lyon in 1914, Irma was a bridesmaid and sang at the wedding service. Hers was the voice that many spoke of afterward as "the beautiful voice of an opera singer coming from the Bosquet.")

FIRE DESTROYS BLITHEWOLD I

Bessie and Marjorie and their guest Irma arrived at Blithewold from Europe on the evening of June 7, 1906. One can only imagine Marjorie and Bessie's excitement at being home, seeing Augustine, William McKee, and Estelle Clements again, and introducing Irma to

---

[1] *Reminiscences of Marjorie Van Wickle Lyon in her 90th Year,* as told to her niece Marjorie Shaw Jeffries. Blithewold Archives.

everyone. Bessie would have been anxious, no doubt, to check on some renovations on the south wing of the house that had been undertaken in her absence in preparation for the summer season, including the installation of new electrical wiring.

The next day, Friday, June 8, dawned bright and clear, with a southwest wind. At around noon, Bessie's maid Katrina called to William McKee that a fire had broken out high up in the ceiling of the third floor of the servants' wing. It appeared to be an electrical fire that was trapped between the ceiling and the roof. Will and Marjorie did what they could with fire buckets, while Katrina ran to summon help. The fire brigade came quickly, but their engines were small and hand-operated. The family had been about to sit down to lunch, and Marjorie wrote afterward *"The table had been set for lunch. I remember the butler had brought out the butter balls and I watched as they gradually faded away."[1]*

The fire was burning very slowly, but the firemen could not muster enough water pressure to reach the flames. They ran hoses down to the Bay and took water from the underground cisterns, but it was soon clear that the house could not be saved. By this time, many people from Bristol had arrived on the scene to offer help, including the employees from the Herreshoff boat-building company who had been working less than a mile away on Ferry Road. They brought their tools and helped organize volunteers to start taking everything out of the house. First to be brought out were personal possessions. China, silver, crystal, and furniture and furnishings were then carried out carefully and stacked on the lawns. One maid carried silver tableware outside in the coal scuttle, and someone else saved May Blossom, Augustine's favorite doll.[2] Marjorie had the task of taking all the glassware out to safety. She used tablecloths to carry the crystal and was very proud that nothing had broken. The men still had time to

---

[1] *Reminiscences of Marjorie Van Wickle Lyon in her 90th Year,* as told to her niece Marjorie Shaw Jeffries. Blithewold Archives.
[2] May Blossom can be seen on display periodically in the Nursery at Blithewold.

start removing fireplaces, bathtubs, paneling, and stairways, working feverishly on the north side of the house even as the roof was crashing down on the south side. Of particular sentimental value was the Blithewold Stone, which had been set into the Living Room fireplace. Bertie Chesebrough (a boat designer at Herreshoff) chiseled it out and carried it to safety, becoming the hero of the day. Estelle Clements wrote in her diary:

> *All Bristol turned out, and Mr. Herreshoff sent his foreman and 30 men with tools, who took out mantelpieces, the library shelves, etc. So most everything on the first and second floor were saved except things in the kitchen and laundry, and some things from the servants' bedrooms. Bertie Chesebrough dug out the Blithewold Stone in the living room mantel. There was no undue excitement and everyone was cool and worked well.[1]*

Many years later, George Howe of Bristol wrote to Marjorie of his memories of that day. He was seven years old, and had been playing with a friend in a garden on Hope Street when he saw the fire engines rush by. The two boys immediately jumped on their bicycles and followed the engines to Blithewold. Young George witnessed the whole drama:

> *I recall well the day of the fire...Harleigh Tingley and I had been roughhousing in the big yard on the southeast corner of Hope and Union Streets, where my grandmother lived, one summer noon, when the fire engines dashed by with horns and sirens blowing. When at the house itself, your mother [Bessie] was greeting her friends with complete self-control, though her house was blazing away behind the clump of trees where she was standing...But I well remember her dignity and regal bearing through what must have been a harrowing experience for her.[2]*

---

[1] Estelle Clements' Diary, June 8, 1904. Blithewold Archives.
[2] George Howe to Marjorie Van Wickle Lyon, January 16, 1974. Blithewold Archives.

John DeWolf was among the many people who came rushing down from Bristol to help. He set to work immediately, soaking sacks with water and spreading them over plantings near the house to protect them.

Blithewold I burning, June 8, 1906

The roof caves in. Note the bathtub on the lawn

Five hours later, when the fire had finally burned itself out, little remained in the smoldering rubble except for the stone chimneys. The family, all their possessions gathered around them on the Great Lawn, suddenly realized that they had nowhere to stay that night. The Gardner House to the south of Blithewold had been rented out,[1] since they had thought they would not need it that summer. Friends and neighbors offered accommodation, and family members were parceled out. Bessie and William McKee stayed at the Burnside house, just across Ferry Road on land now owned by Roger Williams University. Estelle stayed with the head gardener, John Best, and his wife. (John Best's cottage, which still stands in the northeast part of the garden near the Greenhouse, had mercifully been saved. When flames jumped from the trees in the Bosquet to the roof of the cottage, quick-thinking firemen opened up the large underground cistern near the Cutting Gardens and managed to save the cottage.) Augustine and Marjorie and their shocked guest Irma went to stay with the Herreshoffs. The Herreshoff boys fell in love with Irma, but, unfortunately for them, they could not speak a word of French and she couldn't speak English. Eventually everyone moved to the Burnside house, but it was not large enough to accommodate the house-party guests that the McKees had invited before the house burned. William McKee rose to the occasion — he erected a large, beautiful Assyrian tent that he had purchased at the World's Columbian Exposition in Chicago in 1893. Irma indicated that she would like to sleep in the tent, but spent a restless night, *"terrified that the 'Peaux Rouges' (Red Indians) were going to come and murder her in the night because she was sleeping in a tent in America!"*[2]

---

[1] The Gardner house had been rented to the Monks family, friends of the McKees from Boston. Grace Monks was a friend of Marjorie's.

[2] *Reminiscences by Marjorie Van Wickle Lyon in her 90th Year,* as told to her niece, Marjorie Shaw Jeffries. Blithewold Archives.

After the fire, 1906

William McKee (right) standing by the ruined north tower, 1906

BUILDING BLITHEWOLD II

Within a few days, Bessie and William McKee invited an architect to come to Bristol to help them start making plans to rebuild. The architect, Walter Kilham of Kilham & Hopkins, Boston, had just finished the two-year restoration of the McKees' house on Commonwealth Avenue, and Bessie had been very pleased with his work. At first everyone seemed to agree that the house should be rebuilt as an exact replica of the original, using the architectural elements saved from the burning house. Walter Kilham began to sketch floor plans of the house from his and Bessie and Will's memories, and from those sketches he formulated new working plans.[1]

Some months later, however, Bessie had second thoughts: she thought the new Blithewold should be more solid, and certainly more fireproof, so she asked Kilham to submit suggestions for a totally new design. Kilham's partner, James Hopkins, was something of an Anglophile, and he spent part of each year in England where he witnessed the English Arts and Crafts Movement first-hand. The English Country Manor style was revitalized as part of that Movement, and James Hopkins embraced this design as eminently desirable for the wealthy classes of America. The houses were typically built of rough stone with steep pitched roofs and medieval ornamentation, and this was the architects' recommendation for the new Blithewold. The design suggested that both patron and architect were up-to-date in their thinking, and that they subscribed to an acceptable aesthetic taste. The choice of Arts and Crafts style bore witness to Bessie's personality and illuminated her social aspirations. She rejected ostentation and pretension; rather, she wanted the house was to be a comfortable family home, a place where her guests could relax. Kilham & Hopkins' plan was approved, and stone for the façade was brought from the old Van Wickle mine in Coleraine, Pennsylvania. In the interests of safety, extra fireproof

---

[1] Walter Kilham's *"rough floor plan of Blithewold I from memory"* is preserved at Blithewold.

materials were used wherever possible in the construction, and fire-stops were installed in all the interior walls. This is the house that remains today.

Because the family loved outdoor pursuits, the very architecture of the mansion ensured that its occupants were constantly aware of the house's magnificent setting on Narragansett Bay. Blithewold II is long and narrow, built on a north–south axis so that all the main rooms face west to the water. (Since the dining room and the living room are the full width of the mansion, large windows on the east walls allow beautiful views also — of the front lawn and the trees growing there.) French doors lead out to west-facing terraces and porches from all the main first-floor rooms, and large windows frame the glorious sunsets. Off the second-floor master bedroom is a large sleeping porch that was used regularly by the family until as late as November.

Blithewold II under construction, 1907

EUROPE 1908

In the spring of 1908, as builders and decorators were putting the finishing touches to the new Blithewold, Marjorie and Louise Smith returned to Europe, taking Estelle Clements with them. The trip was a Christmas gift to Estelle from Bessie and William McKee. The small party sailed in February from New York on the S.S. *Caronia*, one of the largest and most elegant vessels in the Cunard fleet. Their first stop: Madeira. Marjorie thought that Madeira was the nicest place she had ever seen:

> *We sighted the island at about 4 on Tuesday, and it seemed just like an enchanted isle rising "mist-crowned" from the sea. We gazed quite steadily from four until seven thirty, and even then could scarcely eat any dinner! If I seem to rave over Madeira it's only the way I feel — never was there such a wonderful place, nor such heavenly climate.*[1]

She went on to describe, in enthusiastic detail, the pink and grey rocks, the light green of the sugar cane, and the darker green of the trees. She described hedges of freesia, and masses of begonias, magnolias, heliotrope, camellias, and roses. Estelle Clements described wild canaries singing in the streets and gardens, and the abundant wild, rich purple bougainvillea.

Still on the *Caronia*, they cruised to Gibraltar where they spent a day on land, after which the ship skirted the coast for several days, stopping off at Cannes, Nice, Monte Carlo, and Mentone. Marjorie and Louise enjoyed being with their chaperone Estelle, teasing her that *they* were the ones chaperoning *her* when she spent hours on end sitting with an Episcopal Rector on the boat deck! They reported:

> *Aunt Dellie is a perfect chaperone — so enthusiastic and always ready to do anything. We trot her round in the sun and the rain, from morning till night, and every minute she's*

---

[1] Marjorie Van Wickle to Bessie Van Wickle McKee, February 27, 1908. Blithewold Archives.

more appreciative and excited even than we are. Really, we two girls couldn't have a nicer or dearer chaperone.[1]

Marjorie wrote to Bessie suggesting that the whole family take the same trip on the *Caronia* in 1910, but that then they should stay for at least *six* weeks in Madeira.

The travelers left the ship in Naples, and after a few days spent touring the city they took the overnight train to Rome where they stayed at the Hotel Russie, Marjorie's favorite hotel from her 1903 trip. There they all, and especially Estelle, enjoyed the hotel's Winter Garden:

A most attractive place like a conservatory of glass with a framework of iron. The furniture is of wicker, white and green, and there are many flowering plants and palms put high up on pedestals. The azaleas are large and branching...a band plays for an hour or more after dinner, and some persons have coffee there and smoke.[2]

The Winter Garden at the Hotel Russie, 1906, with "wicker furniture" and "palms high up on pedestals"

---

[1] Marjorie Van Wickle to Bessie Van Wickle McKee, March 8, 1908. Blithewold Archives.
[2] From Estelle Clements' diary, March 5, 1908. Blithewold Archives.

They were joined at the Hotel Russie by Louise's brother Sibley Smith and his wife Ethel. They all bought flowers at the Spanish Steps and filled the washbasins in their rooms with yellow daisies, mignonettes, crimson anemones, white and pink freesias, and ferns. Marjorie acted as *"Baedeker* guide," leading the group to all the wonderful places she remembered — the Sistine Chapel, the Borghese Gardens, and the Piazza di Spagna. They went to Hadrian's Villa, the Villa Borghese, and the Villa d'Este. Every afternoon they had tea and cakes at Aragno's Tea Room, and at the end of their sojourn in Rome they all went to the Trevi Fountain and threw in their pennies to bring them good luck and guarantee their return to Rome someday.

Sibley Smith decided to rent an automobile, *"a fine Richarde Brasier 40 horse power,"* to take everyone on the next part of their journey, a leisurely drive to Orvieto. The automobile trip was deemed a huge success —*"An automobile is the way to see Italy, surely."*[1] They wound their way north through the hill towns of Caprarola, Viterbo, and Orvieto. At Viterbo they walked around the beautiful gardens of the Villa Lante in the pouring rain, and then bought postcards to send home.[2] In a restaurant there, they sat with a *scaldino*, or heater, under the table to dry their skirts and shoes as much as possible as they ate lunch, before setting out again.

Their favorite hill town was Orvieto, where they had to coax their car up the steep and winding streets. Marjorie wrote,

> *Orvieto is unused to Automobiles! We had to wait on the very steepest part while an old peasant woman climbed out of her donkey cart in terror and took to the woods, and an old horse who ran full tilt up the street refusing to be caught or comforted — until someone finally shooed him into a grocery*

---

[1] Marjorie Van Wickle to Bessie Van Wickle McKee, March 28, 1908. Blithewold Archives.
[2] The postcards are now part of the Postcard Collection in the Blithewold Archives.

shop where he hid his head among the preserved fruit and was happy![1]

Reluctantly leaving the car at Orvieto, they traveled the rest of the way to Florence by train. Their large sunny rooms at the Pensione Lelli (on Via Palestro 13) were filled with flowers and had wonderful views. Florence seemed even more magical than Marjorie remembered, and they looked forward to five or six weeks exploring and studying. They immediately picked up their letters from home. A letter from Bessie told them how busy she was in Bristol arranging all the last-minute details of decorating the new Blithewold so that they could all spend the summer there. Marjorie replied,

Oh, Mother, dear, do be careful and not get so many headaches and so much tired. I want to come home and find you well, and ready for a happy summer in the new house. Don't you dare write me a bit oftener than you really have time for. Of course the letters do mean a lot to me — but you're not being tired is infinitely more important. Your grand long letter has come and I am oh, so delighted with it. I know you must have tired yourself to give me all that pleasure — but I don't know whether to scold or not, for I did so love every word of it![2]

Marjorie and Louise arranged to take fencing lessons three times a week, and they all took Italian conversation classes every day. Estelle wrote in her diary, *"I think that I am making some progress."*[3] They studied the colorful history of the Medicis, *"their pomp and processions, their conspiracies and intrigues."*[4] They went day after day to the Uffizi to study the paintings there; to the Santa Maria Novella church to see the Cimabue frescoes; to the San Lorenzo to see the Medici tombs carved by Michelangelo; and to the Bargello to see the

---

[1] Marjorie Van Wickle to Bessie Van Wickle McKee, March 28, 1908. Blithewold Archives.
[2] Ibid.
[3] Estelle Clements's diary. Blithewold Archives.
[4] Ibid.

Donatellos. Most of all, Marjorie loved the frescoes by Fra Angelico at the Convent of San Marco, her favorite one being *The Annunziation* at the top of the stairs leading to the monks' cells. She purchased a print of the fresco from a stand in the piazzetta nearby.[1]

Armed with their letters of introduction, the three women began to make calls on the American ex-patriot community in Florence. They paid a call on Miss Florence Blood, an American artist who lived at Villa Gamberai in Fiesole; there they saw the most beautiful gardens and magnificent views of the hills

At the end of each busy day they went to Giacosa's — the famous tea salon that Marjorie had frequented in 1903: *"Giacosa's is such a gay amusing caffe — we never get tired of going there, drinking our chocolate, eating the delectable cakes, and gazing at the people."*[2] There, they invariably met other traveling Americans and exchanged recommendations of worthwhile trips and good hotels, as well as news from home.

Giacosa's Tea Salon, Florence, ca. 1908

---

[1] Taken from Estelle's diary, and letters from Estelle and Marjorie to Bessie, March and April 1908, Blithewold Archives. The print is in the Archives at Blithewold.
[2] Marjorie Van Wickle to Bessie Van Wickle McKee, April 19, 1908. Blithewold Archives.

One memorable day in April, after Sibley and Ethel had left for San Remo on the Italian Riviera, Marjorie, Louise, and Estelle arranged for a car and driver to take them to Volterra. Before they left, they took a photograph of the red car waiting for them outside the Pensione Lelli. This car would feature prominently in one of the great adventures of their trip.

Estelle, Marjorie, and Louise in the Red Car outside Pension Lelli, 1908

They had a wonderful day. On the way home, though, an incident took place that Marjorie described in detail to Bessie:

> *About six or eight miles from Volterra, in the midst of this wild mountain scenery, our automobile coughed a few times, gasped and stopped: no gasoline! So here we were, stranded in the country. Can you imagine a more perfectly shipwrecked feeling! But nobody seemed to mind in the least. The chauffeur went trotting off up the road and after*

an hour or so came back with a wine bottle under each arm full of "benzina." It was only by great good luck he got those two small bottles full. Of course, they didn't last us long. About a half hour later we slowed up ominously and stopped again. This time the chauffeur was rather in despair and started off to get some oxen to tow us! So the getting up the two or three miles of winding steep road to the top of the hills was done by oxen. We were actually pulled slowly but surely by those patient willing beasts. I have never seen a more amusing sight (we girls walked all the way, so we could admire it!) There was the red car with the chauffeur almost wringing his hands in humiliation, and Aunt Dellie beside him. Then in front, a cart with the little boy beating the oxen, and then the beautiful white beasts themselves led by a man and a rope. Really, that was an experience.[1]

They had another interesting "Italian travel" experience on the day they were to leave Florence by train to go to Venice. Marjorie had been to Cook's the day before to check on the time of departure of the train, and she had been told it would leave at 3 p.m. However, a friend who had just made the trip said 2:38, and Signor Lelli from Pension Lelli said 2:38. Finally, in desperation, Marjorie went to the Bankers: *"Oh yes, there is a train at 1:45 — no I believe it may be 2:45."* So they went to the station early and got on a train at 2:38, only to be hustled out by a guard who said that the train didn't go to Venice and then to be hustled back on at the last minute because it *did* go to Venice, after all! But Marjorie took it all in stride and commented, *"Travelling in Italy is a great sport."*

---

[1] Marjorie Van Wickle to Bessie Van Wickle McKee, April 19, 1908. Blithewold Archives.

Marjorie's postcard of San Marco, Venice

Estelle loved Venice, particularly San Marco: *"Really, that old cathedral with its quaint domes and its glorious coloring stands alone before all the world in its architecture and its charm."*[1] In Piazza San Marco they unexpectedly ran into Marjorie's cousin from Hazleton, Emily Markle, and they all had tea together at Café Florian on the Piazza. Estelle and her two young charges then took a guided tour of the Grand Canal, hearing about its history and then later reading accounts of the glorious palaces. They visited churches and libraries, soaking up the architecture and the art, particularly the works of Veronese and Tintoretto. After Venice, they traveled by train to Padua to see the Giotto and Mantegna frescoes and the Donatello bronzes.

---

[1] Estelle Clements to Bessie McKee, May 4, 1908. Blithewold Archives.

157

The last two weeks of the tour were spent in Paris where Marjorie was delighted to see Irma Nayral again. Also staying at their hotel were Marjorie's cousins May Earle and Gertrude Keller.[1] The young women had a wonderful time together, attending the ballet and the opera and the Nayrals' Matinée Musicale. They had appointments with dressmakers and hatters and the corset lady, who was *"doing her best to make us all three beautiful!"* It was a wonderful time to be in Paris — the horse-chestnuts were in bloom, also the lilacs, the laburnums, and the forget-me-nots. They went often to the Bois de Boulogne where they encountered poppies by the roadside. Marjorie remembered fondly her stay in Paris in 1906 and wished that Dorothy and Priscilla were with her again.[2] By the end of the trip, though, Marjorie and Estelle were surely anxious to return home to spend their first summer at the magnificent new Blithewold II.

---

[1] Gertrude was the daughter of Bessie's sister, Gertrude. It was Gertrude Keller who saved many of Ario Pardee's letters, and wrote the book *"Dear Pa —And So It Goes*. May Earle was the daughter of Bessie's sister Alice.
[2] Marjorie Van Wickle to Bessie McKee, May 12, 1908. Blithewold Archives.

Chapter IX

A NEW BLITHEWOLD

Blithewold II, 1908

A BEAUTIFUL NEW HOME

The new Blithewold, which was ready for occupancy in the early summer of 1908, used some of the architectural elements from the original Blithewold that had been stored in the barn after the fire. Unlike Blithewold I, which had been built specifically as a summer residence, Blithewold II was designed to be used year-round, having electricity throughout and coal-fired central heating, thus taking advantage of modern technology. Bessie and Will McKee now opened up Blithewold regularly during the winter — for Thanksgiving, Christmas, and Easter — and they would often drive down from Boston just for the day. Bessie continued her work in the gardens and helped design new garden spaces. Walter Kilham designed the garage complex that was built south of the mansion near Ferry Road. Two cottages, one at each end of the garage, were built there as staff housing for families.

The Entrance Hall, looking north, 1910

The center hall and staircase of the house were designed in the Colonial Revival style. As you stand in the center hallway you are surrounded by elaborate ceilings, fluted columns, dentil moldings, volutes, and three different patterns of balusters on the staircase. Large French doors open from the west side of the hall onto a Mercer-tiled loggia that in turn leads to a stone terrace overlooking the Great Lawn and Narragansett Bay. The long hallway runs the length of the house from south to north. (It was along this hallway that, many years later, Marjorie's dog, an Irish terrier named

Ballyhaise Bitters,[1] would be sent to announce that it was time to be seated for dinner. The maids in the kitchen would tuck a note under his collar and send him running to the Living Room, where Marjorie would retrieve the note and announce, *"Dinner is served."*)

Bessie chose English Oak for the paneling in the Dining Room. A plate rail above the paneling displays her collection of Delft and other rare pieces of china. Set in the wall over the fireplace is an interesting oil painting that shows a young woman with her suitor (attributed to the Italian Giorgione school).[2] The room is large enough to accommodate the dining table (with its many extension leaves) that was saved from the first house, along with its 18 chairs, matching vitrines, and side tables. A handsome buffet is built into the south wall.

The Dining Room, 1910

---

[1] Marjorie bred Irish terriers.
[2] This painting was recently cleaned by an art restorer.

Dinners were very formal, grand affairs. The ladies were required to wear long dresses, and dinner jackets were 'de rigueur' for the men. Bessie kept a Dinner Party Record Book in which she detailed the menu, the wines served, the floral decorations, and the choice of china, as well as a diagram of where the named guests were seated at the table. This room was the site of hundreds of family celebrations, including wedding feasts, engagement parties, Christmas celebrations, and birthday parties. An interesting tradition evolved at Blithewold in which guests and family wrote poems to commemorate special occasions, with the poems being read at the dinner table. Often, it was the guests' daytime activities — on the Bay, on the golf course, or in the gardens — that were recounted in poem or limerick form, with witty references to all the company present. Hundreds of these personalized tributes are preserved in the Blithewold Archives, some printed out and beautifully illustrated, others scribbled hurriedly in pencil on scraps of paper. In May, 1922, Marjorie wrote a toast to Bessie and Will to be read at their 21st anniversary dinner:

Mother's and Father's Anniversary

Although we did desert you to golf and tennis play

We've hurried back at sunset, to wish you well this day!

May future years all bring you Good Luck and joy and health;

A life chocked full of blessings, and just enough of wealth.

The past was mostly sunny — perhaps a shower or two,

But the future forecast reading says "All the sky's bright blue."

So here's to best of parent and host and hostess gay!

We've come to help you celebrate on this your wedding day.[1]

---

[1] Poem by Marjorie Lyon, May 1922. Blithewold Archives

The Breakfast Porch, 1910

Breakfast and luncheon were often served on the Breakfast
Porch on warm summer days. When Marjorie married George Lyon on
June 1, 1914, the wedding party dined in this room. In spring and
summer the large windows were replaced with screens, making it a
delightful garden-like space. It was kept filled with potted plants from
the greenhouse — camellias, Boston ferns, rubber plants, and palms.
Ivy climbed around the Italian white marble fountain in the niche on
the east wall. A handle in the Butler's Pantry activated the niche
fountain. The green-stained oak table is a draw-leaf style and opens
up to fill the entire room, and above the table is a patinated bronze
and glass grape-form Italian chandelier.

The Blithewold Stone in the Billiard Room of Blithewold II, ca. 1910

Pool was one of the billiard games that peaked in popularity between the 1890s and the 1920s, and the Billiard Room at Blithewold was a center of activity for the Van Wickle/McKee family. The pool table, made of rosewood and oak with ivory insets, was built around 1900. The lamps over the table are bronze with green glass. The Blithewold stone over the fireplace is the one that was saved from Blithewold I, where it had been set into the fireplace in the original Living Room.

Pool was taken very seriously at Blithewold — Schuyler Pardee, Marjorie's cousin, remembers that when he was a young boy kind Uncle Will McKee would allow him to watch the competitions amongst the men, as long as he didn't get in the way. The major players were Will McKee, George Lyon, and Quincy Shaw, but Marjorie herself had the reputation of being able to beat any of them.

This was Marjorie's favorite room at Blithewold, with its stunning views of the Great Lawn and Narragansett Bay, and of magnificent sunsets over the water. The elaborate design on the vaulted plaster ceiling is repeated on the carved oak mantelpiece. A photograph of William McKee's favorite yacht, *Chanticleer,* takes pride of place over the fireplace.

In the evenings, everyone would retire to the Living Room where comfort and hospitality were of paramount importance. In this room, more than in any other, Bessie's eclectic taste in furniture is evident, ranging from a seventeenth-century Dutch cabinet (where games were kept) to a "modern" 1910 Chickering piano. The guests might play parlor games or card games, or listen to music on the Victrola or the music box. Glass-fronted bookcases still hold leather-bound collections, and above them are watercolors by Louis K. Harlow and William Trost Richards. The beautiful classic mantelpiece is said to be from Gloucester House in London, once the residence of the Duke of Cambridge, a cousin of Queen Victoria. On warm evenings, guests could go out onto the West Porch to watch the sunsets, or onto the North Porch to view the gardens and the Bosquet.

The Living Room, 1910

SUMMER FUN

Augustine, Estelle Clements, and Marjorie at Blithewold, 1908

Entertaining resumed in earnest in 1908 as friends and family gathered at the new mansion. Children of all ages ran wild, giddy with the freedom afforded them at Blithewold where their parents were too occupied with each other to pay any attention to them.[1] Pardee cousins still remember exciting and daring (not to mention dangerous) activities, like climbing the west façade of the mansion from the terrace to the roof, using the gargoyles as handholds; playing with the starting-cannon and fireworks; and canoeing out to the passing Prudence Island ferry boat and "hanging on" for a ride.[2] Family legend has it that one day Frank Pardee, Jr., pulled his kayak up next to the ferry, climbed up over the rail of the ferry from his kayak, and went to greet the Captain on the deck. Meantime, panic ensued onboard when the Captain looked over the rail and saw the empty kayak bobbing on

---

[1] Conversation with Schuyler Pardee, Frank Pardee's grandson, summer 1995.
[2] Ibid.

the waves; he assumed at first that its young occupant had come to grief.[1]

Frank Pardee "riding the Prudence Island Ferry"[2]

Another popular challenge was to stand between the center columns on the terrace, and with one jump (and no hands) brace oneself with one's feet against the columns. This took a steady nerve and fine balance and was more difficult than it appears! It was Schuyler Pardee's favorite trick.

Schuyler Pardee "jumping the columns" at Blithewold

---

[1] Conversation with Nancy Pardee Abercrombie, Frank Pardee's daughter.
[2] Magnification of this photograph reveals a figure in the water behind Frank. This may be Augustine. It was known that the two of them enjoyed performing this "dare" together. An enlargement also shows a woman in a hat leaning over the side of the boat to see what was happening.

"THE HELP"

Blithewold and other large mansions of the era were built on the assumption that there would always be a plentiful supply of servants to run the estate. Bessie Van Wickle McKee could not have maintained her large residences without the physical labor, competence, and loyal dedication of several generations of household staff. Bessie was considered a generous and benevolent employer, both considerate and fair. She always referred to her staff respectfully as "the Help" rather than "the Servants." Some of Bessie's employees arrived and departed in quick succession, while others stayed with the family their entire working lives.

Blithewold Staff, 1908

The south wing of the mansion was devoted to the staff, both for work and for living. Besides the kitchens and laundry rooms, the south wing housed a staff dining room, a sitting room, a screened porch, seven bedrooms, and four bathrooms. Three cottages on the estate housed working couples and their children; a small cabin by the dock was home to the captain of the yacht *Marjorie*. Among the most loyal and long-time employees were head gardener John Best, English butler Frank Dallison, chauffeur and estate manager Arthur Rae, lady's maid Katrina Gluck, and cook Tilly McDonnell.

John Best, born in Ireland in 1862, was head gardener from 1898 until his retirement in 1928. John lived with his family, his wife and children Jack and Margaret, in the brown-shingled cottage near the greenhouse known as the North Cottage. John DeWolf designed the Blithewold landscape, but it was John Best who made it a reality. He maintained it for many years, always taking great pride in his work.

Frank Dallison was one of Blithewold's most colorful characters. Born in Leeds, England, in 1870, he began his employment as butler to the McKees in 1907, and he remained in their employ until the mid-1930s. Bessie wrote in December 1907 of him, *"Dallison is fine — better than Ellis in catering, and I like him personally much better. The household is running very smoothly."*[1] He was described as "lofty" and "dignified,"[2] desirable attributes for a proper English butler. His reputation was somewhat tarnished, however, by accusations of drunkenness and infidelity. An undated letter to Mr. McKee reported *"goings on in your house while you are away..."*[3]

Arthur Rae, who was hired as head coachman in 1906, lived first at the Gardner House and later in the south cottage of the garage complex with his wife Ingrid and their children Arthur and Eleanor. As

---

[1] Letter from Bessie to Estelle Clements, December 8, 1907. Blithewold Archives.
[2] From an interview with Eleanor Rae Gladding, October 12, 2007.
[3] The letter is in the Blithewold Archives.

means of transport changed and the McKees replaced their carriages with automobiles, Arthur Rae adapted easily, taking on the role of chauffeur. He was a dedicated, responsible, and adaptable employee, always at the family's disposal. He met trains and ferries and kept track of the voluminous pieces of guests' baggage. He drove the family to social engagements and transported household staff back and forth between the family's homes in Boston and Bristol. He also delivered produce from Blithewold's gardens to the family's townhouse on Commonwealth Avenue, and he was always responsible for the maintenance and fine appearance of Blithewold's many vehicles. (He even cleaned the cars of Blithewold guests and made sure they were filled up with oil and gasoline.) Arthur Rae drove and cared for a succession of large and expensive cars, from the Simplex and Locomobile to a Packard and Cadillac. When he died in 1953, Marjorie Lyon installed a plaque in the Rose Garden commemorating his 47 years of faithful service.

Arthur Rae in the Locomobile, outside the garage in 1913

Katrina Gluck was Bessie's personal maid for almost fifty years. She was with Bessie in Hazleton long before the first Blithewold was built, and she was still with the family as late as the mid-1930s — probably only leaving when Bessie died in 1936. It was Katrina who first noticed the smoke coming from the roof that heralded the total destruction of Blithewold I in 1906.

Tilly McDonnell, Blithewold's legendary cook, ruled the kitchen for more than forty years, often assisted by Mary Dwyer and Peggy Devine. Marjorie Shaw Jeffries, Bessie's granddaughter, recalls that *"Tilly fussed over whatever children happened to be visiting...she was always a very special person for me as she loved children and made us her friends. She would escort me through the kitchen and find little goodies along the way."[1]*

Marjorie's loyal household staff, still at Blithewold ca. 1970
Tilly, Mary, Mary, and Peggy

---

[1]From *Memory Vignettes of Blithewold* by Marjorie Shaw Jeffries. Blithewold Archives.

GEORGE ARMSTRONG LYON

While Marjorie was in Florence in 1908, she received a letter from an acquaintance, George Lyon, forwarded from Boston. George was then living on a ranch in Cody, Wyoming, for a year and was not aware that Marjorie was in Europe. He wanted to know if she would meet him when he returned to Boston even though they had been out of touch for quite some time. He wrote from Big Horn:

> *Dear Marjorie, It has been a long time since I have written to you — so long in fact, that it is rather hard to know how to explain writing now — a man who lets his friends alone so long shouldn't be allowed to make up to them whenever he happens to feel like it.*

Marjorie did allow him to make it up to her, though, and they embarked on a long, sometimes intense, correspondence. George's initial letter from Wyoming shows how far apart their lives had grown. He had gone west for adventure, and he described breathtaking views of the Rockies from the back door of his cabin and the smell of the crisp, crystal-clear air. At the same time he seemed to mock the kind of life he imagined Marjorie was leading:

> *I suppose you're busy with the usual Eastern winter sports, playing bridge, and going to parties and dinners and dances — meeting the same people and hearing the same trivial gossip. I did it until I got sick to death of it all...perhaps you've varied the monotony by getting engaged or married. Or perhaps you don't think it's as much of a bore as I do.*[1]

Marjorie may have felt somewhat chastened by his comments, but in her reply she told him about all her social activities. She had by then become part of a wealthy, carefree, socially prominent group in Boston, just the crowd George seemed to be disparaging. But, she had also been to Europe three times and was now a much more mature

---

[1] George Lyon to Marjorie Van Wickle, April 19, 1908. Blithewold Archives.

and socially comfortable young woman than the one George Lyon remembered.

Thus began a years-long courtship fraught with teasing, begging, and flirting, with George quite clearly falling desperately in love with Marjorie. Marjorie first encouraged and then rejected George, over and over, for the next six years. During that time she was being seriously pursued by at least two other young men, Roger Swain and Mac Sturgis, both from Boston.[1]

George Armstrong Lyon was born in 1878 in Erie, Pennsylvania, son of a Rear Admiral and grandson of an Episcopal Bishop. He went to Lawrenceville School in New Jersey, where he showed promise as a first-class tennis player. After graduating from Yale University in 1900, he went to Germany to study at the universities of Göttingen and Heidelberg. He eventually returned to America to study law at Harvard University. His natural ability in sports led to his nickname "Tiger Lyon," or simply "Tige," which nickname stuck with him for the rest of his life. He also held the distinction of having been tennis captain at both Yale and Harvard. It was probably while he was at law school at Harvard that he met Marjorie. They were certainly acquainted in 1904, but only as members of a large social group; and he was invited to weekends at Blithewold along with other friends from Boston. He joined the law firm of Lazear & Orr in Pittsburgh, Pennsylvania, a company owned by a relative, but he traveled to New York and Boston on business and always had plenty of old friends to meet up with wherever he went. He later abandoned his law career and spent the rest of his working years with Scudder, Stevens & Clark in Boston as a financial consultant. But George was never entirely comfortable in either of his chosen professions. He much preferred his forays into the wilds of America and Canada, hunting and fishing.

After his Wyoming adventure, during which he had reestablished contact with Marjorie, George settled down to working

---

[1] As evidenced in letters to Marjorie and to Bessie.

on making a success of his law career in Pittsburgh. He attempted to arrange a move to Hartford, Connecticut, which would have placed him nearer to Marjorie in Bristol and Boston. He was constantly frustrated in his efforts to establish a stronger relationship with her by the great geographical distance between them. By the time he had made arrangements to be in Boston or New York at the same time that Marjorie was there, she would already have made other plans. She had scores of close friends and cousins and went from one house-party to another, interspersing visits with extended trips to New York to see friends and go shopping, and to enjoy the theater, the opera, and dinner parties. She had many suitors, and several offers of marriage, but she appeared to enjoy her exhilarating single life far too much to be tied down.[1] As Marjorie flitted, free of care, between Hazleton and Boston and between New York and Maine, Cape Cod, Silver Springs, Lake Placid, and Buffalo, George always seemed to be in the wrong place. In February 1910, for example, Marjorie was in New York for a few days and wired George that she would like to see him, but they missed each other again. The following week, when he *was* in New York, she had to be in Boston for her school friend Priscilla Harding's wedding to Englishman Jim Sherrard. *"I was getting Priscilla married up here in Boston, and couldn't possibly be away. It's always like this when you really want to see people. I'm getting discouraged."*[2] The week after that, Marjorie was in New York again to have gowns fitted and to visit her friend Louise Smith, but by then George was back in Pittsburgh.

EUROPE 1910 AND 1911

In the spring of 1910, Marjorie went back to Europe, this time traveling with Bessie and William McKee and her sister Augustine to Madeira. Their chauffeur, Kroh, had sailed to Europe the week before,

---

[1] As evidenced in letters from Marjorie to George in 1909.
[2] Marjorie Van Wickle to George Lyon, February 13, 1910. Blithewold Archives.

taking the McKees' car, a Simplex, with him. He met up with them in Naples, and they traveled through Italy and France, after which they went on to London. They stayed at the Ritz there and attended Edward VII's funeral on May 20. Augustine wrote to Estelle Clements:

The procession didn't begin until 9.30, so we had lots of time to watch the soldiers forming along the sidewalks, and the crowd, and eat our sandwiches, so we wouldn't be "munching when the King came" — it was a splendid sight, the soldiers marched so well that it made you dizzy to look hard at their legs, the gun-carriage with the crown, orb, and scepter, and following behind the King's horse with the boots turned the wrong way, and the little white dog led by the highlander was most pathetic, and while we were crying over the doggy we looked up, and saw that <u>five</u> Kings had passed by without our getting a good look at them. Then we were all mixed up with the princes, although we had learned them most beautifully. We would have given anything to have had them wear cards on their backs, saying 'Emperor of...We recovered in time to know the different queens and princes and Mr. Roosevelt.[1]

---

[1] Augustine to Estelle Clements from the Ritz Hotel, London, May 23, 1910. Blithewold Archives.

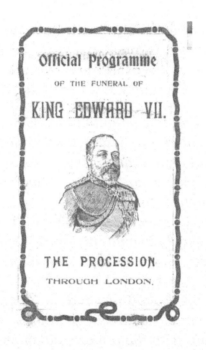

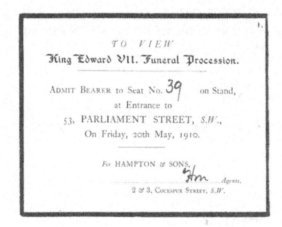

Augustine's ticket to view King Edward's funeral procession, 1910

When the family returned to Boston at the end of May, Marjorie stayed on in London. Now living in England, Priscilla Harding Sherrard and her husband Jim had invited Marjorie to visit them. Marjorie helped Priscilla move into a new apartment and "set up housekeeping." Jim, who was in the British Army, was *"down at*

Pinbright shooting with his men for two days — but he appears in London quite frequently never the less."[1] Jim and Priscilla tried to introduce Marjorie to eligible young men, but Marjorie had other plans, going off to Paris to stay with the Nayrals. Since she planned to be back in Bristol in time for the July Fourth celebrations (sailing on the S.S. *Lusitania*) she wrote to George and asked if he might meet her in New York, at the same time scolding him for not writing to her for three months.

CUNARD R.M.S. "LUSITANIA".

Marjorie traveled home on the Lusitania, *1910* [2]

George Lyon was invited to a large house party at Blithewold for July Fourth, 1910, but he had to get back to his job in Pittsburgh and could not stay long. (The house party, which included Irma Nayral, Irma's brother Pierre, and Marjorie's cousins Schuyler, Frank, Gladys, and Katharine Pardee, continued well into the summer.) George had been hopeful that the relationship might now begin to pick up momentum, but shortly after the visit Marjorie wrote him a letter of apology. Apparently she had been rather dismissive of him while he

---

[1] Marjorie Van Wickle to Bessie McKee, June 3, 1910. Blithewold Archives.
[2] Postcard in the Blithewold Archives.

was at Blithewold and had not replied to his letters after he returned to Pittsburgh. She wrote:

> *Really, I <u>am</u> penitent. And the excuse is the same old one of the strenuous life. Twelve people with us all the time — nineteen for last Sunday, twenty-one for this, and even more for next.*

She went on to describe some of the ongoing frivolities at Blithewold:

> *We have one continuous "rough-house" from morning till night. The only reason I have a spare half hour now is because I have forcibly ejected, from my room, Gladys and Irma. They have gone off with my Italian peasant costume and are dressing Irma up in it to have her picture taken on the terrace. I hear shrieks of laughter from upstairs!*

And she could not resist adding, *"an awfully attractive boy from your town was here with Schuyler."*[1]

Irma Nayral on the terrace in Marjorie's Italian costume, August 1910

---

[1] Marjorie Van Wickle to George Lyon, August 5, 1910. Blithewold Archives.

George felt excluded and miserable, and he wrote to Marjorie to tell her so. Marjorie defended herself:

> *Your letter has just come, and I can read enough between the lines to see that you are a bit offended with your little Bristol friend and don't care much whether you see her again or not. I am sorry. Only I can't help remembering that there have been times when you have hurt me too. So do let's call it square and be friends.*[1]

In August Marjorie was in York Harbor, Maine, staying with Louise Smith, while George was at the Meadow Club in Long Island, taking part in the tennis championships. In September, Marjorie went to the Adirondacks, as she did at the end of every summer, to spend time with many of her Pardee relatives gathered at her Uncle Calvin and Aunt Mary Pardee's country home.

The boathouse at Calvin Pardee's summer camp near Lake Placid, ca. 1910

George Lyon accepted an invitation to join the family there for a few days, and he took this time to finally profess his love for Marjorie.

---

[1] Marjorie Van Wickle to George Lyon, August 10, 1910. Blithewold Archives.

Marjorie, on the other hand, was not confident that she could reciprocate his devotion. After he left, George wrote,

> *Dearest Marjorie, That much at least is certain. I have thought of you and wanted to see you ever since we said good-bye on Monday night. How I wish I could have stayed, and yet it seemed to me as if you were* not *sorry to have me go.*

He went on to tell her that he had again requested a transfer from Pittsburgh to Hartford. It would mean that he would have to travel more, but he would be a step closer to Marjorie. He ended his letter:

> *Oh, my dear, how much I long for you, and yet what right have I to think about you — Even if you cared it means such a long, long wait — and life is going by so fast. But* if *you care, or* when *you care, nothing else will matter.*[1]

Marjorie replied that she was:

> *...awfully far from sure of anything. You will just have to be patient — that was a dear letter you wrote me, and you know how much I wish I could answer it as it should be answered. But I can't pretend — it isn't fair to either of us.*[2]

George finally moved to Hartford and took up residence at the Hartford Golf Club, but once again their schedules clashed. He had to turn down several invitations to Blithewold because of tennis commitments, and Marjorie was still entertaining Irma, taking her on trips to New York City for the opera; to Hazleton to stay with the Pardees; and to Morristown, New Jersey, to stay with the Cauldwells,[3] where Marjorie enjoyed visiting *"the haunts of childhood."* She offered George a few dates when she would be in New York, and added *"If you*

---

[1] George Lyon to Marjorie Van Wickle, September 10, 1910. Blithewold Archives.

[2] Marjorie Van Wickle to George Lyon, September 11, 1910. Blithewold Archives.

[3] Tom and Carrie Cauldwell were old friends of Augustus and Bessie's.

are to be there any of those times, let me know and perhaps we can connect...I'm sorry I'm such a hard person to understand."[1] She teased George with descriptions of a hectic social life: *"Irma and I are being feted continually and we are quite spoiled. We have three invitations for tomorrow."*[2] But she does end her letter with a word of encouragement: *"Don't forget you have promised to come to Bristol for Christmas!"* And in her next letter, *"Don't forget Christmas at Blithewold — if you can possibly make it. We are to have a Christmas tree two stories high!"*[3]

As Christmas 1910 drew closer, Marjorie's social schedule became even more crowded, including a party for 60 people in Boston. She wrote to George:

> *A strenuous life this! But I wanted you to know <u>right away</u> how much we want you at Bristol. It will be decidedly nice to see you. We will have some good times and I'll promise not to be quite worn out before then, even if I have to swear off some parties!*[4]

And the following week, she wrote:

> *Cecile Gifford is visiting me now and we are going to two dances, the opera, the theatre, a few dinners, two weddings, a picnic and an "oratorio" all in one week! Think we will survive? Goodbye till the Christmas party.*[5]

George did go to Blithewold for Christmas, and the "two-story" tree in the entrance hall that Marjorie had promised became a

---

[1] Marjorie Van Wickle to George Lyon, October 14, 1910. Blithewold Archives.

[2] Marjorie Van Wickle to George Lyon, October 28, 1910. Blithewold Archives.

[3] Marjorie Van Wickle to George Lyon, December 1, 1910. Blithewold Archives. This is the first reference to the 18- to 20-foot-tall Christmas tree that became a Blithewold family tradition.

[4] Marjorie Van Wickle to George Lyon, December 12, 1910. Blithewold Archives.

[5] Marjorie Van Wickle to George Lyon, December 18, 1910. Blithewold Archives.

Blithewold tradition. Marjorie and George apparently had time for several heart-to-heart talks during this visit. For the first time they confided their true feelings about many things to each other. Marjorie was beginning to feel that her life was superficial, and she was tiring of the constant rounds of parties. She wrote to George shortly after the holidays,

> *We have been perfectly frank with each other so far. It's the only way to be real friends. And I want you for my friend more than you perhaps realize. Even if we don't both ever fall in love with each other at the same time, we can have pleasure just being together and interested in the same things and let it go at that. I'm going to take your advice and find something to do in the world. I don't seem to be as happy as I ought to be; and trying hard to amuse oneself is pretty poor sport. No more of it in the future.*

But she still didn't know if she really loved George, certainly not in the way that he loved her, and she was confused by her close romantic relationship with Mac Sturgis. She appeared to love George from a distance, missing him when he was away but difficult and distant with him when he was with her. She wrote just after Christmas:

> *As I said before, I am woefully afraid I have no heart and will never fall in love with anyone. Sometimes I love you so it almost hurts, and at other times I don't seem to care at all. So I'm going to give up, and just let's be friends. Be good and dear to me, and don't say "how contradictory" when I tell you that I'm loving you pretty hard tonight and miss you dreadfully!*[1]

George reluctantly agreed to try to be just friends, replying:

---

[1] Marjorie Van Wickle to George Lyon, December 27, 1910. Blithewold Archives.

I am so sorry you're so unhappy but you mustn't be and I'm sure you won't be if you once get into something that will take your attention and time and make you feel that you're contributing to the world with necessary work in some way. I'm sure you would be more contented — and with your love for children and your knack in getting along with them, it should be the easiest thing to get started.[1]

In January 1911, before she had a chance to resolve any of these serious relationship issues, Marjorie left Boston to visit her Van Wickle cousins Anna and May and their brother George Van Wickle[2] in Puerto Rico. Anna and Howard Castle and May and Arthur Hunsden lived on a grapefruit farm about forty miles west of San Juan. It was a restful time for Marjorie — two months of the simple life where the most she did was sit on the porch reading Kipling, play with May's baby, Rosemary, and ride countless miles about the country on *"the dearest, tiniest horses you ever saw."* She slept ten hours every night and felt herself relaxing.

When Marjorie landed in New York in March, George went into the city to have lunch with her. Eight days later she was back in New York. She stayed with her cousin Dorothy Pardee Clark and Dorothy's husband Ben, and wrote to George saying she would like to see him. But just as George was beginning to think that they could move forward in their relationship, he suffered another blow. Marjorie told him that she was leaving for England on April 3 to stay with Priscilla and Jim Sherrard for six weeks. Their first baby, Mary Priscilla, was to be christened and Marjorie had been asked to be her godmother.

The Sherrards had bought a 138-acre farm with a large house in Derbyshire. There were fish ponds, shrubberies, and a tennis lawn, walled gardens, rambling stables, and a farmyard with pigs, cows, and

---

[1] George Lyon to Marjorie Van Wickle, January 9, 1911. Blithewold Archives.
[2] George Van Wickle, Jr. was Marjorie's cousin. He traveled extensively in China before marrying Eugenie Verges (born in Puerto Rico). The couple moved to Boston, along with Eugenie's mother, and had a son, Verges Van Wickle. George, Eugenie, and Verges moved to Seattle in the 1920s.

chickens. The old brick walls were covered with flowering pear and cherry trees. Marjorie greatly enjoyed the down-to-earth country life: but more than anything, she loved the horses. This was hunting country, and Marjorie found that:

> *...a person's whole character, manners and morals are judged by whether he goes well to hounds! The racing, too, is quite part of daily life. We have been to three race meets since I've been here. Jim's horse won a steeplechase a while ago. I adore the very sight and smell of a racecourse and know I should be an inveterate "backer"* [of horses] *if I lived here.*[1]

Marjorie went riding with Jim Sherrard every morning and even helped him paint the new pig sties. The weather was wonderful — unseasonably warm and sunny.[2] They played tennis every weekend, and Marjorie told Bessie, *"I find I play quite as well, if not better than, most English girls."*[3]

Gaddesby Hall, Derbyshire, England;
home of Jim and Priscilla Sherrard, 1911

---

[1] Marjorie Van Wickle to George Lyon, April 1911. Blithewold Archives.
[2] All of England was preparing that summer for King George V's upcoming coronation. Author Juliet Nicolson notes how the beautiful and unusually warm weather added to the general excitement. (Juliet Nicolson. *The Perfect Summer*. Grove Press, 2006, p. 2.)
[3] Marjorie Van Wickle to Bessie McKee, May 15, 1911. Blithewold Archives.

By June 1911 Marjorie was back in Bristol for the summer, encouraging George to be there for July Fourth.

Last night we came home on the midnight train and are so glad to see Bristol again. It certainly is quite one of the nicest places I ever see on my travels! What I really am writing for is to ask you up here for over the 'fourth' of July. We want you a lot. Louise will be here and some other people you know probably, and we are going to have a regular old-time Bristol celebration. I think it's going to be a specially nice reunion this July 4th, and Bristol is planning to be very gay. A dance and a 'bathing lunch party' are to be given all in one day! Gladys and Katharine have arrived at the Gardiner [sic] House.[1]

George did go to Bristol for the holiday and everyone enjoyed themselves, as evidenced by letters between George and Marjorie later that month. In August, George played tennis in the Southampton Tournament and did well; Marjorie, meantime, was in York Harbor, Maine, with Louise once again. She invited George to join them there for Labor Day Sunday, but he needed to be in Philadelphia with his ailing father.

Marjorie must have had time to think about her relationship with George while she was in York Harbor. On August 22 she wrote, somewhat mysteriously, *"George, if you care for me any more than you did at Christmas, please say so, for there would be something I would want to tell you. If we are still just very good friends, it doesn't matter."[2]* George surely must have had his hopes raised at that. In September he joined Marjorie and her friends (including Mac Sturgis and Roger Swain) at the Lake Placid camp where Marjorie celebrated her twenty-eighth birthday. But after George returned home he received a letter from Marjorie that ended simply, (and maybe dismissively), *"Don't*

---

[1] Marjorie Van Wickle to George Lyon, June 10, 1911. Blithewold Archives.
[2] Marjorie Van Wickle to George Lyon, August 22, 1911. Blithewold Archives.

forget that I'm always glad to see you. Goodbye and good luck, from Marjorie."[1]

Summer 1911 had been a glorious, extended season at Blithewold for the McKees and their guests. The mansion and the Gardner guesthouse were full to capacity — as soon as one set of guests left others came to take their places. By the end of October, however, William McKee wanted to return to their city life. Bessie, on the other hand, hated to leave her lovely gardens. Back on September 1, Bessie had asked John DeWolf to come to Blithewold to discuss her ideas for a sunken garden just beyond the North Porch. DeWolf began work immediately, and Bessie very much enjoyed watching his progress. On October 29, as Blithewold was being packed up and closed down for the winter, Bessie wrote to her sister Alice,

We are leaving Bristol tomorrow and my heart is broken over leaving this dear place, but Will is very tired of club life[2] and is longing to have the town house open. We are making a new garden at the north end of the house and I am especially sad to leave before the work is finished — it will have the effect of a sunken garden, and we have built a stone wall about it. And in the face of the wall next to the house will be a fountain and stone steps curving down on either side of the fountain. The wall is nearly done, and the steps, but the wash and basin are not in place. We are delighted with the effect so far and think it will be lovely next summer.[3]

---

[1] Marjorie Van Wickle to George Lyon, September 18, 1911. Blithewold Archives.

[2] William McKee stayed at the Algonquin Club on Commonwealth Avenue during the workweek over the summer, since they closed up their townhouse while they were at Blithewold.

[3] Bessie McKee to her sister Alice Pardee Earle, October 29, 1911. Blithewold Archives.

From left: Marjorie, Bessie, and Augustine,[1]
observing the construction of the Sunken Garden,[1] 1911

Bessie was very happy to have at last found a place for the "North Star" — a set of stones arranged in the shape of a star that had been saved from the north tower of the first house. It had been stored in the barn until they could find the perfect north-facing spot for it. Now it was to be set into the retaining wall of the sunken garden.

> *We have also put in the wall the north star that was in the*
> *north tower of the old Blithewold, we could not get it into the*
> *new home so that it would look towards the north. I am very*
> *glad to have it at last placed.[2]*

Other stones meaningful to the family were set into the same wall.

> *I have a small stone in the wall from your rocky coast — it is*
> *one Augustine fished up when she was climbing over the*
> *rocks, also two from Cape Cod — some quartz crystal from*
> *Coleraine, two stones from the White Mountains, and a*

---

[1] Now known as the North Garden.
[2] Bessie McKee to her sister Alice Pardee Earle, October 29, 1911. Blithewold Archives.

187

number from other places we have been. It is rather fun, I think.[1]

The completed Sunken Garden, 1912, showing the "North Star" set into the lower right part of the retaining wall

A COMPLICATED COURTSHIP

Marjorie seemed to be no nearer to finding her true role in life, but her good friend Louise Smith took a job teaching at a settlement house in New York City. Marjorie wrote: *"Her family have not been heard from. I'm afraid they'll not like it. But I do hope she'll make a success of it and feel of use. It's a nice feeling to accomplish something."* And later, somewhat cynically, *"She surely is getting on well down there in the slums."* But Marjorie was impressed with Louise's dedication to a cause and envied her sense of purpose.

---

[1] Bessie McKee to her sister Alice Pardee Earle, October 29, 1911. Blithewold Archives.

After several unsuccessful attempts by George and Marjorie to synchronize their schedules in the fall of 1911, George finally accepted an invitation to stay with the McKees in Boston at the end of November for Thanksgiving. He and Marjorie had an enjoyable time at the Harvard–Yale game, but something went wrong over the weekend. Tempers frayed and George left in a huff. Marjorie wrote afterward,

> *You've only been gone a half hour — and I miss you desperately. I'm sorry I let you see how hurt I was...and I was foolish to show you I cared. And the only thing that matters is that you've gone. It's disconcerting — for I can't think of anything else. And yet when we are together, we are both so shy or something, that often after you've been here I feel much less acquainted than I did before. Don't you feel that way too? We are not getting what we should out of our friendship and I can't see why. For I do want your sympathy and love so much, and I think you want mine. We are on the wrong track somehow. Let's think up a new scheme before Christmas.[1]*

Christmas 1911 came and went, and Marjorie and George were still apart — George was sick with tonsillitis, but Marjorie didn't find out about it until after the holidays. She decided to spend the winter in Boston for the first time in three years. A rather insensitive letter to George on January 27, 1912, describes her many activities:

> *Tomorrow I go out to Dedham — lunch at one house, coasting or skating all afternoon, then dinner and a birthday party at another house. There have been more dances lately, and I'm still keen on them. Two snowshoe over-Sunday parties are planned and several small dances and theater parties.[2]*

---

[1] Marjorie Van Wickle to George Lyon, November 27, 1911. Blithewold Archives.
[2] Marjorie Van Wickle to George Lyon, January 27, 1912. Blithewold Archives.

But she did redeem herself by inviting him to go to the White Mountains with the family in February.

In September of 1912 Marjorie made her annual pilgrimage to Lake Placid. Visiting her there at the same time were several would-be suitors — George Clarke, Mac Sturgis, Nat Ayer, and George Lyon. George Lyon seems to have won the day, and his letters now became unambiguous love letters. He begged Marjorie to marry him, and she told him that she would give him her decision by Christmas. George wrote, *"I know you are coming to me in the end, and Christmas is going to be the great holiday of my life — and yours too."*[1] Unfortunately for Marjorie, he began writing letters of undying love every day, overwhelming her. She began to panic. And her confusion was compounded by unidentified family pressures. She received an offer of marriage from Mac Sturgis, a man deemed an eminently suitable match for Marjorie by her family. A point in his favor, to the McKees, was that his family belonged to the same social circles in Boston as they did. Although Marjorie loved *being* with Mac, she was not sure that she *loved* him. At the end of September George wrote to Marjorie:

> *I am so sorry you've had so much on your hands. It sounds as if an avalanche had run you down and I think family troubles are the very hardest to cope with. You mustn't think about hurting me by being frank. At first I was sick with fear of losing you but...your job is to listen to your heart and brain and know what they say, and not think of the consequences to anyone else.*[2]

Perhaps the family disapproved of George, or doubted that he was the right husband for Marjorie. We do not know for certain where the 'family troubles' lay.

---

[1] George Lyon to Marjorie Van Wickle, September 22, 1912. Blithewold Archives.
[2] George Lyon to Marjorie Van Wickle, September 29, 1912. Blithewold Archives.

In October, Marjorie decided to go away. She needed to get her thoughts in order. She wrote to her mother *"I do hate to leave you — you see it isn't you that I'm running away from."*[1] She made plans to visit her Aunt Isabell (William McKee's sister) in Greenwood, Virginia, and she asked George not to write to her while she was there. He said he *had* to write to her but that he would tear up the letters instead of mailing them. When Marjorie returned home in December, George went to Boston to see her, again earnestly proclaiming his love. They spent an uneventful Christmas together, after which Marjorie went to Hazleton with the rest of her family to spend New Year's. But her confusion and George's overwhelming persistence had worn her down and she felt totally incapable of coming to any decision.[2]

In May of 1913, in desperation and close to a breakdown, Marjorie went to stay with Priscilla and Jim Sherrard in England, possibly to talk over her dilemma with her dearest friend. She resolved that she would *not* return to Boston until she had made a decision. While she was away, Mac Sturgis traveled from Boston to Blithewold to speak to Bessie, presumably to plead his case. For Marjorie, the distance from all the people pressuring her (and maybe being in the tranquil, bucolic English countryside with the serene and imperturbable Priscilla) helped her make her life-altering decision. She wrote to her mother from Derby:

> *I wish you were here today, for I have written to Mac that I can't ever marry him — and I'm feeling heart sore for the dear boy — and for myself, for I know I am giving up something very wonderful when I refuse his love. But mother dear, I am doing right — hard though it is. For though I have lost the fight I realize that winning would have been impossible, feeling as I do...I should only have been bluffing myself, and I'm glad I see clearly enough now to realize that*

---

[1] Marjorie Van Wickle to Bessie McKee, October 5, 1912. Blithewold Archives.
[2] As evidenced in Marjorie's letters to George and Bessie, in the spring of 1913. Blithewold Archives.

I couldn't ever love him. I love his ideas, his sense of humor, his unselfishness, but not <u>him</u>. So I have written saying "good-bye," and I know I've done right. Do you understand? It wouldn't be square to him to pretend — and I couldn't — George is somehow between us, for try as hard as I could to put him out of my head, I just can't succeed. Maybe I wasn't meant to!! Good-bye, Mother dear — help dear old Mac if you can. If only I could have helped all this! You can tell anyone you like that I am coming home![1]

AN ENGAGEMENT AND A MARRIAGE

Marjorie and George became engaged on August 22, 1913. George was ecstatic:

I have just finished answering five new letters from your relatives and friends, in all of which they tell me how fine you are and what a lucky dog I am. As if I didn't know already that I had won the dearest girl in the world! Why don't you come up to Boston Sat. am., and we'll go out to the Country Club...have lunch together and back to Bristol if you want me (and it is wise).[2]

At the end of the letter, George also mentions his happiness with Marjorie's new photographic portrait. Although from this letter it appears that George was aware of the McKees' disappointment, Bessie and Will soon put all this behind them and welcomed George into the family.

---

[1] Marjorie Van Wickle to Bessie McKee, May 23, 1913. Blithewold Archives.
[2] George Lyon to Marjorie Van Wickle, September 18, 1913. Blithewold Archives.

Marjorie ca. 1913

The decision now made, Bessie and William McKee began to make plans for Marjorie's wedding on June 1 the following year in Bristol. Blithewold was *the* perfect place for a summer wedding. Bessie stepped up work on the gardens to provide a flawless setting for the event. John DeWolf spent the summer working on the Water Garden and the Rock Garden, but by October 1913 he was suffering from heart problems. He died in November at Love Rocks, his sister's home on Walley Street in Bristol.

In November George was ill again with tonsillitis, for which he underwent a tonsillectomy. He went to Atlantic City to recuperate, and by Christmas he was well enough to join the McKees and Estelle Clements at Blithewold.[1] In February Admiral George Lyon, George's

---

[1] The 18 small junipers that decorated the dining room that Christmas were later planted in the Water Garden at Blithewold. From Estelle Clements' diary, December 27, 1913. Blithewold Archives.

father, fell seriously ill, and George went to Philadelphia to be with him. The Admiral died in March and was buried in Erie, Pennsylvania, at the church where George's grandfather had been pastor for forty-eight years.

Because of his father's illness George had missed the annual winter holiday at Peckett's ski resort in New Hampshire. Marjorie went with the rest of the family and invited Mac Sturgis to join the group, as he had done in years past. He declined her invitation, writing, *"You say 'let's begin being real friends again.' I don't believe we ever stopped being real friends but I feel sure we are two friends that had better not meet — not for a long time anyway. Sometime it may be possible, but it isn't now."*[1]

Marjorie and George quickly fell into a pattern of comfortable familiarity, with lots of good-natured teasing as they planned their wedding, their honeymoon (in South America, where they hoped they wouldn't be recognized as a "honeymoon couple"), and their future home. George's letters lost the urgency and panic they had shown only a few months previously. In fact, Marjorie now accused George of being too staid, to which he responded, *"I love you very much although you think me such a serious-minded cuss, and I wish you were here."*[2]

Preparations for the wedding intensified. Shreve's in Boston sent out invitations to Pardee, Van Wickle, McKee, and Lyon relatives — and to a long list of Marjorie and George's friends. Bessie and Marjorie bought wedding clothes, and Marjorie put together her trousseau. George chose his best man, his brother Dr. Vincent Lyon, and his ushers, and gave them gold cufflinks as gifts. Marjorie chose as her bridesmaids Katharine and Gladys Pardee, Irma Nayral and Gertrude Vaughan, and Louise Smith and Doris Earle.[3] Her sister Augustine was her Maid of Honor. To her attendants Marjorie gave the pearl necklaces they wore at the wedding.

---

[1] Mac Sturgis to Marjorie Van Wickle, February 2, 1914. Blithewold Archives.
[2] George Lyon to Marjorie Van Wickle, April 1, 1914. Blithewold Archives.
[3] Marjorie's close friend Priscilla attended the wedding, but she was not a bridesmaid since she herself was already married.

The guests began arriving at Blithewold five days before the wedding, and the house and guesthouse soon filled up. Other guests stayed in private homes or at the Hotel Belvedere in the center of Bristol. (Irma Nayral, who traveled from France and was the first to arrive, entertained family and guests in the evenings with her lovely voice.) On the afternoon of the wedding, the steamer *Sagamore* picked up a large party of guests from Boston who had arrived at the Bristol Ferry by special train and delivered them to Blithewold's wharf.

Will McKee was put in charge of arranging all the gifts in the Billiard Room and talking to the society reporters who were covering the wedding. Meanwhile, extra chefs helped with the catering for the large number of guests. On the evening before the wedding they helped serve dinner to 60 guests aboard Will's yacht *Chanticleer*.

The Summerhouse, decorated for Marjorie's wedding, June 1, 1914

June 1, the day of the wedding, dawned clear and fine, according to Estelle Clements' diary. Three hundred guests gathered in the Enclosed Garden, surrounded by trees, shrubs, and flowers. The *Providence Journal* described the scene:

> *The summerhouse had been transformed into a floral altar with lattice screen in the background, covered with climbing vines and flowers. 16 members of the boys' choir of the Church of the Emmanuel, Boston, marched along the path from the house singing "The Voice that Breathed O'er Eden" to the accompaniment of a pipe organ concealed behind the shrubbery near the floral bower. Then came the bird-like notes of a concealed soprano soloist, Mlle. De Nayral Puybusque, one of the bridesmaids, who sang the prayer "Angelicus." Soon after 4 o'clock the organ pealed out the wedding march from Lohengrin and the procession came down the flower-bordered winding path from the house into the garden. Twelve ushers led, followed by six bridesmaids and maid of honor. The ceremony was performed by Rt. Rev. Boyd Vincent, Episcopal Bishop of Southern Ohio, an uncle of the bridegroom. The scene was very impressive and beautiful, the large party of guests standing on the lawn behind a semi-circular band of white ribbon, while, in the floral bower, the young couple repeated their marriage vows.[1]*

---

[1] *Providence Journal*, June 2, 1914.

Marjorie and George Lyon on their wedding day at Blithewold
Augustine is Maid of Honor

The newspaper reported that the couple left aboard Mr. McKee's yacht, *Chanticleer*, later in the afternoon. In fact, this was a trick played on the guests. After the wedding dinner everyone watched a young couple taking a launch out to the *Chanticleer* and waving to everyone on shore. The guests, who naturally thought it was Marjorie and George leaving for their honeymoon, all waved enthusiastically. Only Bessie and Will McKee and Estelle Clements knew that Marjorie and George were at that moment driving down Ferry Road in Marjorie's Fiat to meet their Cadillac at a predestined spot, which would then take them to Mansfield, Massachusetts, to spend the night. They had made the perfect getaway!

A guest wrote to Marjorie afterward,

How beautifully you fooled us on Monday evening!! Of course we all supposed the people we saw in the launch on the way to the yacht were "Marjorie and George." The festivities continued unabated for some hours after you left, dancing on the porch and in the living room.[1]

Marjorie and George now began their first of many extended trips together. In New York, where they had driven after the night in Mansfield, they stayed for a few days at the Vanderbilt Hotel on Park Avenue before sailing on the S.S. *Tenadores*, by way of Kingston, Jamaica, and the Bahamas to Panama.

They arrived back in New York on June 18: *"We got back yesterday. It <u>was</u> such a good time. From the first day till the last, all fair weather and happiness."*[2] In New York they continued their honeymoon, enjoying the last Yale–Princeton game of the season and attending the gala opening of the new roof garden at the Biltmore Hotel. They prolonged their vacation further by spending a week at the Hotel Nassau in Long Beach, Long Island, *"for some more sun and bathing,"* before returning to Boston to begin their new life together.

---

[1] Helen Ridell to Marjorie, June 4, 1914. Blithewold Archives.
[2] Marjorie to Bessie, June 29, 1914. Blithewold Archives.

Chapter X

MR. AND MRS. GEORGE ARMSTRONG LYON

Marjorie and George rented an apartment at 41 Pilgrim Road, in Brookline, just outside of Boston, as they looked for a house to buy. They furnished the apartment with pieces from Blithewold and the McKees' home on Commonwealth Avenue, and added all the elegant wedding gifts they had received from friends and relatives — gifts of silver and crystal, fine china and lovely linens, pictures and ornate mirrors.

July 1, just one month after the wedding, George was on the road again, working in Hartford and staying at the Hartford Golf Club. He wrote to Marjorie:

> *My Darling Wife, this is the first time that I have ever <u>written</u> it and it seems very sweet. This is the first night we have been separated, and it is too bad that there are to be so many of them. I shall do my best to get back in time for dinner, but if I shouldn't you must not feel disappointed, because I love you and things have to be done.[1]*

July Fourth found the new couple at Blithewold, after which George wrote a sentimental letter to his new mother-in-law, Bessie:

> *I thought it was very dear of you to speak to me so lovingly Sunday night...I should like to call you mother, and have you feel so towards me and have you think of me as your son... The memory of my mother is so precious to me and I have missed her so much that I can't begin to tell you how much it means to me to think that you really want me to be a son to you.[2]*

---

[1] George to Marjorie, July 1, 1914. Blithewold Archives.
[2] George to Bessie, July 8, 1914. Blithewold Archives.

George left immediately after the July 4th holiday for Hartford, and Marjorie returned to their new apartment. The separations were hard on both of them, and George wrote, *"I miss you sadly. I am so happy with you at home that it becomes harder and harder each time to leave you."*[1]

Once the summer season was over and Bessie and Will had left Blithewold to return to Commonwealth Avenue, Marjorie was able to spend more time with them, but still she felt lonely in the city. George was on a grueling schedule of being in Hartford or New York during the workweek, only returning to Boston at weekends. Marjorie tried to amuse herself by playing tennis and golf, or shopping and lunching with friends, but the novelty of having her own home soon began to fade. She began to show signs of melancholy,[2] even though George wrote faithfully from the Hartford Golf Club or the Biltmore or Vanderbilt in New York City. He reminded Marjorie that they had always understood that he would have to spend long periods of time away from Boston.

In January 1915, Marjorie and George saw a house they liked on Acorn Street on Beacon Hill in Boston. They began negotiations to purchase it, but it turned out to be a long, protracted business. They began to think about having children — Marjorie's friend Priscilla had just had her second child — *"A son today. Both doing well"* reads a telegram to the Lyons. George wrote to Marjorie *"They must be very happy over it. I hope we shall be happy in the same way before too long."*[3] In April they joined the McKees and Augustine at the Greenbriar Hotel in White Sulphur Springs, Virginia, for a golfing holiday. George had to leave early to return to work in New York City but wrote, *"The vacation did me a great deal of good. It made me feel very fit."*[4] Marjorie returned to the Pilgrim Road apartment alone.

---

[1] George to Marjorie July 28, 1914. Blithewold Archives.
[2] As evidenced in letters between Marjorie and George in the fall of 1914. Blithewold Archives.
[3] George to Marjorie, January 5, 1915. Blithewold Archives.
[4] George Lyon to Marjorie Lyon, April 26, 1915. Blithewold Archives.

THE WAR IN EUROPE

Marjorie and George spent the month of July 1915 at Blithewold, where the war news from Europe made everyone edgy. Although war had been declared in Europe in September 1914, all sides expected the struggle to be short-lived. Instead, it escalated until it eventually became a global military conflict. New technology added to the horrors: poison gas, barbed wire, tanks, armed airplanes, aircraft carriers, submarines, and machine guns. While everyone in America intently watched what was happening in Europe, the United States government generally supported a policy of isolationism, avoiding conflict while trying to broker peace. On May 7, 1915, the *Lusitania* was sunk off the Irish coast, with 128 Americans among the hundreds lost. British Prime Minister Herbert Asquith hoped that the incident would persuade America to finally enter the war. The U.S. President, Woodrow Wilson, however, refused to act — the American public was not ready for war. But the path to an ultimate declaration of hostilities was now set and America began to prepare for combat.

In August 1915, George Lyon volunteered for war duty and was told to report for basic officer training in Plattsburgh, New York. It was a concentrated course of training, and 1200 men would be expected to learn in one month what normally would have taken more than five. When the men arrived at the training camp, each man was assigned to a company and to a tent (six men to a tent). They received a mattress and pillow, a cot, three blankets, and a poncho, as well as a rifle, bayonet, cartridge belt, canteen, knife, spoon, fork, haversack, and metal plate. George wrote:

We lost our civilian identity and became a crowd of recruits. My company is H and we have 121 men in it. There are over 1200 in all. The men have been all mixed up and are bunked together without regard to associations. It is interesting to see how soon one becomes just a private even though he may be mayor of New York. The uniform is a great leveler, and it is pretty hard to tell what walk of life a man comes

*from, or what his advantages have been, when all are
dressed alike.*[1]

The camp was situated on Lake Champlain half-way between
Plattsburgh, New York, and the Hotel Champlain. On the first day
George chose to specialize in map-making, which included *"trenches
and fortifications,"* but he also spent time in drilling and in practicing
how to use the rifle. All the men prepared for the end-of-course 80-
mile hike with full equipment, *"duplicating as far as possible actual
war conditions. Various military problems will be worked out en route."*
He warned Marjorie not to expect frequent letters. His daily schedule
began with reveille at 5:45 each morning and assembly at 6. Mess call
was 6:30, call for a four-hour drill at 7:25, mess at 12, a three-mile
march in the afternoon, and then lectures. So went the days, every
minute tightly scheduled until lights-out at 9 p.m. In between drills,
they attended inspections and more lectures. The only respite was on
Sundays, when breakfast was at 7 instead of 6 a.m., and in their
sparse leisure time the men could swim in the lake. George told
Marjorie that there was a telephone at the camp through which he
could *possibly* be reached, but there might be a several-hours wait.

Conditions at the camp became worse instead of better, and on
August 20 George reported that he had spent four hours that day
crawling on his belly with a 42-pound pack and his rifle on his back.

> *...under a hot sun and over rocks and through thickets,
> with six or seven miles of tramping thrown in and digging
> trenches six feet deep, two feet wide...which, together
> with the various and sundry duties that come under the
> head of routine, make a pretty free day — and I am dog
> tired.*[2]

---

[1] George Lyon to Marjorie Van Wickle Lyon, August 12, 1915. Blithewold
Archives.
[2] George Lyon to Marjorie Van Wickle Lyon, August 20, 1915. Blithewold
Archives.

Still, he was able to express sympathy for Marjorie, who was suffering from hay fever and resting at Blithewold. He ended the letter with *"Target range at 6:30 tomorrow morning which means up at 4:30 — so I must get to bed."*

On August 25, Theodore Roosevelt arrived at the camp to give the men a pep talk. *"Mr. Roosevelt has just given us an hour's talk this evening in which he went after the Professional Pacifists with characteristic vigor, and told us how noble we were."* At the time George was preparing himself for the rigors of the dreaded "hike," which was to begin the following day, August 26, at 4 a.m. — eight or nine days of maneuvers: *"It will be tough going but a very helpful experience no doubt."* George generously thanked Marjorie for her support during the past few weeks, apologizing for his absence, and explaining that he had felt obliged *"to help along the vital cause of preparedness in this country...you did your part right loyally and patriotically and without fuss, and I feel so grateful and proud of you."* He was looking forward to camp ending and being home in time to enjoy Labor Day before going back to work.[1]

Although Marjorie and George began negotiations for the Acorn Street house in January, they were still waiting in September to hear if their offer had been accepted. Marjorie wrote to her mother *"Still haven't heard from 4 Acorn. I'm afraid I'm going to be pretty much disappointed. However, it's so nice having George home — nothing material matters."*[2] But the sale eventually did go through, and George and Marjorie began extensive renovations.

In early February 1916, Marjorie had abdominal surgery[3] at a Boston hospital, followed by a long recuperation period. Even after several weeks' convalescence she still needed rest to regain her full health. At George's urging she went for an extended visit to The

---

[1] It was probably at this time that George changed his career path and started working for Scudder, Stevens & Clark in Boston, a financial consulting company.
[2] Marjorie Lyon to Bessie McKee, September 15, 1915. Blithewold Archives.
[3] The reason for the surgery is not known.

Kirkwood Hotel in Camden, South Carolina. Camden, a popular winter getaway for Bostonians, offered polo and steeple chasing. Built in 1903, the hotel was a rambling, white, shingled, resort-style structure with a good golf course. Several of Marjorie's Pardee cousins went to stay with her there to keep her company, and the women passed the time picnicking, hunting for wild flowers, riding, golfing, knitting, reading, and playing tennis. Marjorie quickly felt stronger and started to regain weight. Back in Boston, George was suffering through the severest winter on record — freezing temperatures and more than six feet of snow. He kept busy supervising the work on the new house, writing to Marjorie:

> *The house is getting along splendidly. The pantry is about done and the laundry. In the dining room all of the white woodwork is in place and the library has the paneling and book shelves in. Our room has the floor half down...it begins to look like a real house.*[1]

Meanwhile, the war news from Europe was grim. Irma Nayral's[2] brother Pierre was at Verdun. *"It seems as if he <u>couldn't</u> come out of that alive,"*[3] wrote Marjorie to her mother.[4] In Derby, England, Priscilla Sherrard was looking after the farm and her two young children while her husband Jim was in Gallipoli with the British Army. She wrote to Marjorie,

> *I try to look after the farm at which, my dear, I am not a success! The place has only the aged left on it — old Temple the gardener, and two men over 60 in the stables who have to support each other and are frightened of the horses! I expect I have more strength than most of them, but never mind. I have been near 2 Zeppelin raids, but a deafening noise from the explosions was as near as they came to me.*

---

[1] George to Marjorie, March 17, 1916. Blithewold Archives.
[2] Irma was Marjorie's friend from Paris who had been a bridesmaid at her wedding.
[3] Pierre Nayral did survive the war.
[4] Marjorie to Bessie, March, 1916. Blithewold Archives.

It's a year since Jim left and I only hope and pray it won't be long before the few people who are left will be home and happy once more.[1]

AUGUSTINE'S DEBUTANTE SEASON

Marjorie and George finally moved into their new home at 4 Acorn Street in early June of 1916. It was a cold beginning to summer in Boston, and Marjorie reported sleeping in the new house with two blankets, a coat, a sweater, tights, and George's golf stockings on. But they were thrilled to be in their own home at last. One of Marjorie's favorite diversions was moving furniture around until she was pleased with the effect. She wrote to Bessie, *"The guest room is all fixed up now and looks adorable. When are you coming to spend a night in it?"*[2]

Bessie and Will were at Blithewold for the summer, and Marjorie and George joined them there for a while. Bessie was busy planning special social events for Augustine, who had just graduated from Miss May's School in Boston and had joined the group of debutantes who were making their debut in the 1916–1917 season. Since Bessie had allowed Marjorie to escape *her* debutante season, she was determined to launch Augustine in grand style. There were numerous "pre-season" events for the young people throughout the summer, including sailing weekends at Blithewold.

---

[1] Priscilla Sherrard to Marjorie, March 25, 1916. Blithewold Archives.
[2] Marjorie to Bessie, June 10, 1916. Blithewold Archives.

Augustine and friends sailing on Chanticleer *on Narragansett Bay 1916*
Augustine is in the center

Tennis at Blithewold, ca. 1916

Marjorie and Augustine on the bowsprit of Chanticleer, *ca. 1916*

Augustine dancing on the deck of Chanticleer, *summer 1916*

Apparently Marjorie was not anxious to be a part of Augustine's social year. She had rejected the tradition of having her own coming-out season in 1903 and had never regretted it. She and George chose this time to leave Boston on a trip west that would last eight months. Living in very primitive conditions in Wyoming, they must have felt happily disconnected from all the obsessive preparations back East. Family letters from home were full of the news of Augustine's parties and balls, shopping trips to New York, and gossip about her circle of friends. Augustine herself reported playing golf at the Country Club with Quincy Shaw, and talked of how well they got on. Quincy Adams Shaw, Jr., was the only son of a wealthy Boston family. (An ancestor was Robert Gould Shaw,[1] and Quincy's grandfather was a wealthy art collector who had donated a large collection of Millet paintings and Donatello marble sculptures to the Museum of Fine Arts in Boston.)

The young women being presented to society were from socially prominent Boston families, and were all members of the "Sewing Circle."[2] The young men chosen as escorts for the season were either brothers or cousins of the debutantes, or Harvard students known to the families. The parents of each young woman were responsible for hosting several social events over the season. As the season progressed, Augustine received invitations to dozens of balls, teas, dances, theatre parties, dinners, and luncheons.[3] Bessie, in turn, invited Augustine's friends to a large formal dinner and the theater on November 15, and to a lavish ball to be held later in the month at the Somerset Hotel on Commonwealth Avenue. William McKee gave

---

[1] Robert Gould Shaw was the colonel in command of the all-black 54th Regiment during the Civil War. An elaborate memorial on Boston Common honors his service.

[2] The first Sewing Circles had formed in Boston during the Civil War when young women "of good families" got together to roll bandages. The group ultimately merged with the Junior League, a women's social organization aimed at improving communities through member volunteerism and the building of members' civic leadership skills.

[3] The album Augustine kept of all her invitations for the year is preserved in the Blithewold Archives.

Augustine a lovely platinum and diamond watch as a "coming out" present.

Augustine Van Wickle, ca. 1917

On November 14, as the Lyons were entering Arizona, Marjorie wrote to Bessie from the train, *The California Limited,* telling her mother that she would be thinking of them all *"on the great Day tomorrow!"* She knew that both Bessie and Augustine were excited and nervous about their first big event in Augustine's honor, the dinner and theater. What Marjorie did not know, however, was that a death in the family had changed all their plans. Bessie's oldest sister, Alice Pardee Earle, had died at her home in Whitemarsh, Pennsylvania, on November 9. The formal event was cancelled and invitations were quickly retracted. Bessie and William McKee then traveled by train to Whitemarsh to attend the funeral. When they returned a few days later, however, they decided that the smaller event, the dinner and theater excursion, could proceed. On the evening of November 15, twenty-six young men and women gathered at the McKees' home on Commonwealth Avenue for a subdued but elegant dinner. The ball was rescheduled for January 24th.

The Ballroom of the Somerset Hotel, January 24, 1917,
decorated for Augustine's debutante ball

Augustine's Ball at the Somerset Hotel[1] on January 24, 1917, was a huge success. Augustine wrote a letter to Marjorie describing the festivities. The evening began with a dinner for 42 at the McKee home on Commonwealth Avenue, after which everyone went to the Somerset Hotel to greet other guests and begin the dancing. All the young men wanted to dance with Augustine, including her special beau, Quincy Shaw. *"My dancing really was a joke as I couldn't get more than six or eight steps with one man when often three would come*

---

[1] The Somerset Hotel was one of the very best venues for Boston parties. *"The Somerset was smaller than the newer Copley Plaza, older than the Ritz, and more equipped for chauffeured cars than the Vendôme."* Honor Moore, *The White Blackbird.* W.W. Norton & Company, 1996, p. 57.

at once to cut in — the one going fastest getting me!"[1] There was a break for supper, and then more dancing until four in the morning, when breakfast was served. By all accounts, Augustine was "radiant" and "a delight to look at" in her beautiful white gown — silver-colored silk covered with a layer of white tulle, with pink roses caught between the layers.[2]

After the ball Augustine had a chance to relax and rest on her laurels for a while. Dances were suspended for three weeks because the Harvard boys had to work on their exams. Augustine was gloomy, writing to her sister, *"on account of midyears — it really is very dull and sad. I think I'll go to Bristol for a few days."[3]* In the same letter she thanked Marjorie for the photographs from Honolulu: *"Has George had his hair shaved? Is he trying to be a football star, or what? It really isn't bad!"*

George, in Hawaii, 1917

---

[1] Letter from Augustine to Marjorie, January 25, 1917. Blithewold Archives.
[2] From reports in the Boston and New York newspapers. Blithewold Archives.
[3] Letter from Augustine to Marjorie, January 25, 1917. Blithewold Archives.

The debutante season finally came to a close, and the attention of Augustine and her friends and family turned to more serious matters. As part of a general preparation for war, the Y.W.C.A. in Boston offered practical courses to the public. Augustine signed up for motor mechanics and wireless telegraphy courses. Her friend Emma signed up for canteen cooking. Bessie herself was volunteering at the local hospital and working at the church making surgical dressings. Estelle Clements was knitting socks for the soldiers.

Chapter XI

THE TRIP WEST, 1916

Marjorie and George began what turned out to be an eight-month trip west on August 27, 1916, when they took a train to Montreal where they picked up the Canadian Pacific Railway to cross Canada. Three days later, between Fort William and Winnipeg, Marjorie wrote to Bessie describing their accommodations. *"We are very comfortable on board. Our compartment is palatial for a train. We sleep like logs the whole night through and do justice to three very good meals a day. There is an observation car where we sit a good deal."*[1]

Marjorie stepping off a Canadian Pacific Railway train, 1916

---

[1] Marjorie to Bessie, August 30, 1916. Blithewold Archives.

They passed through forests of white birch and fir trees and by lakes and rivers until they came to the Wheatlands near Fort William, where they saw more grain elevators than they ever knew existed, *"rising above the towns like the sky-scrapers of New York."*[1] When they arrived in Banff, Alberta, on September 3, they left the train for a 12-day tour of Banff and Lake Louise. They took long walks through the woods and rode horses up into the mountains. At a preserve they saw buffalo, yak, mountain goats, and sheep. At Lake Louise, they found themselves in the loveliest place they had ever seen. Marjorie described the walking trails: *"There is moss on the trails and the smell of spruce...and beside them are the towering majestic mountains with their snowy line against the sky. We are having such a good time."*[2] They rode to Moraine Lake and the Valley of the Ten Peaks, where they were startled to meet a *"big black bear"* ambling among the rocks, *"perfectly unconcerned."*[3] They also saw a lynx and many marmots. At the hotel they played golf and lawn bowls. On another day they set off on ponies up Saddleback Mountain and down into Paradise Valley.

Marjorie hated to leave the area and Lake Louise — *"It will always be one of the brightest spots in my memory"*[4] — but they rejoined the train on September 19 to complete their ride across Canada. They arrived in Vancouver, British Columbia, *"exactly on time! Cheers for the C.P.R.!"* At Stanley Park they admired the wonderful giant trees — Douglas firs, spruces, cedars, and hemlocks.[5] They visited Victoria, British Columbia, for a few days, leaving it reluctantly to take the boat to Seattle, Washington. Not liking Seattle at all,[6] they hurried on to Portland, Oregon, and from there to Cody, Wyoming, where they would begin a 6-week adventure — living in the wild.

---

[1] Marjorie to Bessie, August 30, 1916. Blithewold Archives.

[2] Marjorie to Bessie, September 11, 1916. Blithewold Archives.

[3] Ibid.

[4] Ibid.

[5] Ibid.

[6] *"There's no love lost between me and Seattle."* Marjorie to Bessie, September 19, 1916. Blithewold Archives.

THE WILDS OF WYOMING

In the relative civilization of Cody, Marjorie and George went to the trading store to stock up on clothing, food supplies, and hunting equipment for their adventure. They bought blankets, quilts, and pillows; 100 pounds of potatoes and other necessities; and even a few treats such as crackers and cheese, jam, and figs. They were driven with all their equipment 50 miles out to meet their pack horses and to pick up Merrill, their guide. Merrill's wife cooked a fine dinner for them: broiled elk, pickled beets, potatoes, beans, bread, jam, sliced peaches and cream — *"all on the same plate, and no napkins!"* Their meal was followed by country music — piano, mandolin, kettle drum, bells, bones, and castanets. George sang and Merrill "clogged." The next morning the group set off with 18 ponies (nine pack ponies, four loose ponies, and five saddle horses), 25 miles up into the mountains to their camp, 9,000 feet up on Thorofare Creek near the Yellowstone Reservation. The plan was to live in tents for five weeks, riding, tramping, hunting, and fishing. It promised to be a challenging escapade, but Marjorie was more than ready for it, writing excitedly to Bessie, *"This certainly is the life! I never dreamt I'd be lucky enough to have an experience like this. The only sign of civilization I've noticed is that we try to keep our boots dry."*[1] In the same letter, Marjorie described their camp:

> *At present I am lying in our tent. The flap is open and snow is coming down outside. On a line through the center of the tent hang most of our belongings. Shoes and duffle bags in one corner, wood (which I just chopped) in another corner. Two beds, two camp stools, and two stakes driven into the ground to hold wet shoes — that is our complete inside equipment. Outside the tent door is a convenient pine tree (we nail a box to it for brushes and combs, soap, etc.) also 3 small oblong tin cans for tooth brushes and shaving brushes, and many nails for our mirror and other laughable belongings. Beside the tree stand 3 sturdy stakes of*

---

[1] Marjorie to Bessie, October 2, 1916. Blithewold Archives.

convenient height and on them rests a very sturdy hand basin. A canvas bucket and a tin cup are handy. Our beds too are so comfortable. We spent a whole afternoon cutting pine tips for them. Then we spread our tarps out in a sunny spot. On top of the tarps we laid our blankets...well, it's luxury <u>really</u>. You can believe that we sleep 10 hours nearly every night.[1]

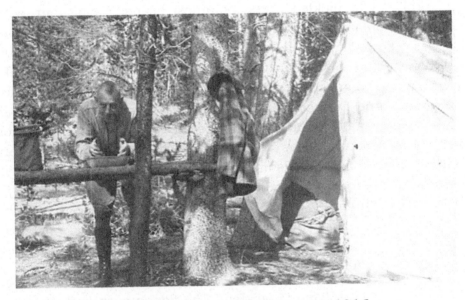

George washing outside the tent, 1916

Their cook and Merrill slept in a nearby tepee. The cook tent was the general meeting place — the scene of storytelling, shoe-greasing, reading, cooking, and dish washing. Their meals consisted of whatever animals they shot, mostly bear and elk, accompanied by *"...every vegetable or soup that ever came out of a can, jam, tea and coffee, biscuits, home-made bread, sauerkraut, sausages, fish cakes, and Irish stew — We certainly live high."*[2]

---

[1] Marjorie to Bessie, October 2, 1916. Blithewold Archives.
[2] Ibid.

The first morning George went hunting. He came back later in the day with a large black bear, six feet from tip to tip. The next morning they woke to find that snow had fallen in the night, so they all went off hunting, following the animal tracks, moving camp every few days, all the time following the trails. At one camp they were astonished to see the game warden, who had brought mail for them from Cody. While he hadn't the slightest idea as to their whereabouts, he thought he would take a chance and go looking for them. He found them less than a mile from his own camp.

George (right) with the "big grizzly," 1916

On Sunday October 15 George shot a moose and an elk. The cook was happy with some fresh meat to supplement their sardines and codfish. By October 25 winter was definitely setting in and the guide was afraid they would get snowed in. Marjorie, however, was not concerned; she thought it would be an adventure to be snowed in, even liking the idea of staying for the whole winter. She wrote to her mother that she had tracked a grizzly bear for 3 or 4 hours:

> *I never had so many thrills. Up mountain ridges, over creeks, into deep snow and ravines as fast and as silently*

as we could go, I gripping my gun. But no bear. He must have heard us on the snow crust. Finally we had to acknowledge that we were beaten. Too bad. I would have liked to get a shot at a grizzly...we've tracked mountain lion too, and wolverine.[1]

In 1916 Wyoming was considered an idyllic place, popular particularly with wealthy New Englanders. It bore a certain cachet for the elite, offering the quintessential wilderness experience. It appealed to a spirit of adventure and risk-taking that recalled an earlier, simpler existence before America shifted from an agrarian to an urban society.

But even in the wilderness the war in Europe was never far from George's mind. Marjorie commented, *"Just think, we don't know* anything *— not even if the war is over."*[2] Despite their enjoyment of the expedition, they were quite prepared to cut short their trip in the event that America went to war. George felt keenly that it was his patriotic duty to enlist immediately.

As their hunting trip drew to a close, Marjorie and George began preparing for their long trek out of the wilderness and, reluctantly, back to civilization. In Cody, they arranged for two crates *"containing trophies of the chase"* to be shipped back to Boston. (Some of the animal heads would ultimately be donated to the Museum of Science in Boston.)

From Cody, Marjorie and George took the train to Miles City, Montana (site of the Battle of Little Bighorn in 1876), to look up George's cousin Craig McDowell and his wife Fannie. The McDowells met them at the station and drove them 63 miles east to their 3000-acre ranch, where George and Marjorie stayed the night. Craig raised cattle and horses and enough crops for their own use. Because the weather had turned bad, the trip back to Miles City was treacherous. Once back in "the city," however, they were able to go to the movies,

---

[1] Marjorie to Bessie, October 25, 1916. Blithewold Archives.
[2] Ibid.

play bridge, drink beer and highballs, and listen to the presidential election returns (Woodrow Wilson was the clear winner).

They maintained their good humor and sense of adventure despite a long and sometimes arduous return journey[1] — they missed several connections and spent many hours in train station waiting rooms. The thermometer dropped to 22 degrees below zero and they were 13 hours late getting into Denver. They traveled more or less uneventfully, however, through Montana, Wyoming, Colorado, Nebraska, South Dakota, and New Mexico. At one point, as they passed through Albuquerque, New Mexico, they saw interesting Indian villages that had mud houses with fodder piled on the roofs and fenced corrals. The next stop after Albuquerque was the Grand Canyon in Arizona; *"I'm looking forward to its good fresh air after all these trains!"*[2]

Marjorie and George experienced a truly memorable visit to the Grand Canyon. After the long train trip and much stormy weather, they were enjoying the clean, cool days of sparkling sunshine: *"And the <u>colors</u> there! There was yellow limestone, pink sandstone, gypsum of red, black basalt, grey granite."*[3] They immediately set off to follow the first trail — the Bright Angel Trail — going more than seven miles down the trail and then back up, walking most of the way and dragging their mules with them. Their time in Wyoming had toned them and strengthened their endurance, and Marjorie did not feel in the least bit tired, *"being in such good shape."*

On their fourth day at the Canyon they set out on what Marjorie considered their best trip, the visit to Hermit's Camp. A carriage drove them along the rim of the canyon to the start of the Hermit Trail, where they picked up mules and set off down the trail, seven miles to the bottom, past Cathedral Stairs and The Serpent, and thus to the Hermit's Camp. There they left their mules and walked 1½

---

[1] As evidenced in Marjorie's letter to Bessie, November 14, 1916. Blithewold Archives.
[2] Marjorie to Bessie, November 14, 1916. Blithewold Archives.
[3] Marjorie to Bessie, November 26, 1916. Blithewold Archives.

miles down to the river, a good steep walk with rocks to scramble over and a stream to wade across. They spent the night back at Hermit's Camp and were off early next morning for a 25-mile trip along the Canyon floor, around promontories, up and down rough trails, and then back up the Bright Angel Trail. During their time at the Grand Canyon they went shopping for Christmas gifts, sending home a large package that included a cowboy hat and belt for Augustine, a Navajo rug for Bessie,[1] and an Indian headdress for Will. That night they headed by train to Los Angeles.

Coming down Bright Angel Trail.
Marjorie walking, George on horseback behind, 1916

Los Angeles was all hustle and bustle and efficiency, *"warm and sunny — flowers everywhere."* At the Hotel Alexandria, Marjorie and George were amazed at the wonderful food and the speed and quality

---

[1] The Navajo rug is at Blithewold.

of service, *"You can have anything done for you — and always quicker and cheaper than at home."*[1] They had arranged for their Cadillac (fondly nicknamed "Caddy") to be shipped to Los Angeles from Boston. At first they found the speed of the traffic intimidating, but they soon overcame their nervousness and enjoyed driving on roads infinitely superior to those they were accustomed to in New England. They traveled to Pasadena, Pomona, Redlands, San Pedro, and Venice, admiring the orange groves, eucalyptus, pepper trees, walnut groves, and vineyards. But they began to tire of the flat terrain and longed to see mountains again, so they drove up to the top of Mount Wilson, had dinner at the 6000-foot summit, and returned to their hotel by starlight. The next leg of their trip would be to Hawaii, where they planned to spend the Christmas holidays.

HAWAII

Marjorie and George left Los Angeles on November 26 to sail to Hawaii on the *Great Northern*, with "Caddy" safely in the hold. It was a rough crossing, but George and Marjorie were among the few who did not get sick. George played poker *"all the time,"* and Marjorie read and walked and played deck sports. Thanksgiving Day came and went during the voyage, with little acknowledgement. They landed at Hilo on the morning of December 3 in pouring rain, but they went to see the falls and admired the profusion of flowers: hibiscus, calla lilies, poinsettias, bougainvilleas, hydrangeas, fuchsias, and heliotrope. Their first destination was the top of the Kilauea Volcano, well above the vegetation line. It was a bleak, desolate landscape of black hard-baked lava punctuated by clouds and spouts of steam. Their driver took them almost to the rim. Marjorie and George got out and walked, very slowly and cautiously, toward a huge hole.[2] A strange cackling sound added to the drama; suddenly they found themselves on the edge of the crater itself.

---

[1] Marjorie to Bessie, November 26, 1916. Blithewold Archives.
[2] Marjorie to Bessie, December 7, 1916. Blithewold Archives.

George peering over the crater at Kilauea, 1916

Four hundred feet below them and two-thirds of a mile across, all they could see was an expanse of burning lava,

> *...a grey mass, slowly seething and boiling. The biggest and most appalling thing I have ever seen...hills and valleys of grey molten lava, rivers, cracks of red fire, lakes, fountains, and geysers of roaring crackling flame. As we watched, great sections of cooled lava were sucked down into the cracks and new fountains of flame burst out; wild waves of fire dashed against the craggy sides of the crater; all is wild — inferno-like.*

They sat there, mesmerized, for hours. When the sun set, the crater's rim was only a vague outline in the near-complete darkness: *"only the rivers and fountains of fire shone out, brilliant and unconquerable.*"[1] In a daze, they made their way down the mountain and back to their ship for the overnight sail to Honolulu. Marjorie and George found Honolulu to be an interesting little city, with a few good American shops and many Japanese bazaars. They had planned to stay at the Moana Hotel, but they found it old-fashioned and noisy (owing to hotel construction nearby). Instead they rented a small cottage named Hale Kai (Home by the Sea), which had a sitting room, bedroom, and bathroom; a nice porch with a front yard full of flowers, palms, a fig tree, and a bougainvillea vine; the back entry had a place to hang their wet bathing suits. And best of all, it had a view of the sea. Marjorie made it feel like home with flowers, Japanese prints, and a new lamp, *"and with the rag rugs on the floor and the nice rocking chair and couch and our books, we are as comfy as you please."*[2]

Living room of Marjorie and George's cottage at Hale Kai, 1916, showing Marjorie's flowers, Japanese prints, and new lamp

---

[1] Marjorie to Bessie, December 7, 1916. Blithewold Archives.
[2] Ibid.

Their original plan was to stay over the Christmas holidays and then return to the mainland. George took out a temporary membership at the local country club, but they were discouraged by the wet weather, having to drive all over the island in the relentless rain, and even play golf in the rain and mud. Just as they began to despair — becoming rather homesick and bored and considering an early retreat — the weather changed. The sun finally appeared and now they were able to play a lot of golf and attend parties and dinners at the club, and meet lots of people, including an old Yale friend of George's. They loved swimming in the huge waves and were persuaded to try surfboarding and outrigger canoeing. Before long they decided that not only would they *not* be leaving the island early, but they would be *extending* their stay. They began to follow up on the letters of introduction from friends and family that they had brought with them and were soon wrapped up in the society life of Honolulu. They accepted invitations to receptions and teas, art exhibits, musical evenings, dinners and dances, and house parties. *"We have been very society! So, Augustine is not the only gadder!"*[1]

The day before Christmas, Marjorie and George received letters, cards, and packages from home. They saved them all for the next day and went out to a Christmas Eve party. Christmas Day began with an hour's surfboard riding, then church at the Episcopal Cathedral, and then more surfing, followed by *"a huge and very galumptious Christmas dinner, roast pig and everything else including Christmas toys and candy"* at the home of new friends. Then it was out to the country club where everyone danced around the Christmas tree. They played nine holes of golf and danced some more, then went to the Alexander Young Hotel for another Christmas dinner — this time just the two of them. They finally read all the Christmas letters and cards from home, and declared that it had been a *"very worth remembering"* Christmas Day.

---

[1] Marjorie to Bessie, December 18, 1916. Blithewold Archives.

On January 2 George wrote a long letter to Bessie and Will in which he described all their activities. He told them that he and Marjorie were particularly enjoying the surfing.

About the best fun that we have enjoyed here is surf-board riding which we indulge in practically every day at Waikiki Beach. We are slowly becoming proficient at it and now can catch almost every wave. It is a thrilling and exciting sport.[1]

Between Christmas and New Year's, George went off on a five-day fishing trip to Maui. He and Marjorie scheduled a six-day return trip to the island of Hawaii together but at the last minute decided not to go: *"It's just too nice here and we decided we couldn't bear to leave the surf-riding!"*

Marjorie surf-riding, 1917

In January Marjorie and George extended their vacation again, deciding to stay *"several weeks longer. We have grown to have a great liking for the place."[2]* The weather was by now absolutely perfect — *"I*

---

[1] George Lyon to Bessie, January 2, 1917. Blithewold Archives.
[2] George Lyon to Bessie, January 12, 1917. Blithewold Archives.

never knew such days anywhere." When the moon was full they drove about to look at the mountains and the surf in the *"beauteous moonlight."* On January 7 they witnessed a total eclipse of the moon, which *they* liked but which terrified many of the Chinese people on the island.

Toward the end of their Hawaiian trip they made arrangements by an exchange of telegrams to meet Bessie, William McKee, and Augustine at the White Sulphur Springs resort in West Virginia at the end of March, where they would stay for a month. In the meantime, they heard that there was new activity at the Island of Hawaii's volcano, so they loaded "Caddy" onto the ship and sailed across to Hilo. They drove around the island during the day, then after dinner set off to the volcano over the sharp lava roads. Still twenty miles away, a pillar of fire was visible in the sky. When they reached the crater, they found that the lava had risen significantly, making it even more eerie and frightening than it had been before.

George and a Professor Jaeger at the edge of the volcano, 1917

But their idyll was about to end. On February 1 they heard that Germany had resumed unrestricted submarine warfare. President Woodrow Wilson severed diplomatic ties with Germany on February 3, and the American people were put on notice that the United States might declare war at any moment. George cabled the McKees, saying that if war were declared they would return to Boston immediately. Under a heavy war cloud, Marjorie and George left Honolulu on the S.S. *Matsonia*. *"The* Matsonia *is crowded to capacity as a result of the breaking off of diplomatic relations. There was a rush for accommodations as soon as the possibility of war and its meaning was realized,"*[1] wrote George to Bessie.

The Lyons' Cadillac being loaded onto the S.S. Matsonia, *1917*

---

[1] George to Bessie, March 8, 1917. Blithewold Archives.

Although Marjorie wondered what news awaited them in San Francisco, the couple agreed that unless there was a declaration of war they would continue with their plan to meet the McKees on March 27 at White Sulphur Springs. They spent a few days in San Francisco looking around the city that George had lived in with his family when he was twelve, contemplating with amazement the steep hills down which he used to *"coast on his wagon."* They both went shopping for new clothes and George had the Cadillac serviced. San Francisco was cold and wet, and they were happy to head south to Santa Barbara. Unfortunately, the coast road was impassable because of heavy spring flooding, and they had to drive more than 500 miles on inland roads, sometimes feet deep in mud.

George driving on the rain-soaked road to Santa Barbara, 1917

SANTA BARBARA AND WHITE SULPHUR SPRINGS

Once in Santa Barbara they settled in for three weeks at the luxurious Hotel Potter, *"squandering all our remaining substance."* They met up with many friends and acquaintances, describing Santa Barbara as largely a Boston colony. *"It's rather gay, and <u>society</u>! Santa Barbara seems like a bit of the East transported out here."*[1] The Misses Barnes (Hattie and Isolene) from Bristol were staying at the same hotel and sponsored George and Marjorie for temporary membership at the Santa Barbara Golf and Country Club.

Marjorie golfing at the Santa Barbara Country Club, 1917

---

[1] Marjorie's diary, March 4, 1917. Blithewold Archives.

The Lyons loved the mountains, the trees, and the blue hills of the Southern California city. For three glorious weeks they played golf and tennis every day; they took lessons, played in tournaments, and lunched at the club, fitting in as much activity as they could each day: *"As you see we have lived more or less at the Club. Some days we lunch there — arriving at 9:30 and leaving at 6 or so PM! Sport clothes are fashionable at any and all times here."*[1] It was definitely a happy time!

On March 19 they reluctantly began to pack their belongings for the next leg of the journey. The Cadillac was shipped home to Boston, and they boarded a train that would take them through California, Arizona, Texas, and Mississippi. They disembarked in New Orleans and spent two days at the Hotel St. Charles, enjoying fascinating tours of the city. Back on the train they passed through Montgomery, Alabama, and Kentucky and Ohio, arriving at White Sulphur Springs, West Virginia, early in the morning of March 27. Bessie was waiting for them on the steps of the hotel and they all had a joyful reunion. *"My but we were glad to see her!"* wrote Marjorie in her diary. George immediately checked out the golfing facilities, while Marjorie and Bessie sat happily on the porch reading and knitting, and catching up on many months of news.

---

[1] Marjorie to Bessie, March 16, 1917. Blithewold Archives.

Bessie McKee knitting on the White Sulphur Springs Hotel porch,
March 1917

The young couple looked forward to four long, lazy weeks with family, including Marjorie's cousin Katharine (Kitty) Pardee who joined them for a while. William McKee and George fell into a pleasant routine of horse-back riding, golfing, and tennis, while Marjorie and Kitty rode into the mountains where they saw *"such gorgeous views — with the sea and the misty islands beyond."*[1] They also took long walks. One day the two young women prepared a picnic for everyone by the stream on White Sugar Hill. They built a fire and cooked chops

---

[1] Marjorie's diary, March 27, 1917. Blithewold Archives.

and bacon and made coffee, while Marjorie and George entertained the group with tales of their wilderness adventures.

The picnic on White Sugar Hill.
George and Kitty center; Bessie right, 1917

Over the years Marjorie and George would take many more trips together. They appear to have been happy and compatible traveling companions, as evidenced by their enthusiasm and excited letters home. They occasionally traveled with friends but most often they went alone, although they did enjoy meeting new people and took advantage of letters of introduction. On their wilderness hunting trips, they established good relationships with guides and cooks, often using the same ones on subsequent trips. They would also often arrange to meet up with the same hunters on different trips. Conditions on the hunting trips were harsh, but Marjorie took great pride in being able to keep up with the men. She had great stamina and was a strong, capable hunter, respected by her fellow huntsmen.

Chapter XII

AMERICA ENTERS THE WAR

On April 6, 1917, while Marjorie and George and the McKees were still at White Sulphur Springs, America declared war against Germany. Still stinging from the sinking of the S.S. *Lusitania* and seven American merchant ships, President Woodrow Wilson finally capitulated to European pressure after he was handed an intercepted telegram from Germany to Mexico. In the telegram, Mexico was urged to join Germany and Japan in an alliance to fight against the United States. In that way America would be occupied with its own war at home and would be reluctant to assist the war effort in Europe. In return, Germany promised Mexico its support in reclaiming Texas, New Mexico, and Arizona after the war. America mobilized its forces and began sending troops to Europe. This war would be called "The War to End All Wars" — more than 70 million military personnel would be mobilized throughout the world, and 15 million would be killed.

On April 9, George left White Sulphur Springs to go to Washington to see about his *"preparedness job."* From there he went to New York to talk about a job he had been offered as head of the New York Red Cross, which he was strongly urged to take. But he had already put in his application for Cavalry or Infantry Captain, and he had his heart set on serving in the U.S. Army. He returned to White Sulphur Springs to think about his future, to play more golf, and to await the results of his physical examination. Then it was time to start the journey back to Boston. The McKees and the Lyons hired a car and a driver and motored through the Shenandoah Valley to Basick, Virginia, where they stayed overnight with William McKee's sister Isabell Hidden and her husband William at their farm. The Hiddens raised Rhode Island Red chickens, pigs, cows, and horses, and grew oats, corn, and apples.

George, Will McKee, Will Hidden, and Bessie, on the porch
of the Hiddens' farmhouse, April, 1917

The next morning they drove to Greenwood and took the train to Washington. It was exciting to see the hundreds of flags and French and English soldiers milling about. They had tea at the White House as guests of President Wilson,[1] and then were driven back to their hotel in the White House automobile, a Pierce. They traveled by train again to New York: *"It was impressive to see the flags everywhere and soldiers guarding each bridge, reservoir, factory, etc."*[2] Arriving back in Boston the following day, Marjorie and George were happy to be back in their own home at 4 Acorn Street. The last sentence in Marjorie's trip diary is *"Back home after just eight months."* But life was about to become very challenging, and Marjorie and George would spend most of the next two years apart.

Within a few days of their return to Boston, George was called to Fort Meyer, Virginia, for Officers' Training. He was one of 2,000

---

[1] Woodrow Wilson's wife was from Rome, Georgia, and William McKee, who was a strong supporter of Wilson's presidency, may have known her there.
[2] Marjorie's diary, April 29, 1917. Blithewold Archives.

recruits chosen from a pool of 5,000 applicants for a three-month course that would determine which men would be fit for what rank. The most capable and fit men would become captains. For three months they drilled, attended lectures, went on 25-mile hikes (with heavy packs), and were tested in every possible physical and mental capacity. They would go on exercises that simulated war conditions, from which many recruits were left gasping for breath and facing dismissal. George was assigned to Company 9. Each company barracks held 160 men in double-deck cots, with their own mess and bathroom facilities. George reported being quite comfortable at the start, although he had trouble getting enough sleep. His cot was near the door to the mess kitchen and next to the bathroom, which meant that his scant sleep was disturbed constantly. He had to be up at 5 every morning and his whole day was tightly scheduled until lights out at 9:45 pm. Superiors rotated the men's roles and positions, so that each man was observed at different levels of the organizational hierarchy.

George at Camp Meyer, 1917

On a more personal level, George sent his laundry home every week. Marjorie took care of it and quickly sent it back, along with any extras he requested. His one luxury was Baker's chocolate, and Marjorie sent him great quantities of it. His few hours off-duty on Sundays he spent playing tennis at a nearby club.

In the middle of May Marjorie went down to Fort Meyer for a weekend, bringing fresh supplies and extra socks that Bessie had knit. George was shocked by Marjorie's pale and thin appearance. He wrote to Bessie, asking her confidentially what she thought might be wrong. He thought she looked very run-down: *"Is she doing too much, or worrying about me, or what do you think the trouble is?"* He questioned his own decision to volunteer for duty: *"Perhaps my duty isn't here after all. What do you think? Is the house too much for her, and would it be better to close it up and relieve her of that work? As you see I am a good deal upset and troubled."*[1] George and Bessie and even Marjorie herself made frequent references to Marjorie's health over the next few years. She always suffered from hay fever in the summer and appeared to succumb to despair on occasion. But at the same time she also had great stamina and determination, as demonstrated by her energy and endurance on the many rigorous trips she took with George.

By June the work at the training camp was becoming more strenuous. George was feeling the intense heat and swarms of mosquitoes and flies made sleep even more elusive. He reported that: *"Many men were eliminated from the camp either for mental or physical deficiencies. I hope to stick it longer."*[2] He passed his first examinations with top marks, however, and to celebrate he arranged to meet Marjorie in Washington for the July Fourth weekend. They spent two days together, making what plans they could and wondering what their futures held. Marjorie was taking classes in motor mechanics and chauffeuring in Boston, and they both wanted to take language

---

[1] George to Bessie, May 17, 1917. Blithewold Archives.
[2] George to Marjorie, June 9, 1917. Blithewold Archives.

lessons to improve their French, with the idea that if George got sent to France, Marjorie might also qualify to do useful war work there.

As the summer progressed conditions became even worse, but George became hardened by the rigorous demands. He took pride in the 25-mile marches and standing around in the trenches in pouring rain. He went on a night maneuver, suffering through the heat, humidity, dust, rain, mud, and sweat. To him these things were part of his patriotic duty. *"It is the greatest sacrifice,"* he said, as the temperature soared to 104 degrees in the shade. At the end of July George was rewarded for all his hard work: he was one of only seven in the company slated for a captaincy. Not only was he to be a captain, but he ended his training with the highest marks. His superior told him that if they were allowed to give higher rankings, George would certainly have been made a major. George was very happy with his title of captain, however, and left the training camp on August 15 having achieved his goal. He returned to Acorn Street to await his assignment. He was 39 years old and desperately wanted to go to France and see *"some action."*[1]

COLUMBIA, SOUTH CAROLINA

At the beginning of September George heard he was not to go to Europe after all. He was being sent to Camp Jackson, seven miles from Columbia in South Carolina, where he would help train new recruits. He was disappointed, but he knew that this was also important work and he was determined to do the best possible job.[2]

---

[1] As evidenced in George's letters to Marjorie, summer of 1917. Blithewold Archives.
[2] Ibid.

Captain George Armstrong Lyon, 1917

Marjorie, too, was disappointed. She had hoped to follow George to France and offer her services to her country in any way possible. Instead, to support George and to ease his life at camp in South Carolina, she decided to move to Columbia. On September 10, just two days short of her thirty-fourth birthday, she traveled down by train from Boston via New York, having left instructions for her car to be shipped to her in South Carolina. She intended to stay for as long as George was stationed there. On her arrival in Columbia she checked herself into the Jefferson Hotel while she looked around for a more permanent place to stay. Her initial impression was of a quaint town at a high elevation and with nice air.[1] She thought it would be fun settling into a brand-new place. The countryside was pleasant, with rolling lowland and plenty of trees. The hotel was *"slow, and backwoodsy in some ways, but on the whole good. The room is very nice,"* even though she had to *"get the maid and a boy and the vacuum*

---

[1] Letter from Marjorie to Bessie, September 13, 1917. Blithewold Archives.

cleaners all at work before I dared unpack — but now all is well! The bathroom is white tiled and really grand."[1] On the morning of September 12, her birthday, Marjorie found a large bouquet of flowers in her room. When George arrived after lunch he found the room a bower of roses, *"thanks to his thoughtfulness."* George was *very* glad to see his wife, taking her out in his hired Ford to the camp to see his quarters and to meet his friends. As a Captain he had his own room, nicely furnished with a cot, a carpet, two wooden chairs, a wooden desk, a bookshelf, and a window. It must have seemed very luxurious after his recent accommodations at Fort Meyer. They later drove out to the Ridgewood Golf and Country Club for a special dinner. The lovely sunset over the pines added to the enjoyment. When at the end of the evening Marjorie commented that it was a lovely ending to her birthday, George was shocked — he had not remembered her birthday! He promised to visit her again the following Sunday, when they hoped to play golf at the Ridgewood Club after their clubs arrived from Boston.

After a few days Marjorie decided that she liked Columbia and would look for Red Cross work there, but first she needed to find a place to stay. She eventually found a boardinghouse in a suburb of Columbia (at 2315 Taylor Street) run by Mr. and Mrs. Murdaugh, where she could board and have her meals. The room was large, and she would have the use of a bathroom on the same floor. There was also a stable for "Caddy." The only possible problem might be that the Murdaughs had eight young children. Marjorie, nevertheless, took the room and became fond of the whole family. She read to the children in the evenings and came to love them dearly.

Marjorie met people in the town and was soon asked to take charge of the Home Services Institute of the Red Cross, with the title of Head of Civilian Relief Work. With the new camp just outside of town, there would be a growing need for such services. She was given an office with a telephone and a typewriter; her small support staff would assist her in the work of helping 31 local families. Part of her day was

---

[1] Letter from Marjorie to Bessie, September 13, 1917. Blithewold Archives.

spent in the office supervising her staff and writing reports, and part visiting her families to see what they needed and how she could help them. They were all military families with special needs — husbands away fighting the war or, sometimes, war widows.

In November, Marjorie received a letter from her school friend Louise Smith, who had gone to France as a military driver. In her letter Louise described her strenuous and stressful work. She and her colleagues worked 24 hours on and 24 hours off during attacks. All "off" time was spent working on the cars. She described difficult conditions: bad food, no beds, and the strain of driving at night without lights over hilly, muddy roads full of shell holes. She generally found herself in front of the artillery, and only 1½ to 6 kilometers behind the first lines. The wounded were carried in from the field by stretcher bearers, given first aid, and then put into cars to be driven back to the first available hospital. In the beginning two women would drive each car, but as the war progressed there were more casualties and not enough drivers, so Louise found herself driving alone on newly recaptured roads. She was often under shell-fire herself.[1] Marjorie immediately took up the idea of doing similar necessary work when George was sent to France.

Marjorie was too busy to go home to Bristol for the family Thanksgiving (where Bessie and Will reported *"snow and moonlight"*). She spent her time instead taking Thanksgiving baskets around to some of her families, assisted by her co-worker Mrs. Wey. Meanwhile, things out at Camp Jackson were not good — a deadly epidemic of measles and pneumonia took three lives in George's regiment alone. But he was still able to take a few hours off to visit Marjorie and to go for a Thanksgiving drive.

The weather was getting colder in South Carolina, with temperatures hovering around zero. George had no heat in his quarters and was grateful for the warm socks and sweaters that Bessie sent him. At night Marjorie slept in *"stockings, tights, a*

---

[1] Letter from Louise Smith to Marjorie, November 1917. Blithewold Archives.

sweater, four blankets, a spread and a fur coat!"[1] The Cadillac's radiator froze and then burst. At Camp Jackson there was another epidemic, this time of meningitis, which threatened to keep all the men quarantined over the holidays. George and Marjorie, though, received good news in early December: George would get 14 days' leave over Christmas, if he had no meningitis germs in his throat. They planned to leave Columbia on December 20, and take the overnight train to New York. The McKees, meanwhile, had proudly hung a "Service Flag" outside their house on Commonwealth Avenue to indicate that someone in the family was serving in the military. The day after George left camp, the meningitis epidemic escalated and quarantine was declared. All further leave was cancelled and the remaining officers and men had to spend Christmas and the following two weeks in camp.

Marjorie and George arrived in Boston on December 22. On Christmas Eve, the whole family drove to Blithewold and spent an idyllic Christmas vacation there. Marjorie wrote:

> *What a wonderful time we had. And wasn't it lucky we could all be together in dear Blithewold. I wonder if the old place realizes how much I love it?*[2]

And George added his own thanks:

> *Didn't we have a dandy time at Bristol? Blithewold certainly is a delightful haven to drop anchor in, and it was so nice to see you all and be with you.*

---

[1] Letter from Marjorie to Bessie, December 14, 1917. Blithewold Archives.
[2] Marjorie to Bessie, January 4, 1918. Blithewold Archives.

George in uniform, on the Loggia at Blithewold, Christmas 1917

After a very long and tiring return train journey, George and Marjorie arrived back in Columbia six hours late, to find three inches of snow on the ground and temperatures around zero. It was a wonderful Christmas vacation, but they were happy to be back in South Carolina and to resume their work. Marjorie reported to Bessie:

The Murdaughs certainly were glad to see us — just as dear and cordial as they could possibly be. The children sat on top of me and beside me, and we had to tell them all about everything! Then George, after a good supper, went out to Camp (I motored him with such regret) and we got back to our jobs.[1]

Conditions at the camp improved in February, but the epidemics had now spread to the town. All the theaters, schools, and churches were closed, but the Red Cross office had permission to continue its important work. Marjorie was assigned 39 new families during January, bringing the total number of families served to 121. Bessie, Augustine, and Estelle Clements knitted more socks, hats, and sweaters for George and sent gifts of yarn and needles to the Murdaugh children (Marjorie was teaching them to knit sweaters for themselves).

In March the McKees and Augustine traveled south to visit. Bessie and Will stayed at the Jefferson Hotel and Augustine stayed at the Murdaughs' house with Marjorie. After a few days of sightseeing in Columbia, the travelers went on to Aiken, a fashionable "wintering" resort 40 miles from Columbia popular with wealthy people from the northeast. Marjorie and George joined them there for a week. (The Daylight Saving System had just been introduced and the couple were grateful for the extra hour of daylight for the trip back to Columbia: *"I love the way the clock behaves now."*[2]) After Marjorie and George left them, Bessie, Will, and Augustine traveled up to the Greenbrier Hotel in White Sulphur Springs for more golf and horseback riding.

By April 1918, George was getting anxious to go to Europe. *"George hopes to get some new men for his company and then the whole Regiment has gotten orders to get their packing boxes ready in anticipation of Overseas Service. George is so encouraged."*[3] It couldn't come soon enough for George. He expected to be in France by July: *"We are all overjoyed at the end of the waiting."* In May he and his men were sent to Camp Sevier in Greenville, South Carolina, to await final orders. Marjorie quickly wound up her work at the Red Cross in

---

[1] Marjorie to Bessie, January 4, 1918. Blithewold Archives.
[2] Ibid.
[3] Letter from Marjorie to Bessie, April 20, 1918. Blithewold Archives.

Columbia, leaving Mrs. Wey in charge. *"I did weep when I said good-bye...Columbia has a warm place in my heart certainly — and especially the Murdaughs."[1]* Mr. Murdaugh accompanied Marjorie on the 6½-hour drive to Greenville to meet up with George, during which *"we passed hundreds of motor trucks and mule wagons on the way...these are such unusual times. It's literally a question of 'What next?'"[2]* In Greenville, she took a room at the Hotel Imperial. The *"lovely room"* on the fifth floor had a view of the Blue Mountains in the distance, and she soon filled it with flowers. Not knowing how long they would be in Greenville, she signed up for a business course, struggling to master the typewriter and shorthand. She also applied to the War Department for service in Europe, anxious to do *her* part. She emphasized her intimate knowledge of the French language, her successful work with the Red Cross in South Carolina in which she directed many workers, her knowledge of motor mechanics, and her willingness to offer her services free of any expense to the American government. She even offered to ship her own car over to Europe. She was bitterly disappointed, however, to hear back from the Department of State that the War Department prohibited the issuance of passports that would enable mothers, wives, or daughters of officers or enlisted men in the armed forces to visit European countries for any kind of relief or hospital work. Even trained nurses, although desperately needed, were being refused. Marjorie protested the decision but was told only that should the policy be changed she would, owing to her superb qualifications, be considered. The Red Cross tried to use their influence to have them make an exception for Marjorie, but failed. *"Apparently there is no chance whatever of my being allowed to do work in Europe. George being an officer cuts me out. I am disappointed."[3]* As soon as his assignment at Camp Sevier was over, George was given leave to settle his affairs at home, and he and Marjorie drove back to Boston together. After attending to George's business in Boston, they joined the rest of the family at Blithewold.

---

[1] Letter from Marjorie to Bessie, May 18, 1918. Blithewold Archives.
[2] Ibid.
[3] Letter from Marjorie to Bessie, June 7, 1918. Blithewold Archives.

Marjorie wrote to Bessie: *"It was the very best vacation we've had — and nice to have it so, as it may be the last we'll have together for a while. You were all so dear to us, and everything was perfect. I do so love Bristol."*[1]

AUGUSTINE AND QUINCY ADAMS SHAW

In July, after Marjorie and George had left Blithewold, Augustine became seriously ill with diphtheria, considered a deadly disease at the time. The entire household received "antitoxins" and Augustine was confined to her room. When Will McKee's sister and brother-in-law came to visit for the day from Boston, they were advised not to go into the house, but to eat their meals separately from the family on the Breakfast Porch. Their visit did have its dramatic high point, however — a large destroyer sailed by Blithewold on its way into the harbor, terrifying the maids, who were sure it was a German submarine. (This was actually not implausible, since on June 3 a German U-boat had sunk several ships off the Rhode Island coast.)

Augustine's life was now to take a new turn. As soon as she had recovered from her illness she wrote to Marjorie, telling her that Quincy (Quinny) Shaw had proposed marriage and she had accepted. He had already spoken to Bessie and Will McKee. Bessie was delighted, but Will thought they were too young — Augustine was not yet 20 years old and Quinny was still a student at Harvard. Because he was being sent to Officers' Training Camp, though, the young couple wanted to become engaged before he left. Marjorie, however, was very much opposed to an engagement, making the point that Quinny had yet to prove himself. Will McKee at first agreed with

---

[1] Letter from Marjorie to Bessie, June 7, 1918. Blithewold Archives.

Marjorie although he later changed his mind, and the resulting split in the family had repercussions for years to come.[1]

Quincy Adams Shaw, Jr., ca. 1918   Augustine Van Wickle, 1918

In August of 1918 Marjorie was alone with her fears for George's safety and still upset about Augustine's haste to marry Quinny Shaw. She wrote to the McKees on August 25, apologizing in advance for upsetting them by speaking frankly. But, she argued, none of them knew much about the Shaw family other than their social prominence, and she was worried not only about Quinny's youth but his father's mental instability. (In fact, it did become clear later that manic-depression [now called bipolar disorder] ran in the Shaw family, dating back to Robert Gould Shaw, a hero of the Civil

---

[1] As evidenced in letters from Marjorie to Bessie, from Marjorie to Augustine, and from Marjorie to William McKee. Also, in notes written by Marjorie, January and February, 1919. Blithewold Archives.

War. Diagnosis and treatment were ominously elusive in those days, but from what Marjorie *did* know she had good reason to be concerned.) All she asked at the moment, however, was that Augustine be persuaded to wait two years before becoming engaged or marrying. She felt that the wait would be good for both Augustine and Quinny, but added that Bessie and Will should make it clear that they would give their full consent at the end of the two years. She wrote *"At first I thought it might be too late to do anything, but I don't believe that it is. You are the only ones who can do anything."*[1] Marjorie assured them that Augustine was unlikely to do anything rash, like running off, but that the wait *"would make a woman of her, and what's more, a man of Quinny."* Marjorie's pleas fell on deaf ears. Three days later Augustine announced her engagement to Quincy Adams Shaw, Jr. At the end of August Quinny was sent to Camp Jackson in Columbia, South Carolina.

FIGHTING IN FRANCE

In July 1918 George had been sent to Camp Mills in Hempstead, New York, to receive his orders and prepare for imminent departure for Europe. At the end of the month he wrote a touching farewell letter to Marjorie:

> *My Very Dear Wife, This is a farewell note to tell you how much I love you, and to speak of one or two other things. I don't want to make you feel sadder than need be at our leave-taking, and I know you have been ready for it for so long. I hope, and expect, to come back, and the chances are that I shall, but of course I may not. If I should not, don't mourn for me, my dear girl, and don't bind yourself to my memory too long. I mean by that, that I want you to marry again. I will cable you on arrival if possible. I am so glad to*

---

[1] Letter from Marjorie to William McKee, August 5, 1918. Blithewold Archives.

be finally on the way to do my part. Goodbye, my dear wife, and may God bless and keep you safe for my home-coming. Devotedly, George.[1]

He also wrote to Bessie,

This is to bid you goodbye. I hope you know, my dear Mother, how strong my affection for you and the family — but especially for you — has grown. I am so happy to go. It has been fierce to wait all this time, to know that I was among the first in the Service and yet still here, and so many of the others over there...Take care of my wife. She needs support and love. Cheer her up and help her not to worry. I know she thinks I am doing right, and I shall come back please God.[2]

With George away, Marjorie felt the need to find useful work. In October she offered her services to the northeastern branch of the Red Cross and was promptly offered a temporary position in the Harwichport, Massachusetts, headquarters of the Red Cross Home Service for the Cape Cod area. Its Secretary was to take an "Institute" course in Boston, so Marjorie took his place for six weeks. Because she did such an excellent job there, she was next sent to northern Vermont to organize a Home Service Department in that area. She spent the first seven hectic days in Vermont interviewing committees and soldiers' families in different towns, giving lectures, and sleeping in a different bed each night.

On the war front, the next generation of Pardees was serving their country. Israel and Alice Pardee's son Marvin Pardee was in France, reporting that *"Our boys are surely doing wonderful work over here, fighting like fiends."*[3] Dorothy Pardee Clark's husband Ben Clark was also in France, enduring horrific conditions — *"Nothing which has*

---

[1] Letter from George to Marjorie, July 31, 1918. Blithewold Archives.
[2] Letter from George to Bessie, July 31, 1918. Blithewold Archives.
[3] Pardee Family Newsletter, December 1918. Blithewold Archives.

been written describes the horrors of it all."[1] Young Harry Keller, Gertrude's son, had been honorably discharged from the army and was returning home to complete his college studies. Helen Pardee Foulke's husband Herbert was in the fighting near the front in France. One of Calvin Pardee's grandsons, Herbert Warden, was fighting with the Tank Corps that was helping to break the Hindenburg Line[2] in France; another grandson, Calvin Pardee III, was with the Civilian Air Patrol. Anne Pardee Allison's son-in-law, Thatcher Nelson, was serving as a Captain in the American army. And on the Van Wickle side of the family, Marjorie's cousin Morgan Van Wickle was fighting in France.

George's letters home from France described brutal fighting conditions. In October he was in the trenches in Tonnere, southeast of Paris, with hopes of getting to the Front soon. From Tonnere they embarked on a long and difficult march through mud and rain, with:

...roads jammed with artillery and trucks and men, great dumps of supplies and ammunition everywhere, the country absolutely desolated. You can't conceive of desolation more complete. In the shelled towns — and they had all been shelled — hardly one stone above another.[3]

They arrived at Sommedieue near the middle of November and were sent into the frontline trenches:

We were shelled all the way up to where we deployed...my company was without any shelter, and advanced for six hours under continuous machine gun and artillery fire. The men behaved magnificently, and I was amply repaid for all the work and energy I've put into getting a well-disciplined company. I had over 25% casualties, and mighty near went over myself. Machine gun fire is not so bad — you don't

---

[1] Pardee Family Newsletter, December 1918. Blithewold Archives.
[2] The German line of defense, thought to be impregnable.
[3] George to Marjorie, October, 1918.

realize what the sing of the bullets means, but there is no question about the terror of high explosive shells.[1]

They went into action again at daybreak the next day. The men were just getting ready to move out through a heavy fog when the shelling and machine-gun fire suddenly stopped. There was complete silence for a moment or two. It was eleven o'clock on the eleventh day of the eleventh month. Armistice had been declared — the war was over. George's regiment now had to hike 125 miles back to General Headquarters. Other U.S. troops were not so lucky: on the morning of November 11, 320 American soldiers were killed and 3000 more were wounded at Meuse.[2] The final toll after more than four years of hostilities was 15 million dead.

Back in the United States, meantime, the influenza epidemic had spread across the country. By the end of 1918, 675,000 Americans had died of the disease.[3] The deadly virus ultimately spread throughout the world, killing a total of 50 million people before it subsided in 1919. The Pardee Family Newsletter of December 1918 passed on news of the well-being of family members in the last few months of 1918, as well as their whereabouts. Several family members had suffered from the flu, but all survived and everyone was taking special precautions.[4]

---

[1] George to Marjorie, November, 1918.
[2] Juliet Nicolson, *The Great Silence.* Grove Press 2009, p. 27.
[3] Lindsay Redicon, *The Forgotten Killer.*
[4] Pardee Family Newsletter, December 1918. Blithewold Archives.

Chapter XIII

PEACETIME

George did not immediately return home when the war ended, writing to Marjorie that he would be lucky to be home within six months. Even though the war was "officially" over, George was in Chaumont, France (southeast of Paris, north of Dijon) in January 1919. As a member of the General Staff in the Operations Section he was charged with reading through documents which he found intensely interesting.[1] His new work and living conditions were in stark contrast to his recent life with the troops. Instead of a damp trench he had a big, warm office with clerks, stenographers, and orderlies, to do his bidding. He described his accommodations as very luxurious.[2] The house had most recently been used by a French Colonel who had secured the services of the best Parisian chef, so George was well-fed for the first time in months. The house became a kind of select club, and George enjoyed the company of visiting former ambassadors, generals, colonels, and a former attorney general. After-dinner conversation around the fire included talk of Pershing and Foch, Pétain and Haig, Wilson and Lloyd George, *"and other Great Personages bandied about by men who know them, in the most informal fashion. Can you imagine anything more fascinating?"* George, who had been craving meaningful intellectual exchange and stimulation, found that *"many of them look on me with a certain envy because I have been on active service with the troops!"*[3]

George was invited to be part of a team that would tour the battlefields. Superiors gave the group a Cadillac and sent them out *"to do the job."* They visited St. Mihiel, Verdun, Le Mort Homme, the Argonne forest, Grand Pré, Rheims, Fismes, Château Thierry, Mézy,

---

[1] As evidenced in George's letter to Marjorie, January 21, 1919. Blithewold Archives.
[2] Ibid.
[3] Letter from George to Marjorie, January 21, 1919. Blithewold Archives.

Châlons, Clermont, La Voie Sacrée, and Bar-le-Duc. They went over the ground where George's company had seen action and even through the German trenches. George noted ironically that *"flowers were growing everywhere..."* In August 1919, George Lyon was awarded the prestigious Croix de Guerre by the French government for his bravery and endurance during the war.[1]

THE FAMILY DISAGREEMENT CONTINUES

At home in Boston, Marjorie was still upset about Augustine's plans to marry Quincy Shaw. She wrote to her uncles and aunts, trying to explain the serious division in the family and to give her side of the dispute. She felt very strongly that Quinny was too immature, had not even graduated from college, and was not established in any profession, nor had he proved himself in any substantial way.

> *My suggestion is that a boy whose Mother has led a very gay society life and whose father has broken down physically and mentally, should want to prove his own character before marrying. A probation year or two of more or less manual labor at the Michigan mines[2] would strengthen him physically — which he needs — and ought to develop the strength in his character. At present he is just a very nice boy. A year of not having her own way would be fine for Augustine. I love Augustine so much and you all so much, I wanted you to understand how I feel. Though I realize it's none of my business, and absolutely Mother's decision.[3]*

Unfortunately, Bessie intercepted the letter without Marjorie's knowledge, and added her own vehement arguments. The rest of the

---

[1] The official document is in the Archives at Blithewold.

[2] The mines were the Calumet and Hecla Mining Company copper mines near Lake Superior, Michigan, that were owned by Quinny's father, Quincy Adams Shaw, and his brother-in-law Alexander Agassiz.

[3] From rough, penciled notes from January and February 1919 that were found among Marjorie's papers. Blithewold Archives.

family agreed with the McKees that it was too late to change plans, and Marjorie alone bore the strain of trying to be her sister's keeper.

In the spring of 1919, Marjorie had been appointed to the position of Supervisor of Personnel for the Boston chapter of the Red Cross Home Service, where she got to use all the valuable experience she had accumulated over the previous 18 months. Quincy Shaw had been discharged from the army and was back at Harvard, and he and Augustine were planning a June wedding. Letters from Marjorie to Bessie suggest that there was still friction between Augustine and Marjorie. Bessie was busy with preparations for the wedding, which would take place in Boston, with a reception at their home on Commonwealth Avenue. In April the McKees, along with Augustine and Quinny and his parents, went to White Sulphur Springs for a brief respite. While they were there Marjorie received the most joyful news. George was coming home! He expected to arrive in Boston around the middle of May. In a letter to Bessie written from Chaumont, George expressed his delight at finally having his discharge papers *"in my top left pocket, over my heart."* Although he expressed a desire to spend the summer at Blithewold *"having a good time without a thought of anything serious until next fall,"* heavy on his mind was the rapidly deteriorating relationship between Marjorie and her mother and Augustine over Augustine's upcoming marriage. He had been greatly distressed and *"so afraid that just what happened would happen."* In the letter he jumped to Marjorie's defense, suggesting that the rest of the family thought, falsely, that she was behaving irrationally. He offered explanations:

> *...my dear Mother, you must not let there be any estrangement between Marjorie and her family. She is a woman in a million...with a heart of pure gold and more good sense than I could ever hope to have, and the highest ideals of honor and duty. [You] must see to it that there is no break in what has always been such a sane, healthy, and loving family circle, for Marjorie has gone through a great deal, like the brave woman she is, and is pretty unstrung and wrought up over it all...because of worrying over it and thinking so*

much about Augustine's affairs and worrying so hard, and not having me with her. She loves you all deeply and it would be a real calamity, as well as a most foolish thing if even the shadow of an estrangement is allowed to become established. I'll be home soon to help out.[1]

Despite the family strain, everyone came together and rejoiced when George arrived home at the end of May. He and Marjorie immediately began to pick up the threads of their interrupted life together, making the decision to spend the summer relaxing at Blithewold, out of the way of the wedding preparations taking place in Boston.

AUGUSTINE AND QUINNY MARRY

Augustine and Quincy married on June 24, 1919, but the occasion was not without drama. The week before the wedding, Augustine took ill with a bad case of ptomaine poisoning. At first it was doubtful that she would be able to endure the physical and mental strain required of her on her wedding day. One day before the celebrations were to begin, however, though she was pale and thin, the doctors gave their blessing — on the understanding that she should not do any more than was absolutely necessary.

The wedding ceremony was held at the Old South Church in Boston, where William McKee was a Deacon. Estelle Clements wrote:

The Church and the house were lovely with flowers, the bride lovelier. Her dress perfect, and her expression as she turned down the aisle exalted with happiness so wonderful that people caught their breath as at the sight of something not of this world.[2]

---

[1] George Lyon to Bessie, April 22, 1919. Blithewold Archives.
[2] Estelle Clements' diary, June 24, 1919. Blithewold Archives.

The church was a mass of greenery, pink roses, and pink hydrangeas; and every pew was hung with a gilt basket filled with pink roses and blue larkspur. Bessie's cousin Helen Riddell wrote:

> *The bride was a dream of beauty. Her gown (made by Fox, N.Y.) was of satin and lace, but such satin and such lace!! Flounces of it on the skirt, and a wonderful veil of it. Brussels' Point old lace...it fell over the long court train and was caught with orange blossoms. I've seen many a Bride's gown, but none so regal as this one. There were seven ushers and seven bridesmaids, the latter in the most exquisite gowns of pink chiffon tulle and lace trimming.*[1]

A reception for 645 guests took place at the McKee home on Commonwealth Avenue. Bessie and Will had wanted to have an extension built onto the back of the townhouse to accommodate the party, but a construction strike in Boston disrupted that plan. Instead, thanks to the generosity of the family next door, the McKees had staging erected on the front of the two adjoining houses so that the drawing room of the neighboring house could be used. Guests could step out of one drawing room onto a shared balcony and into the drawing room of the other house. Late in the afternoon Augustine and Quinny left in a shower of rose petals to drive to the Shaws' country estate in Eastham, Cape Cod, to begin their honeymoon.

After the wedding, Marjorie and George retreated to Blithewold. At the end of the summer, George wrote to Bessie:

> *I couldn't half tell you, dear Mother, how much pleasure the summer at Bristol has given us. You have been so sweet to us both and it has been a real joy to rest amongst those for whom I have much affection, and in your lovely peaceful home.*[2]

---

[1] Letter from Helen Riddell to Lucia, a Pardee cousin, June 30, 1919. Blithewold Archives.
[2] George Lyon to Bessie, August 24, 1919, Blithewold Archives.

A FAMILY REUNION AND A TRIP TO NEW BRUNSWICK

For many years the entire family gathered at Calvin and Mary Pardee's vacation estate in the Adirondack Mountains near Lake Placid. Calvin loved nothing more than to be surrounded by his family, and he invited all of Ario Pardee's descendants (sometimes as many as 65) for an exhilarating reunion week every year. He had purchased 14,000 acres of woodland that included two beautiful mountain ponds, Clear Pond and Copper Pond, and an excellent 11-mile trout stream.[1] He planted 150,000 trees, mostly pines, and constructed a two-mile mountain road along a ridge. The new road commanded magnificent views eastward across Lake Champlain to the Green Mountains in Vermont. Alongside this road Calvin built rustic cabins[2] and camp sites with lean-tos and fireplaces to accommodate the family gatherings. He named his camp Hale Brook Park.

The Pardee siblings. *From left: Calvin, Barton, Alice, Anne, Bessie, Edith, Gertrude, Israel, and Frank*

---

[1] William G. Foulke, *Pardee Family Reunion: Reminiscences.* Blithewold Archives.
[2] Calvin named his own cabin, the largest, "Eagle's Eyrie."

At each reunion new in-laws and new babies were introduced and welcomed. The adults stayed in the cedar log cabins and the younger cousins camped. The Pardee sisters and sisters-in-law would sit and knit and read, talking nonstop, delighted to be together exchanging family gossip, while the men fished, shared business news, hiked, played golf, raced around the lake in boats, and arranged baseball games. The children ran from one activity to another, renewing friendships and soaking up that special secure feeling that came from being part of a large and privileged family. The gathering itself was so important to the Pardee family that the young cousins discussed whether or not they could ever marry anyone they would not feel comfortable bringing to Hale Brook Park.[1]

With all their men safely home from war, the Pardees organized a grand family reunion for August 1919.

Reunion at Hale Brook Park, outside Eagle's Eyrie, 1919. From left, Barton Pardee, Frank Pardee, Augustine, Bessie, Gladys Pardee. Seated on the porch, Calvin Pardee and William McKee. Bessie's sister Edith is standing on the right

[1] Constance Pardee Collinge and Edith Pardee Van Buren. *Dearest Family,* Private Printing, 1992, p. 34.

This reunion in 1919 was one of family togetherness in which they offered thanks for each other, their safe reunion, their health, and their prosperity. They arrived in *"flocks and shoals,"* fifty-seven all told. The "57 Varieties," someone called them.[1] (And also mentioned was the fact that there were almost as many cars and each one different!)

Immediately after the 1919 Hale Brook reunion, Marjorie and George left on a five-week trip through the White Mountains and on to New Brunswick, Canada. They drove through Franconia Notch and then east to Bretton Woods, where they stayed at the Mount Washington Hotel: *"I have had no hay fever since the day we got to Bretton Woods,"*[2] wrote Marjorie. At the hotel they played golf and prepared their car (a new Mercer[3]) — oiling, greasing, and cleaning spark plugs — for the demanding journey ahead that would take them north into New Brunswick, Canada, and into the Canadian wilderness. They drove through Fort Fairfield, Maine, and Perth, New Brunswick, and then along the Tobique River to Miller's Post Office, an old farmhouse where they stayed overnight.

---

[1] From the Pardee Newsletter, summer 1919. Blithewold Archives.
[2] Letter from Marjorie to Bessie, August 29, 1919. Blithewold Archives.
[3] The Mercer automobile was one of the most popular sports cars of the decade. The Mercer company was owned by cousins Ferdinand and Washington Roebling, engineers who had been successful in suspension-bridge building. Washington Roebling had died on the *Titanic* in 1912, but his cousin Ferdinand continued with the company until he died in 1919. At that point the company merged with Locomobile and Crane-Simplex.

The Lyons' Mercer at Miller's Post Office,
New Brunswick, Canada, 1919

Here they met their friends Gay and Tom Pierce[1] and their four guides. The following morning they left the car at the Post Office and set off upriver, canoeing 14 miles that day. Once ashore they set up tents and cut balsam branches to soften their bedrolls that night. The next day the river was stiffer and narrower, with rapids and twists. They canoed all day, and then set up camp again. They swam, watched the sunset, and played poker after supper. On September 2 they arrived at Second Bathurst Lake and set up a home camp. From there they went out to temporary camps, returning to the home camp periodically to collect fresh supplies. They fished and hunted every day to supplement their dry rations — *"We had partridge for breakfast, fish*

---

[1] Gay Pierce was Marjorie's school friend Gay Dexter, sister of Julian and Dorothy Dexter. Bessie and Will were friends of Gay's parents in Boston. Gay's father may have been the writer and antiques collector, George Dexter. His books on antique collecting are in the Blithewold library.

for dinner and venison for supper."[1] One day George caught "*100 or so trout.*" Another day Marjorie paddled 22 miles down the river to Portage Brook where she caught four fish; George went bear hunting, walking 18 miles up the Micmac Indian Trail. Every day for three weeks, they set off in different directions, hiking and canoeing, in search of good fishing and hunting grounds. It rained every day and the weather was getting cold, but occasionally the sun shone through. They enjoyed glorious views across the lakes to the mountains: *"Up at five. Went down the Bogan, hunting all the way. Lovely sunrise colors and mist on the Lake. Absolutely calm."*[2]

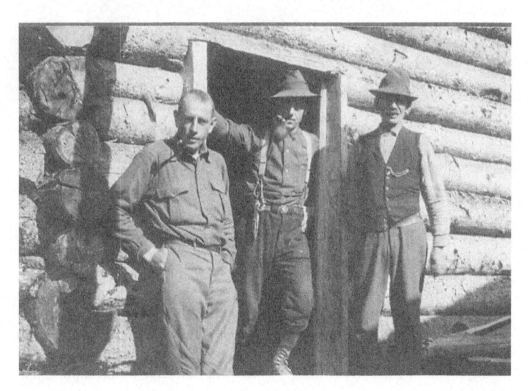

George, left, at the hunting camp in New Brunswick, 1919

---

[1] Marjorie's diary, September 6, 1919. Blithewold Archives.
[2] Marjorie's diary, September 15, 1919. Blithewold Archives.

The return journey was an adventure, paddling downstream with their canoes full of their equipment, sometimes over the rapids, and finally back to Miller's Post Office. The drive home was glorious:

> *a lovely ride. Colors of the trees best we ever saw; brilliant sunshine, too. Passed St. John's River, Androscoggin, Penobscot, and finally Penobscot Bay and the Islands. Penobscot Bay was very blue. There was a fresh breeze, but glorious sunlight. Had lunch in a pretty wood — ice cream cones later and chocolate and buns at Bangor!*[1]

When they arrived back in Boston they spent the night at the Touraine Hotel while arranging to have their house opened the following Monday. In the meantime, they would spend the weekend at Blithewold: *"...to Bristol, and the trip was over,"*[2] wrote Marjorie.

1920 — LIFE GOES ON

In April, 1920, Marjorie had a surprise visit in Boston from John Best, Bessie's gardener at Blithewold — he had brought her flowers from the gardens. *"John Best has been to call — and brought the loveliest pansies and violets and lemon verbena, rose geranium, ferns, and even a few sprays of heliotrope."*[3] It was as if he were bringing Blithewold to them in Boston. A wonderful treat.

When Quincy Shaw graduated from Harvard in 1920, his father sent him to work at the family's copper mine in Calumet, Michigan. Augustine saw it as a huge adventure and adjusted well to being so far from home. She soon became pregnant but lost the baby, owing to "complications." Marjorie went out to stay with them in their new home, and it seemed that the sisters had put their differences behind them.

---

[1] Marjorie's diary, September 24, 1919. Blithewold Archives.
[2] Marjorie's diary, September 26, 1919. Blithewold Archives.
[3] Marjorie to Bessie and William McKee, April 29, 1920. Blithewold Archives.

Meanwhile, Will had been under great strain — his company, A. W. Tedcastle, was not doing well and he had borrowed money from the family to keep it going. By this time, both Marjorie and Augustine were supporting their Mother financially.[1] Augustine wrote to Bessie, *"I am only too glad to be able to help you both out. It certainly is a shame that A. W. Tedcastle & Co. is having such hard times."*[2] In August and September of 1920 George and Marjorie made good on earlier promises to take Bessie and Will to New Brunswick with them. For a while the McKees were able to forget everything unpleasant and enjoy the outdoor life in New Brunswick.

On the Tobique River, New Brunswick, Canada, September 1920
Bessie, center, George, and William McKee

---

[1] As evidenced in letters between Bessie, Augustine, and Marjorie, in 1920. Blithewold Archives.
[2] Augustine to Bessie, January 24, 1921. Blithewold Archives.

Bessie wrote to Marjorie afterward:

I think with a pleasant warm feeling about my heart of the fact that you and George wanted to have us take this trip with you. It was certainly very dear of you both...it has been a wonderful experience and I would not have missed it for anything, and I have had a lot of pleasure out of all these new experiences.[1]

Baking bread at the camp on the Tobique River, September 1920
George, Marjorie, and Bessie

CALUMET 1921

The winter of 1920–1921 was unusually severe in Augustine's new hometown of Calumet, Michigan. In January 1921 she was pregnant again and wrote home that *"I am going to have a little baby in*

---

[1] Bessie to Marjorie, September 7, 1920. Blithewold Archives.

August."[1] Her morning sickness, however, became debilitating, and she became weaker and weaker. Bessie went out to Calumet, brutal winter conditions notwithstanding, to be with her daughter. The pregnancy eventually had to be terminated to save Augustine's health, and it took her several months to recover. In September Marjorie wrote, *"We were delighted with the latest news that Augustine was really better. She has had such a long, tedious time of it."[2]*

---

[1] Letter from Augustine to Bessie, January 24, 1921. Blithewold Archives.
[2] Letter from Marjorie to Bessie, September 30, 1921. Blithewold Archives.

Chapter XIV

BRITISH COLUMBIA, CANADA, 1921

In August 1921 Marjorie and George set off on another hunting trip, this time to the Cassiar region of British Columbia. They were gone for ten weeks, six weeks of which were spent on a hunt in a remote area far from civilization. Their journey began with the trip from Montreal to Vancouver on the Canadian Pacific Railway, after which they took a steamer to Prince Rupert, British Columbia. They traveled north into Alaska, stopping at Ketchikan where they saw salmon climbing upstream.

Salmon climbing upstream, Ketchikan, Alaska

In Wrangel, Alaska, they met up with a group who went up the River Stikine with them in a gas boat. The river trip took them back into British Columbia to Telegraph Creek — a mostly Indian town — where they bought hunting licenses. From there they set out on their six-week adventure, taking 12 horses and a colt. They made their first

camp about seven miles up the trail, after which their Indian guides
led them through the woods to Buckley Lake.

Camp on the Stikine River. George in hat on left, 1921

All along the way they looked for game — hunting and trapping.
They crawled down deep, rocky ravines on their hands and knees, and
climbed up ice cliffs and across glaciers. They shot rams and goats
and the occasional sheep *("good to eat"),* but they were looking forward
to being in bear country. They walked, climbed, and rode, crossing
and recrossing rivers, scaling ridges, surviving on sheep meat,
potatoes, bread, tea, dried fruit, porcupine, and caribou. They were
163 miles into the wilderness when they finally confronted the big
game they were looking for, with George killing a grizzly and Marjorie a
big caribou.

George at camp on Sheep Mountain, 1921

September 12 was Marjorie's birthday, and she celebrated by shooting a *"huge grizzly,"* the biggest their Indian guide had ever seen — 9 feet 4 inches tall. The bear meat could not be consumed right away, so Marjorie's birthday dinner was ptarmigan (small Alaskan grouse) and groundhog. As a special treat they also had *"the porcupines we killed, roasted by hanging them on a string for many hours over the fire, Indian fashion."*[1]

They were traveling about 18 to 20 miles a day, setting up crude camps as they went along. They occasionally passed Indian families on the move, and sometimes spied other hunting groups miles away on different trails. By September 20 the temperatures were dropping and it began to snow. They had now traveled 280 miles, mostly on foot, and they lightened their load by leaving "caches" of their belongings in trees along the way, to be collected later.

---

[1] Marjorie's diary, September 12, 1921. Blithewold Archives.

Marjorie outside their tent at cache camp, 1921. (Note the caches hanging from the trees.)

George and Marjorie and their "trophies," 1921

At the beginning of October their travels finally brought them back to Telegraph Creek, where they took pictures of their trophies. They met up with other hunting groups and compared stories and "bags." Marjorie and George were very proud that *their* "bag" was so impressive.

Meeting other hunting groups, Telegraph Creek

They traveled by gas boat back to Wrangel, passing glaciers and waterfalls on the way, and then went on to Vancouver, arriving there on October 3. They said goodbye to their fellow travelers and took the boat to Victoria. At their favorite hotel, they splurged on a luxurious room, cleaned up, and went to the theater. *"Such fun to be dressed up and going out!"* wrote Marjorie. They dined on tomato bouillon, stuffed crabs, green corn, and salad — a delightful shock to their systems after wilderness rations! By the following day they were already missing the mountains, so they drove up into the hills of Victoria to enjoy more magnificent views.

All too soon it was time to return to their lives in New England. They took the train back to the American side, then traveled from

Seattle across the Cascade Mountains and into Chicago where they spent the day touring the city. Marjorie noticed huge changes since she had last been there with her parents, Augustus and Bessie, for the 1893 World's Columbian Exposition. Their next stop was Cincinnati, where they spent a few hours with George's uncle, Boyd Lyon, and then on to Philadelphia to see George's brother Vincent and his wife Clara. The midnight train from Philadelphia to Providence, and then the early morning train to Warren, reunited them with the family in Bristol. They had been away for ten weeks, and it was a very happy welcome home indeed to be greeted by the large group of Pardees who were gathered at Blithewold.

Chapter XV

GOOD TIMES AND BAD

1922 – ECONOMIC RECESSION

In 1922 William McKee's sister Isabell Hidden and her husband William began borrowing money on a regular basis from the McKees. They had been badly affected by the winter freeze of 1921, which had not only killed their entire apple crop but had weakened their trees to such an extent that the harvest of 1922 was less than half of what they normally saw. William Hidden kept careful notes of how much he borrowed from the McKees, and he promised to repay them when he could.

> *I believe that eventually we will work out of our troubles, though I do hate to be such a drag on you. Apple picking is only three weeks or so away. Prices seem low, and I may put my fruit in cold storage for two or three months until the glut of fruit is cleaned up, getting some temporary accommodation on it since funds are low, though I had much rather sell outright.*[1]

By the end of that year, William McKee's own company, A. W. Tedcastle & Co., was refinancing and showing signs of further decline. Arthur Tedcastle's ambitious move to expand the company in order to take advantage of the wartime boom had placed the firm's affairs in jeopardy because the boom was followed by a postwar recession.[2] Tedcastle had taken out large loans to finance what he thought were lucrative wartime contracts to supply leather combat boots to the military, but he had miscalculated the flow of financing. Because of the heavy repayments that now had to be honored, he lacked the

---

[1] Letter from William Hidden to William McKee, August 25, 1922. Blithewold Archives.
[2] Nash K. Burger. *The Road to West 43rd Street.* University Press of Mississippi, 1995, p. 49.

funds immediately after the war to keep up with the annual fashion changes in shoes. Nash Burger, Tedcastle's chief salesman for many years, commented that he received samples of new shoes that were *"not up-to-date and would sell poorly."*[1]

But family gatherings and outings continued. The McKees, the Lyons, and the Shaws spent February 1922 at Peckett's Ski resort in New Hampshire, along with other relatives and family friends.

Sleighing at Peckett's, February 1922

And at the beginning of the following August the whole family convened at Hale Brook Park for their annual family reunion. A large group of Pardees then went to Blithewold to continue their vacation there. Bessie wrote to Marjorie:

---

[1]Nash K. Burger. *The Road to West 43rd Street.* University Press of Mississippi, 1995, p. 49.

...father...is out on the sleeping porch...and Uncle Izzie is looking on from a comfortable rocker smoking his cigar. Gladys, Helen, Lee and Elizabeth are on the north porch. Aunt Alice and Aunt Dellie are napping.[1]

Marjorie and George left Hale Brook Park after the reunion to sail to England (on the S.S. *Washington)* to visit Priscilla and Jim Sherrard and their children for several weeks. The highlight of the trip was participating in the Quorn Hunt.

The Quorn Hunt, Derbyshire, England, 1922

No sooner had the Lyons returned from England than they left for their third trip to New Brunswick, Canada, for some fishing and hunting. Such was their love for this area that they went back to the same sites several times, hired the same guides, and strengthened their friendship with the Miller family. The Millers, who lived at Miller's Crossing, took care of the supplies and equipment for the Lyons' challenging forays into the wilderness. Marjorie and George

---

[1] Letter from Bessie to Marjorie, August 25, 1922. Blithewold Archives.

went back to New Brunswick for a fourth time in October 1924, and again in 1927.

For Augustine, 1923 began badly. She spent at least two months at the Austen Riggs psychiatric hospital in Stockbridge, Massachusetts.[1] She had suffered two more miscarriages and the whole family was concerned about her health.

HAWAII WITH THE PARDEES

In January 1925, Marjorie accompanied her Uncle Israel (Izzie), Aunt Alice, and their daughter, Helen Lee[2] on a trip to Hawaii. The original plans included the McKees and George, but at the last minute both Will and Bessie were unwell and did not feel up to the long and arduous journey. William McKee was no doubt feeling the strain of his company's decline, and *"working too hard"* as a result. Bessie was under a doctor's care for a broken or sprained wrist. George, too, was unable to join the party, so Marjorie accepted the invitation to go with the Pardees and act as their guide to the Hawaiian Islands. The itinerary was almost identical to the one that Marjorie and George had followed on their 1917–1918 trip. The party of four left Boston by train on January 10 on the first leg of their long journey, traveling via New York, Chicago, the Grand Canyon, Pasadena, and Los Angeles, to San Francisco. During a stopover at the Grand Canyon, Marjorie and Helen, with a guide and mules, took the 7½-hour trip down the Bright Angel Trail while Israel and Alice took a leisurely two-hour drive along the Rim. The group barely missed a big snowstorm that they could see sweeping toward them across the Canyon.

Back on the train, they spent the next morning in the observation car as the train crossed the Sierra Madre Mountains and

---

[1] From letters from Augustine to Estelle Clements, January and February, 1922. Blithewold Archives.
[2] Helen Lee Pardee was so named to differentiate her from her older cousin, Helen Pardee, daughter of Calvin and Mary Pardee.

headed toward Pasadena where they rested for a few days — walking and playing golf, dining with friends, and going to the theater. In San Francisco they stayed at the Fairmont Hotel. *"San Francisco is surely the most naturally beautiful city in this country,"* wrote Marjorie in her diary on January 20.[1] Their five-day sail on the S.S. *Matsonia* from San Francisco to Hawaii was pleasantly uneventful, the sea smooth. Once they settled into the cottages in Honolulu they began a vigorous program of touring, swimming, surfing, and golfing. Marjorie took out a local driving license, and then hired a car so that they could visit all the friends that she and George had made in 1918. *"We had dinner at the Swanzys' house on Manoa Road. Dinner was served on the porch. Mr. and Mrs. MacMorris (who we met eight years ago) were there again and Mr. and Mrs. Morgan."*[2]

Israel Pardee and his wife, Alice Lee,[3] in Honolulu, 1925

---

[1] Marjorie's diary, January 20, 1925. Blithewold Archives.
[2] Marjorie's diary, February 7, 1925. Blithewold Archives.
[3] Israel Pardee's wife Alice was always referred to as Alice Lee to differentiate her from Bessie's older sister, Alice Pardee Earle, and Alice Ross, Frank Pardee's second wife. In 1913, there were seven Alices in the family. In Marjorie's 1913 photograph album there is a photograph of "The Alices" at the Pardee Reunion.

In February, Marjorie, Israel, and Helen accepted an invitation to visit the Hawaiian Pineapple Company's cannery. (Marjorie had a letter of introduction to Mr. James Dole from a Boston friend.) In her diary Marjorie described the cannery, and noted that it was the largest in the world:

> *Flat cars bring the pineapples from the plantations. The crates are fed to a ginoca machine, which, with various knives, takes off the top and bottom, peels and cores the fruit; and then girls (gloved, capped and aproned) remove any specks left. Then along comes the slicing machine; then girls packing the cans, then a machine that syrups each can; then an exhaust that removes the air from the can; then a lid-putting-on machine; then a cooper (which takes ten minutes); then gasoline and lacquer machine for cans; then water cooler; then twenty-four hours rest; then test by tapping; then wrapper-putting-on machine; then boxes packed; then machine that nails them; then wiring machine, and at last the crates are ready! 40,000 crates was the largest daily output, and over 2,000,000 were shipped last year. Everything is immaculate.[1]*

On car trips around the island they saw sugar plantations and agricultural plantings of rice, taro, papaya, mango, avocado, and sisal. They also visited the northern part of the Island to see the largest wireless receiving station in the world.[2] In between the various sightseeing trips, Helen and Marjorie made social calls, improved their surfing skills, and played golf and bridge.

By the end of February, however, Marjorie was suffering from severe homesickness. She missed George and her mother dreadfully: *"I feel frightfully far away,"* although she refused to let her feelings spoil her time with the Pardees: *"We are really having a good time and*

---

[1] Marjorie's diary, February 14, 1925. Blithewold Archives.
[2] Built by the Marconi Wireless Company. The farthest long-distance wireless communications were between Ireland and San Francisco and Honolulu in 1914. (*New York Times*, January 28, 1914.)

I would love it if I weren't so homesick." To distract herself, Marjorie made lists of the flowers and shrubs and trees that she saw,[1] (including the greenhouse flowers of the Island) to send to her mother. She admired the Alamanda Vine and the plumbago, and a flower called "cup of gold," which *"pops open with a real little noise and spreads into a cup-like flower with brown stamens and markings inside."*[2] It was on this trip that she first learned about the night-blooming cereus, which only blooms in June. Marjorie later grew the plant in the greenhouse at Blithewold. She would invite friends and neighbors from Bristol to witness the unique phenomenon — a species that blossoms into a beautiful flower for only a few short hours, and only in the middle of the night.

Helen and Marjorie, wearing leis, outside their cottage in Honolulu, 1925

---

[1] Night-blooming cereus, hibiscus, plumbago, poinsettia, begonia, oleander, cup of gold, Alamanda, mimosa, acacia, ohia, plumier [sic], ixoria, bougainvillea, ginger plant, lehua, kukui, koa, coffee, guava, ironwood, fern, breadfruit, papaya, banana, coconut, royal palm, hau, African tulip, lauhalla, algeroba, banyan poncianna , bombax elipticum, and mesquite.   Compiled from the diary that Marjorie labeled *Trip to Hawaiian Islands, 1925.* Blithewold Archives.

[2] Marjorie to Bessie, February 3, 1925. Blithewold Archives.

The Pardees and Marjorie returned home in April. Marjorie wrote of her relatives, *"They were all three the sweetest traveling companions. We never had a single scrap. Uncle Izzie hardly grumbled even when the coffee was stone cold...Well I certainly always did love them — and even more after this trip."*[1] Marjorie hoped that they could all go again, but next time she hoped that the party would include George, Bessie, and Will.

A TIME OF CRISIS FOR MARJORIE AND GEORGE

After Marjorie arrived home in Boston she immediately began preparations to join George in a much-anticipated golf trip to the Greenbrier Hotel in White Sulphur Springs, West Virginia. Bessie and Will were not in Boston, being away on vacation in Havana, Cuba, but Marjorie was able to see her sister before she left. Augustine was in Boston awaiting the birth of her first child. She had suffered several miscarriages, but she had at last carried a baby to term. Augustine Pardee Shaw was born in Boston on May 29, 1925, by caesarian section. For a few confusing weeks the baby was known as "Augustine Two," but she soon became "Dee," the name by which she was known for the rest of her life. Owing to complications, however, Augustine and the baby remained hospitalized for more than seven weeks.[2] Meanwhile, at Greenbrier, Marjorie and George played golf and tennis and went for long horseback rides on the resort's trails.

In July it was George's turn to take a vacation, a fishing trip with friends. He traveled with Marjorie to Hale Brook Park, and left her with the Pardee family who were gathered once again at Calvin Pardee's camp in the Adirondack Mountains. From there he set out on the long journey to a remote spot on the Gaspé Peninsula to fish for salmon. George's letters home during that trip suggest that Marjorie had been ill, and he was worried about her:

---

[1] Letter from Marjorie to Bessie, April 13, 1925. Blithewold Archives.
[2] Estelle Clements' diary, July 16, 1925. Blithewold Archives.

I am anxious and worried about you for you seemed so tired and forlorn last weekend. I wish you would get rested and strong. It's mostly nerves I suspect but there is no doubt but that you are below par and miserable a great deal of the time. I wish I knew what to do for you. I hope the Doctor will have some ideas.[1]

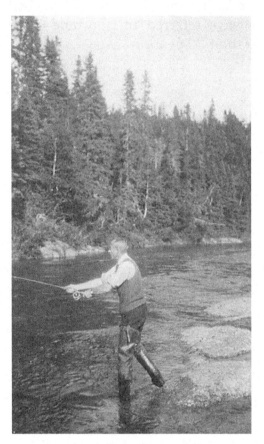

George fishing for salmon on the Gaspé Peninsula, 1925

George sent his first catch, a 10½-pound salmon, down to Hale Brook Park for the family to enjoy. After he decided to extend his stay into the following week he sent a large salmon to his office, *"as a kind*

---

[1] George to Marjorie, July 13, 1925. Blithewold Archives.

of propitiatory offering coincident with telling them I was going to stay here longer, and I hope it works."[1]

Marjorie and George had been looking to purchase real estate in or around Boston for some time. In 1925, they found a beautiful, large, sturdy-looking house on five acres at 209 Newton Street in Brookline, whose gardens backed onto the Brookline Country Club. ("209," as they always referred to it, would remain their principal residence for more than 30 years.)

209 Newton Street, Brookline

It would have been a perfect family house, but the Lyons were beginning to accept the idea that they would not have children. Perhaps infertility was the cause of Marjorie's physical and mental distress and her several hospitalizations. They discussed adoption again, and began to take advice on how to go about it. But they kept putting off the decision, hoping that they might still have their own

---

[1] George to Marjorie, August 2, 1925. Blithewold Archives.

child. (Bessie, Augustine, and Marjorie all had reproductive difficulties; this may have been hereditary, though the generations before and after them apparently had no such problems. Bessie's mother had ten children, and both Augustine's daughters had children without complications.) Whatever its cause, the failure to produce children seemed to be evolving into a crisis for Marjorie and George.

The next summer, 1926, Marjorie retreated to her beloved Blithewold, hoping, no doubt, that being in her favorite place would help her to relax and sort things out in her mind. On June 28 George wrote to her from Boston, insisting that he loved her more than ever and that she should not question his devotion.

> *I feel that I am often cold, undemonstrative, unappreciative of you and harsh to you, and all this I regret...but I've been under a good deal of pressure in the last 2 years and feeling physically pretty well down. Children would have made a great difference to us both, but as we can hardly expect them now, that fact has got to be accepted and made the best of.*

He went on to assure Marjorie that she was a valuable member of society, doing a good job with her Red Cross work and her golf club responsibilities. He felt that they should support each other.

> *You owe me something towards making life pleasant and worthwhile for me, just as I do for you, and that in itself is a sufficient end to justify living for both of us. If I can make you happy, even though I may never be successful at business or otherwise, it seems enough in a way, and there ought to be some such feeling on your side too.*

Marjorie apparently was thinking that there ought to be more meaning to her life, and she was seriously questioning her own, and George's, lack of career accomplishment. George himself seemed to acknowledge the disappointments. He protested:

Perhaps we haven't the capacities for the more important proceedings. The more one thinks of it the clearer it seems that, after all, the effect we have on those who surround us is the really important justification for living — not what we accomplish....It seems to me we have a great deal to be thankful for, compared to many others I know and we ought to make the best of it.

He ends the letter by saying:

I love you dearly, I cannot manage without you, I need you, your criticism and your support, more than ever. It is beyond me to talk much about such things but they are nonetheless true.[1]

A few weeks later, after the Fourth of July festivities at Blithewold, Marjorie and George set off on another wildlife adventure, this time to Alaska. Their trips into the wilderness were a source of great pleasure to them both, being away from any pressures of family and work. They shared a love of camping, fishing, hunting, hiking, canoeing, and testing themselves under harsh conditions. On these adventures, coming to depend on each other for survival, they brought out the best in each other. (In April 1925, Marjorie had written to her mother, *"George and I have had so many good vacations together. It's nice we like to do things together, isn't it? It seems to me we are extra congenial."*) At the beginning of this latest trip to Alaska, Bessie sent Marjorie a "bon voyage" letter in which she told her how much she, Bessie, appreciated having them at Blithewold over the summer: *"Blithewold means so much to me and I rejoice that my children care so much for it too."* (Bessie, in fact, was soon to receive star-rated recognition for her horticultural efforts in Blithewold's gardens.)

---

[1] George to Marjorie, June 28, 1926. Blithewold Archives.

FOURTH OF JULY 1926 AT BLITHEWOLD

The 1926 Fourth of July holiday was a memorable one at Blithewold. According to tradition, the family assembled at the estate for several days, and friends came from Providence, Bristol, and Boston. Every year, on the morning of the Fourth, they would gather at the Cabots' house, "Four Eagles," on Hope Street in Bristol, a choice spot on the parade route. They would have breakfast there and then stand or sit on the front steps of the beautiful colonial house, cheering on the crowds of Bristolians marching in the longest-running July Fourth parade in the country.

Outside Cabot house on Hope Street, Bristol, July 4. George (with cane) is on the left; Marjorie is at the far right, talking to Wallis Howe, 1926

After the parade everyone adjourned to Blithewold for the "Day Fireworks." The staff served a picnic on the lawn, and the men lit Japanese fire-lanterns especially imported for the occasion. The lanterns were capsules that were fired off like rockets into the air. As they floated slowly down to earth, they opened up into large, brightly colored tissue-paper shapes, to the delight of the children. They were in the form of flowers and animals, and as they drifted in the wind the children ran across the Great Lawn trying to catch them and claim them as trophies, mementos of the day. Neighbor children and the children of the Blithewold servants were invited to join the Pardee children. Chauffeur Arthur Rae's daughter, Eleanor, remembers, *"My memories of those Fourths are some of my happiest. The 'Big House,' as we called it, would be overflowing with guests. The events of the afternoons were the highlights of my childhood."*[1]

Children chasing "day fireworks" at Blithewold, July 4, 1926

On this particular July Fourth, there was even more excitement in store for the family and friends gathered on the lawn at Blithewold. A family friend from Boston, Julian Dexter,[2] brought his World War I airplane, a Curtiss Jenny, to Bristol and landed it on the Great Lawn. Taking it up again, he performed aerial tricks and took adventurous guests up for rides. Marjorie, however, was more daring — after giving her a brief lesson, Julian took Marjorie up on her very first flight and allowed her to take the controls. At one point, he taxied the plane to the top of the rise of the Great Lawn near the Mansion and set off toward the Bay, gathering speed as he went, barely making lift-off as

---

[1] From Eleanor Rae Gladding's essay, *Fourth of July at Blithewold in the Twenties.* Blithewold Archives.

[2] Julian was the brother of Gay Dexter Pierce, a friend of Marjorie's from Miss Vinton's school in Connecticut.

he approached the water.[1] Eleanor Rae wrote, *"What excitement he created when he landed on the 'Big Lawn'! I can remember the thrill I felt when he took off, roaring down the lawn towards the water, just barely skimming over the lone apple tree that grew close to the shore."*[2]

Julian Dexter's World War I plane, a Curtiss Jenny, on the Blithewold lawn. Marjorie center, Frank Pardee right, July 1926

Later in the evening, again according to tradition, the adults dressed for dinner and there was dancing and traditional fireworks. Augustine's daughter, Marjorie Shaw Jeffries, has shared her recollections of the evening activities, as seen through the eyes of a small child:

> *...the house was ablaze with lights, and strangers wandered about all over the downstairs. They glided in their evening dresses and jewelry, talking and laughing, while my sister Dee and I stayed close to each other, unnoticed. As the sky darkened, the crowd flowed outside*

[1] This event was captured on a home movie, preserved in the Blithewold Archives.
[2] From Eleanor Rae Gladding's essay, *Fourth of July at Blithewold in the Twenties.* Blithewold Archives.

to stand on the terrace overlooking the lawn. Some stepped carefully down the steps onto the lawn in their high-heeled, fancy party shoes and long, elaborate dresses, while their escorts, replete with tuxedos and highly polished black pumps, guided them by the elbow around the shrubbery to stand and watch the fireworks display. When the noise began, we put our fingers in our ears and watched for a few minutes, but the tension of waiting for the explosions was too much for me and I ran upstairs and hid in my dark bedroom on the opposite side of the house.[1]

"YOU HAVE AN ARBORETUM HERE"

At the beginning of August 1926, while walking along the southern path that led to the water, Bessie and Will noticed that a tree whose name they didn't know was blooming for the first time: beautiful white blossoms on an otherwise ordinary-looking tree. The tree had already been there when the Van Wickles bought Blithewold in 1894, perhaps planted by Mr. Gardner, the previous owner, some 50 years earlier. John DeWolf could not classify the tree when he was asked about it in the early 1900s. Now William McKee decided to take one of the flowers to the Arnold Arboretum in Boston for identification. Professor Charles Sprague Sargent, the Arboretum Director, was immediately *"tremendously interested"* and sent for the chief botanist.[2] The two decided that the tree was of Chinese origin, a *Cedrela Sinensis*, an extremely rare species. They knew of only two others in the country, and neither of them had ever bloomed. They called in Professor Ernest Henry Wilson,[3] who was equally excited over the

---

[1] From *Memory Vignettes of Blithewold* by Marjorie Shaw Jeffries. Blithewold Archives.

[2] Letter from Bessie to Marjorie, August 3, 1926. Blithewold Archives.

[3] Ernest Henry Wilson was a botanical explorer who traveled extensively in China in the early 1900s, photographing and collecting rare and exotic plant specimens, first for Kew Gardens in England, and then for the Arnold

"find" and was anxious to see the tree for himself. He and famous botanist Alfred Rehder[1] made plans to travel to Blithewold later in the week. They would photograph the *Cedrela*, and also the Giant Sequoia growing in the Enclosed Garden. Bessie wrote to Marjorie in great excitement:

> *Father, Mr. Wilson and Mr. Rehder arrived about 10.30 and we have had a delightful day...Both men are pleasant, and what a good time they had. They were frankly amazed to find so lovely and interesting a place here — and kept saying "why, you have a second Arboretum here. We never dreamed there was a place like this!" Mr. Wilson only brought four plates with him and kept regretting that fact. So he wants to come down again later when the seed of the Cedrela has ripened. Then he says he will bring a lot of plates — for he said there was so much he would like to photograph. We went over the entire place and they loved it. Mr. Wilson was captivated by the Bosquet, he wanted to linger there. They went back about 4 pm and left me tired but happy.*[2]

On August 10, Ernest Wilson wrote to Bessie, *"So rich in good things did we find your place that I am looking forward to another visit later in the autumn."*[3]

Arboretum of Harvard University. He became known to his colleagues as "Chinese" Wilson.

[1] Alfred Rehder was a colleague of E. H. Wilson, and the two men traveled what was then known as the Orient seeking new plants.

[2] Letter from Bessie to Marjorie, August 3, 1926. Blithewold Archives.

[3] Letter to Bessie from Ernest Wilson, August 10 1926. Blithewold Archives.

*Botanical explorer
Alfred Rehder at
Blithewold, August
1926*

GRANDCHILDREN AT BLITHEWOLD

To add to her joy, Bessie was delighted to have her first grandchild staying with her at Blithewold that summer of 1926. A home movie shows Bessie and Will picking up Augustine and her one-year-old daughter Dee from the railway station, then playing with her on the Blithewold lawn at the July Fourth celebration. Dee was a beautiful, happy baby, and Bessie regretted any time she had to spend away from her, even for the annual retreat to Hale Brook Park to be with her Pardee relatives.

Bessie with granddaughter Dee Shaw at Blithewold 1926

Bessie, Dee Shaw, and George Lyon on the Blithewold dock,
summer 1927

Augustine with Dee and Marjorie Shaw, 1928

In June, 1928, Augustine gave birth in Boston to her second child, a daughter named Marjorie Pemberton Shaw — Marjorie after her aunt, and Pemberton after her paternal grandmother. The new baby was sickly as an infant, and Dee now had to share her place in the limelight. Young Marjorie quickly became her Aunt Marjorie's favorite niece. The baby was nicknamed "Mar-Pem," to differentiate between her and her aunt of the same name. Augustine and Quinny, who had moved back to the Boston area so they and their daughters could be closer to their families, built a house on Sears Road in

Brookline on 16 acres of land (near the country club), given to them by Quincy's father in 1925.[1]

Marjorie Lyon with Marjorie Shaw at Blithewold, 1929

Around this time Augustine lent William McKee $50,000[2] to invest in strengthening his company. The company *did* rally for a short time, but, unknown to any of them, a greater disaster — the Great Depression — was about to spell the end of A. W. Tedcastle.

---

[1] From Estelle Clements' diary, May 17, 1925. Blithewold Archives.
[2] This loan is referred to in a statement of the A. W. Tedcastle Company's assets and liabilities prepared by George A. Morin and Associates, Attorneys, Accountants and Tax Counselors, dated March 28, 1928. Blithewold Archives.

In 1929 Marjorie and George Lyon again started worrying again about their apparent inability to have children. With time running out, they once more looked into the possibility of adopting. In 1930 George received an encouraging letter from his friend, Henry Coffin, urging him to consider the Alice Chapin Adoption Nursery in New York City. Coffin had adopted two infants from this agency, and heartily recommended it: *"Mrs. Chapin is in the way of finding little children who need homes and whose antecedents are such that there is every prospect of their becoming capable members of society."*[1] In other words, the children would most likely be from good families and genetically sound. Either Marjorie or George (or perhaps both) still had reservations about adoption and they did not follow up on the recommendation. Or perhaps they were, by then, too old to be considered as adoptive parents. In August Marjorie was hospitalized again in Boston at the Phillips House, part of Massachusetts General Hospital. Why she was there is still unknown.

---

[1] Letter from Henry Coffin to George Lyon, March 27, 1930. Blithewold Archives.

Chapter XVI

FINANCIAL CRISIS

The first recorded evidence that the McKees were in severe financial trouble was a March 1931 letter written by Bessie to George in which she asked for more money. In the letter, she wrote,

> *I am hoping not to have to ask for another dollar this year. If I do, it will not be until the fall...It certainly is not pleasant for me to have to ask any help from my children, you can understand that, but Marjorie and Augustine have always been very sweet about wishing me to live as I have always been accustomed.*[1]

DISSOLUTION OF A. W. TEDCASTLE & COMPANY

The McKees' extravagant lifestyle and the upkeep of two very expensive homes were beginning to take a financial toll. With the rise of labor unions and the introduction of personal income taxes before World War I, families like the McKees were far less able to accumulate and retain great wealth. The Tedcastle Company was in serious difficulties, but instead of trying to get his money out in order to repay his family's notes in 1929 (when the company rallied for a time) Will McKee soldiered on, convinced that good times would return.[2] In April 1931, however, the American stock market embarked on a steady slide that would not end until World War II. The Great Depression had begun, and the McKees would not recover. In December, Marjorie,

---

[1] Letter from Bessie to George Lyon, March 6, 1931. Blithewold Archives.
[2] William McKee was not the only one to believe in the company's viability. Head salesman Nash K. Burger also held on, sure that the company would ultimately turn around. His son reported that Mr. Burger lived on his savings for several years while waiting for better times, which never came. Nash K. Burger. *The Road to West 43rd Street.* University Press of Mississippi, 1995, p. 49.

Augustine, George, and Quincy met with the McKees at 284 Commonwealth Avenue to discuss the liquidation of the Tedcastle Company. With the humiliating possibility of bankruptcy uppermost in his mind, William McKee accepted $25,000 from Marjorie and Augustine to begin the process of closing down the Company. The agreement was that $10,000 went to reducing the Company's loan from the Second National Bank in Boston, and the remaining $15,000 to pay some of what the Company owed to manufacturers, as well as *"any other immediate pressing indebtedness."*[1]

A. W. Tedcastle building, Boston

In the documents William McKee signed he agreed that the Company would now devote itself entirely to liquidating and would not undertake any new business. Moreover, the Company had to agree that it would not borrow any more money or assume any new

---

[1] Memorandum addressed to William McKee and signed by himself, Marjorie and George Lyon, and Augustine and Quincy Shaw, December 17, 1931. Blithewold Archives.

obligations; George Lyon and Quincy Shaw would also have full access to any or all of the Company's books and records at any time. Real estate companies were asked to assess the values of the 284 Commonwealth Avenue house and Blithewold, in the hope that one of them could be sold quickly. In the early summer of 1932, Marjorie and Augustine bought 284 Commonwealth Avenue from their mother for $15,000 each (though the funds only went to pay existing debts). Bessie also transferred ownership of Blithewold to her two daughters, to offset her debts to them and to relieve herself of the burden of its taxes and maintenance.[1]

FAMILY TURMOIL

The die was now cast, and family relationships began to deteriorate. Marjorie and Augustine exchanged angry letters over the best way to manage their mother's sensitive finances, while George and Quincy undertook all responsibility for dealing with taxes and lawyers and real estate agents. Bessie's nerves began to fray. At one point she protested, perhaps facetiously, to Marjorie, *"Your lion is pretty growly and roars so that he frightens us..."*[2] Augustine could not forgive her stepfather for bringing about Bessie's financial downfall and wanted to cut him out of all family discussions and negotiations. Marjorie, always the peacemaker and the voice of reason, insisted that for their mother's sake they should respect William McKee's pride. She wrote to her sister that they should:

> *...not forget the 31 years of happiness and cheerful kindliness he has brought into our lives...Also his unfailing love and courtesy to Mother...He was dead wrong, of course...But money isn't everything. The long years of association, love, and trust do count to me. And Mother will never benefit by all we are planning to do for her, unless*

---

[1] As evidenced by a letter to Bessie, Marjorie, and Augustine from Quincy Shaw, explaining tax implications, September 24, 1932. Blithewold Archives.
[2] Bessie to Marjorie, May 31, 1932. Blithewold Archives.

Father is considered a part of the plan. No family plan ever succeeded without taking into consideration all the members.[1]

Augustine eventually acquiesced, but she insisted that she would not advance any more money until the McKees found a way to reduce the Bristol expenses. They all began to work together again, but Bessie was forced to send all household expense bills to George and Quincy for payment. Perhaps not surprisingly, Bessie was hospitalized in August 1932. On September 1, Quincy wrote to Bessie referring to the fact that she would be given a personal monthly allowance of $1,000, and William McKee $200.[2] Quincy and Augustine and George and Marjorie decided to cancel the notes endorsed by the Tedcastle company that they held.[3] They made the decision that in order to stem the flow of rapidly diminishing funds and to try to settle Bessie and Will's affairs, Blithewold would have to be sold. It was a wrenching decision because it was the place beloved by them all. But the real estate market was already dead, and there were no offers for Blithewold.

The next month tensions flared again, and Bessie accused George of delivering a low blow to her husband. George protested vehemently, insisting that the measures he had taken were essential to the well-being of the family, and that no one had benefited more from what had thus far been accomplished than William McKee himself. *"Although we have a great deal of sympathy for him, he has suffered no injury or injustice, and we all think he is behaving childishly. It is also as unreasonable as it is unfair to have him focus his ill feeling upon me, for I have done a great deal for him."*[4]

Even amid all the family turmoil, Marjorie remembered that September 20, 1932, marked what would have been Bessie and

---

[1] Marjorie to Augustine, June 15, 1932. Blithewold Archives.
[2] Quincy Shaw to Bessie, September 1, 1932. Blithewold Archives.
[3] Letter of confirmation of the transaction from Scudder, Stevens & Clark, to George Lyon, December 29, 1932. Blithewold Archives.
[4] George to Bessie, September 8, 1932. Blithewold Archives.

Augustus's Golden Wedding Anniversary had it not been for his untimely death in 1898. She wrote a tender, poignant letter to her Mother, offering a moment of calm and reflection on this special day:

Mother dearest, I'll be thinking of you so hard tomorrow — on your Golden Wedding Day. Wouldn't it be wonderful if dear Papa were really looking down at you, and his beloved Blithewold? How interested and pleased he would be with it all. I'm sure he'd approve the Place, and all the fine changes you have made. Also, I'm very sure he'd approve you and your mature grace and charm and your wonderful vitality. I wish he could see us all. He'd like 209 Newton St. too, I think. But best of all he'd love his two jolly granddaughters. Well, perhaps he is looking down...I never cease to be grateful that I can remember my Father so well, and so many of his ways, and his fun-making. Wasn't he a dear![1]

Marjorie and Augustine were now the owners of 284 Commonwealth Avenue *and* Blithewold, as well as their own homes, so they were responsible for the maintenance, monthly expenses, and taxes on all of them. A concerted effort began to sell one or other of the McKee properties. They consulted agents and solicited appraisals. Blithewold, including the land to the south, was generously appraised at $95,000, but the real estate agent added, *"While this property is well located and commands an excellent view of Narragansett Bay, I do not consider that it could be sold at this time at the price stated above. We all know that there is no market for real estate at present."*[2]

A second plan thus needed to be formed. The Commonwealth Avenue house might be easier to sell, although probably at only a quarter of its real value. At the same time, since the land at Blithewold could easily be divided, they would attempt to sell the 30 acres to the south of the house that included the Gardner house and the

---

[1] Marjorie to Bessie, September 19, 1932. Blithewold Archives.
[2] Letter from Arthur Drew, Real Estate Agent, November 10, 1932. Blithewold Archives.

clubhouse. The thirty-acre parcel was sold in August 1933 to an agent who assured the McKees that he was working on behalf of a client from Chicago, a Mr. Porter, who wished to build a home on the land. The deal was struck, and the family realized $17,500, although the assessed value was $23,500.[1] The McKees moved to Bristol in the late summer of 1933, which simplified life somewhat. Blithewold, with its remaining 40 acres became their permanent, year-round home. Although the townhouse on Commonwealth Avenue was leased out, it had been appraised for tax purposes at $80,000 and was offered for sale at $25,000 (the reasonable expectation being that they would only realize $20,000). A children's speech school[2] had leased it with an option to buy, and the family fervently hoped that the school would soon decide to buy and meet at least the $20,000 price.

THE MCKEES TAKE A TRIP TO EUROPE

Within a few months, everyone's humor improved, which would seem to indicate that the school did indeed buy the property, easing financial pressures all around. In February 1934, Bessie and Will set off on a two-month cruise to Europe and Egypt, possibly to celebrate the final settlement of their affairs. Certainly, family letters from this point are warm and affectionate again.

---

[1] The McKees discovered later that the agent's client was actually the Columban Fathers of the Catholic Church, who would use the Gardner House as a home for young Catholic priests in training. In 1954 the Fathers demolished the old Gardner house and built another that is now used as a home for retired Catholic priests who have spent their careers in the foreign missionary field. The Fathers and Blithewold, Inc. to this day maintain a friendly and mutually beneficial relationship. The clubhouse remains on their property, and the Fathers extend generous access to the facility for research by Blithewold staff. The captain's cottage that had been on the southern edge of the property was destroyed in the hurricane of 1938.
[2] The Copley School of Expression, Boston Speech Foundation, 284 Commonwealth Avenue. Letter to George Lyon, October 2, 1933. Blithewold Archives.

Bessie and Will left New York on the snowy morning of February 8, 1934, sailing on the deluxe R.M.S. *Statendam.*[1] The trip began with bad weather — snow squalls and rough seas — but by the fifth day the weather had become fair and much warmer. The McKees left the past four unhappy years behind them and enjoyed luxurious travel once again.

Their first stop was Madeira, the second Gibraltar. In Seville, Spain, they went to the Alcazar Cathedral and the Geralda Tower. They then drove overland to Cordoba and Granada, meeting the ship again in Malaga. Although they disliked their next stop, Algiers, they happily visited Monaco, Nice, and Malta. They went ashore in every port and saw interesting churches, museums, and other tourist attractions. After sailing to Beirut, Jerusalem, Haifa, and Port Said, they finally arrived in Cairo. From Cairo they took a train to Luxor and Karnak, sailed down the Nile, visited the Egyptian Museum and the Tomb of Kings, and went shopping in the Bazaars — an itinerary that would have left the most intrepid traveler gasping. They even rode on camels at the Pyramids and the Sphinx.

Bessie riding a camel in Egypt, 1934

---

[1] The Holland America Line, built in 1929.

On March 10 they reboarded their ship and sailed to Rhodes, passing the Dardanelles and Gallipoli. By the time the ship anchored in Istanbul they were exhausted, so they decided not to go ashore. They rested, wanting to save their energy for Athens where they would arrive the following day. By this time, Will was suffering badly from gout and was walking with difficulty, but he was still very anxious to see the sights of Athens. He climbed the Acropolis in his bedroom slippers because he could not get his shoes on over his painful feet.

Bessie (seated) at the Acropolis in Athens, March 1934

The next leg of the journey was a cruise to Yugoslavia and Venice, after which the ship went south to Corfu and Sicily. The continuing hectic pace began to take its toll once again, and they missed, due to exhaustion, several highlights of the next part of the trip, including Pompeii and Cannes. The last leg of their journey took them to Holland and then back to Southampton to prepare for the sail home to the United States in early April of 1934. They were rested enough after their arrival in New York to travel south to visit William McKee's sister and her husband in Virginia, before going home to Bristol.

Chapter XVII

A NEW ERA AT BLITHEWOLD

The McKees' first summer as permanent residents of Bristol flew by in a flurry of activity; guests came and went and overlapped from May until the end of November 1934.[1] Bessie and Will enjoyed motoring over to Harwichport on Cape Cod (Massachusetts) to visit Bessie's sisters Anne and Edith. In September 1934, when Bessie's sister Gertrude Keller and her son Harry were visiting Blithewold from Hazleton, they all took the opportunity of going to Harwichport so that the four surviving Pardee sisters could be together. Harry Keller took a photograph of the sisters there, probably the last. All the sisters except Bessie were in ill health.

The four surviving Pardee sisters in Harwichport, September 1934
Edith, Gertrude, Bessie, Anne

---

[1] As evidenced by entries in the Blithewold Guest Book. Blithewold Archives.

Will and Bessie had hoped to drive down to Hazleton before winter set in, to visit with everyone there. But family letters suggest that their Bristol social life was very busy and they didn't know if they would be able to make it before the first snow.[1]

AUGUSTINE AND QUINCY DIVORCE

By 1934, Augustine and Quincy Shaw were having serious marital problems. Quincy wanted to marry a much younger woman, Margery Cheney. The two had met when Margery came to stay with her sister, who lived next door to the Shaws on Sears Road in Brookline.[2] Augustine left Massachusetts and moved with her children to Pennsylvania, where she lived in a rented house in Chestnut Hill to be near her cousins, the Earles. It was at that time that she met Robert Toland[3] whom she would later marry. While waiting for her divorce to become final, Augustine moved back north to Blithewold with her two children, living there for a year.

Bessie and Will McKee were more than happy to have their daughter and granddaughters with them. For seven-year-old Marjorie it was an idyllic summer at Blithewold. She learned to swim well enough to reach the float attached to the dock — a huge achievement for her, of which she was justly proud. She also learned to row well

---

[1] Letter from William McKee to Bessie's brother, Israel, October 4, 1934. Blithewold Archives.

[2] Quincy Shaw and Margery Cheney married in 1936 and lived in the house on Sears Road where they raised two daughters, Alexandra and Anne. The Cheneys had owned a successful silk manufacturing company in Manchester, Connecticut, but had lost much of their their wealth in the Depression.

[3] Robert Toland lived in Whitemarsh, Pennsylvania, in a house named Aubrey, next door to Church Hill Hall where the Earles lived — the house Calvin Pardee (Bessie's older brother) had built for his family when they left Hazleton.

enough to take her grandfather Will out to his boat, *Wild Swan,*[1] a Herreshoff-designed 23-foot gaff-rigged sloop.

Dee and Marjorie went to the Wheeler School in Providence for the 1935–1936 school year, driven the 17 miles each day by Bessie's chauffeur, Arthur Rae. Young Marjorie thought the experience quite an adventure, and though she was not particularly happy at the school she loved the freedom of living at Blithewold and having the undivided attention of her grandparents. Dee, three years older than Marjorie, was angry and resentful at the upheaval in her life, and she hated having to leave her home, her friends, and her father.[2]

Marjorie Shaw practicing her rowing to the Wild Swan, *1934*

[1] *Wild Swan* was built in the 1890s for Augustus Van Wickle by the Herreshoff Boatbuilding Company in Bristol, Rhode Island.
[2] Interview with Marjorie Shaw Jeffries, October 20, 2009.

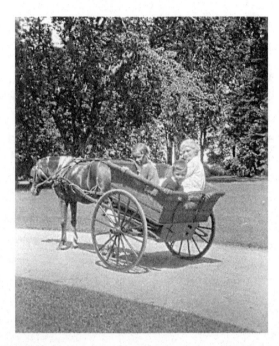

*Dee Shaw with Bessie's maid, Katrina,
in the donkey cart at Blithewold, 1934*

*On the terrace at Blithewold, summer 1935. Back row from left: William
McKee, Marjorie Lyon, two unidentified women, George Lyon. Front row:
Isabell Hidden, Bessie McKee, Marjorie Shaw, Dee Shaw, and
Augustine Shaw*

The winter of 1935–1936 was particularly cold and Blithewold was blanketed in ice and snow. Marjorie Shaw Jeffries remembers that during that winter the Bay was:

...a mass of white, chaotic slabs of ice scattered here and there. I learned much later that people walked over the Bay to Poppasquash that winter. I feel slightly cheated that I did not do that. But we had our own amazing scene. We went down to the Water Garden and put on our skates. It wasn't very big, of course, but I was only seven, though I did know how to skate. Dee at 10 was much more advanced and found the space very constraining. Then someone realized we could actually skate on the grass. We erupted from the pond, delighted with this novel happening. Under the trees the crust broke through occasionally but once we had moved beyond the nut trees at the edge of the lawn it was perfect. Then the game became one of scrambling up the slope to just below the house and seeing how far we could coast without moving a muscle. We screamed downhill, and because the lawn sloped gradually all the way to the water, we went an amazingly long distance.[1]

Dee Shaw skating at Blithewold, February 1936

---

[1] *Memory Vignettes of Blithewold*, by Marjorie Shaw Jeffries, Blithewold Archives.

The west-facing façade of Blithewold,
pictured during the icy winter of 1935–1936

Christmas 1935 was a joyful time despite the new family circumstances. The McKees brought a 20-foot-tree in from the garden and erected it in Blithewold's two-story entrance hall, a tradition that had begun in 1910. Hundreds of twinkling lights covered it, to the delight of the grandchildren. Bessie invited her friends from the Bristol Garden Club to hold their annual Christmas party at her home, and they all joyfully drank wassail and admired the tree and its decorations.[1] The Shaw children were relaxed and happy in their newfound security and family warmth — they were with their mother and their adoring, and adored, grandparents. As Christmas Day drew nearer their excitement grew. And it was a good time for Marjorie Lyon, too — she wrote in the Guest Book, *"Christmas Party with the biggest tree we ever had. Katrina[2] still here to put the old balls and decorations on the tree. A happy Christmas party! Mother was the heart*

---

[1] From an article by Julia Drury in the *Bristol Phoenix,* February 14, 1936.
[2] Katrina Gluck was Bessie's maid for almost 50 years.

and soul of it all!"[1] Seven-year-old Marjorie Shaw Jeffries remembered the holiday clearly:

> *Christmas came and the house was full of secrets and decorations. The tree stood in the front hall reaching up two stories. I have little memory of individual decorations, just the immensity of the tree. The billiard table was covered with presents, an awesome sight. My Mother, Grandfather, and Grandmother presided with dignity over the festivities. Dee and I were dressed in our best and allowed to eat with the family on Christmas Eve.[2]*

Little did the Shaw children, or anyone, know that their world was about to change again, irrevocably.

END OF AN ERA — DEATH OF BESSIE MCKEE

Less than a month after that wonderful Christmas, Bessie tripped on the staircase at Blithewold coming down for dinner, breaking her leg badly. Although she was given the best of care in a Providence hospital, her injuries were insurmountable. She died three weeks later on February 4, 1936, just a few days after her seventy-sixth birthday. She was buried at the Juniper Hill Cemetery in Bristol. In an article in Bristol's St. Michael's Church Parish magazine it said of her:

> *For more than a quarter of a century, Sunday morning saw her in her pew whenever she was in Bristol, without fail. No Parish activity escaped her notice and friendly interest, and no Parish endeavor failed to elicit her generous support. Many of our people knew at first hand the gracious hospitality of her beautiful home, and cherish the vision of*

---

[1] From the Blithewold Guest Book, December 1935. Blithewold Archives.
[2] *Memory Vignettes of Blithewold,* by Marjorie Shaw Jeffries. Blithewold Archives.

*quiet and gentle dignity granted them there. She was gifted
with understanding large enough to encompass two worlds,
the ancient regime of New England, and the modern world.
She walked in both with no sacrifice of integrity, finding life a
reflection of her own serene mind.[1]*

The *Bristol Phoenix* published an article by Bessie's friend, Julia
Drury, who reported sadly that *"the shadow of a great sorrow has
fallen over Blithewold. After a few short weeks of anxiety and illness,
the mistress has gone away. We can't believe that the trees and flowers
she so loved and tended will go on growing without her."[2]*

The whole family was heartbroken. William McKee lived for
another ten years but he never recovered his stamina or his zest for
life.[3] In April he wrote to Alice Lee Pardee, widow of Bessie's brother
Israel, describing life at Blithewold without Bessie. He was desperately
lonely, he said, but took great comfort in his grandchildren,
particularly young Marjorie, who adored her grandfather. She would
follow him around, watching him cut wood for the fire and pile it in
the barn. She would sit by his side in the Living Room as he read the
newspaper or a book and ask him endless questions. He taught her
about the Native American Indians and their tenacity, what wonderful
dancers they were, and what great warriors. She also accompanied
him as he busied himself around the property. One day, while the two
were out walking, he noticed that one of the large stone caps on the
wall along Ferry Road had been pulled off (a favorite trick of the young
people of Bristol). He recounted the incident in a letter to Alice:

*I stooped over and tried to pick it up, forgetting that I had
passed seventy years of age and could not pick up quite as
big stones as I used to. I tried two or three times to lift the*

[1] Parish Magazine of St. Michael's Church, Bristol, February 1936.
Blithewold Archives.
[2] The *Bristol Phoenix*, February 14, 1936.
[3] As evidenced in many letters from William McKee to his relatives
throughout this period. Carbon copies of his letters were kept and are stored
in the Blithewold Archives.

stone to the top of the wall and missed it, the last time stumbling over something and falling all over myself. Finally, I picked the stone up and got it on the wall. Little Marjorie said "There, you are just like the Indian dancers. You said you would do it and now you have done it."[1]

But Will was about to lose the comfort of his grandchildren, too. In 1937, Augustine married Robert Toland in a quiet ceremony at Blithewold. Her daughters Dee and Marjorie were bridesmaids and wore long pink tulle dresses.[2] Her new husband had four children of his own, somewhat older than the Shaw girls, but the children all got on well. And they all loved Augustine.[3] Too soon for Will, Dee and Marjorie went with their mother to their new home in Whitemarsh, near Philadelphia, and Will McKee was left alone with his memories.

Augustine riding with daughters Dee and Marjorie in Pennsylvania, ca. 1936

[1] William McKee to Alice Lee Pardee, April 1, 1936. Blithewold Archives.
[2] Now in the Blithewold costume collection.
[3] Interview with Marjorie Shaw Jeffries, March 16, 2001.

The same year that Bessie died, Marjorie Lyon had a car accident in Boston that ended up compromising her mobility for the rest of her life. Her badly injured right knee needed surgery, and although the procedure went well, an infection set in while she was still in the hospital. Unfortunately, her doctor was on vacation at the time, and Marjorie was reluctant to complain about the pain to another physician.[1] By the time her own doctor returned and checked the wound, it was a mass of infection. He immediately put her on antibiotics, and she soon felt well again and free of pain. Her knee was completely fused, however, and it remained stiff and unbendable for the next forty years of her life.

Marjorie after her accident, with George, 1936

---

[1] Interview with Marjorie Shaw Jeffries, March 16, 2001.

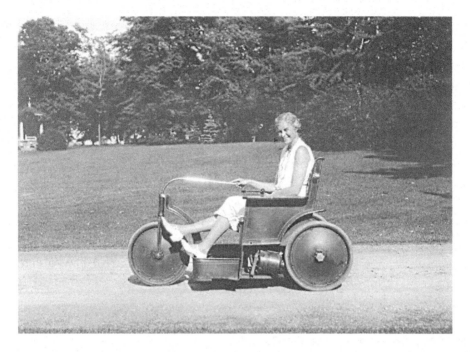

Marjorie in an electric golf cart at Blithewold, leg outstretched, ca. 1936

All photographs of Marjorie taken after this time show her either seated, her right leg supported on a footstool, or standing stiffly, a walking stick often hidden behind her back. Her cousin Jill Pardee bought her an electric golf cart so that she could more easily get around the gardens at Blithewold. With the cart she could collect flowers from the cutting gardens each day. She even insisted that she could still tend the gardens, although she had to sit awkwardly on the ground with her right leg stretched out in front of her. Her niece Marjorie said, *"She managed without complaint, to tie her shoe, drive a car, garden, swim, kayak and golf."*[1]

Marjorie's days of hunting in the wild, hiking twenty or thirty miles a day over rough terrain, and sleeping on the floor in Spartan conditions were now clearly over. She found, however, that she could

---

[1] *Memories of Marjorie Randolph Van Wickle Lyon* by her niece Marjorie Shaw Jeffries. Essay, Blithewold Archives.

still manage travel to Europe — with special help from the airlines and the staff at the first-class hotels she had patronized for years. She resumed an earlier interest in painting and started to take lessons in Boston. In April 1938, armed with her art supplies, she traveled to Amsterdam on the *Statendam,* visiting Brussels, Paris, London, and Monte Carlo. With a footstool to support her stiff leg, she sat at her easel and painted to her heart's content. (On her return to Boston and Bristol, Marjorie used those color sketches as the bases for lovely watercolor paintings on full-sized art paper, framing many of them.[1])

In Monte Carlo Marjorie met up with Irma Nayral, whom she had not seen since her wedding day at Blithewold in 1914. *"Irma at Station. I cried a little — well it _was_ 24 years!!"* Marjorie wrote in her diary, *"Very little change in her."*

WILLIAM MCKEE'S LAST YEARS

Bessie's death in 1936 marked the end of the golden era of Blithewold. Without Bessie's gracious influence, and her absence as the keeper of family unity, Marjorie and Augustine allowed their mutual antipathies to rise to the surface. Neither one felt the need, nor the desire, to seek out the other's company.

After Augustine and her children left Blithewold to start their new life in Whitemarsh, Pennsylvania, William McKee's health deteriorated rapidly, to the point that he could no longer live at Blithewold alone. He moved to the Algonquin Club on Commonwealth Avenue in Boston, where he was a lifetime member. Although his gout had become much worse, he wrote to Augustine in the fall of 1937 to say that he was looking forward to spending Christmas in Whitemarsh with them. At the last minute, though, he was too frail to make the

---

[1] A large collection of Marjorie's paintings are preserved at Blithewold, including full-sized framed works of art and hundreds of her smaller-format colored sketches.

journey. But he told them he hoped to be well enough to spend the following summer with them at Blithewold.

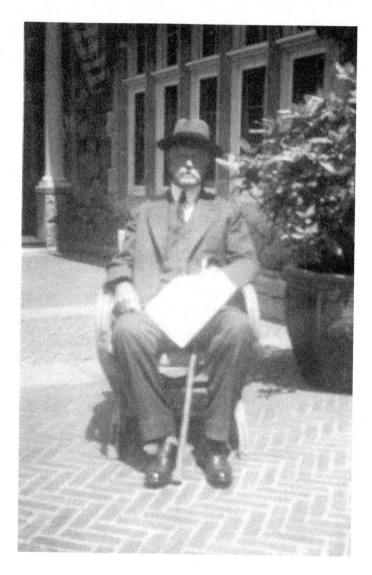

William McKee at Blithewold, 1941

By 1941 Will could not walk at all. He was admitted to Faulkner Hospital in Jamaica Plain, where he would spend much of the following five years. A part-time secretary would come to the hospital and type the letters that were his only means of contact with his friends and family. The carbon copies of that correspondence leave the letters' readers with a clear account of a very lonely, diminished life. It fell to Marjorie to care for him. She visited him every day, while Augustine visited sporadically from Philadelphia. He spent his time reading and listening to music. In October 1943, he wrote to Israel's widow, Alice Lee Pardee:

> *I am completely free from pain. I have been here on my back in bed nearly a year now and no one seems to know just exactly what is the matter with me. The trouble is I cannot walk, and as a matter of fact, I cannot get out of bed without help. Marjorie comes in every day. Augustine was here today from Philadelphia. I would love to have them both together.[1]*

His last comment seems to suggest that the sisters made a point of not visiting at the same time. They still shared ownership of Blithewold, but they spent little time there together. They both attended family celebrations and reunions, but it was common knowledge amongst the family that they no longer shared much affection.[2]

On Christmas Day 1943, Marjorie collected Will from the hospital to bring him to her house for dinner, a huge effort but one he appreciated. He planned to go to Bristol for the month of July 1944 while Augustine and her children were there,[3] but by the end of May

---

[1] William McKee to Alice Lee Pardee, October 1943. Blithewold Archives.
[2] Comments to the author from several family members, including Nancy Pardee Abercrombie, Frank Pardee, Schuyler Pardee, and Marjorie Shaw Jeffries.
[3] As part of the divorce agreement between Augustine and Quinny Shaw, Dee and Marjorie Shaw were expected to spend the month of July every year with Augustine at Blithewold.

314

he was beginning to doubt he could make the journey. *"Just now it seems as if it would be a great undertaking to get dressed and move out of here,"*[1] he wrote to Augustine.

William McKee at Marjorie's house in Brookline, 1945

In 1946 Will spent the months from January through June at the Kenmore Hotel in Boston, with nursing care. At the end of June, when it became clear that he had very little time left, the family transferred him, with great difficulty, to Blithewold. He was a broken man, having exhausted his health, his enthusiasm, and his resources. He wished to end his days at Blithewold, the place he loved best and where he had been so happy. He died there on July 6, 1946, at the age of 82. He left a letter of farewell in which he quoted his favorite poem, "Crossing the Bar," by Alfred Lord Tennyson, along with a list of friends and relatives to whom he wished Marjorie to send copies. He was buried alongside Bessie at Juniper Hill Cemetery in Bristol. The many condolence letters sent to Marjorie are testimony to a much-

---

[1] William McKee to Augustine, May, 1943. Blithewold Archives.

loved man who was known to all, young and old, as "The Commodore."
Of the many tributes, the most eloquent and wistful was:

> *I hate to think that generation has nearly all gone. They*
> *were all part of such a gracious, peaceful, unhurried*
> *life...and in spite of personal difficulties they seemed as if*
> *they knew how to cope with the difficulties and put them*
> *in their place and make living calm and good in spite of*
> *everything.*[1]

Ironically, two days after his death a $10,000 check in William
McKee's name was received from his brother-in-law William Hidden's
lawyer. Will was a beneficiary of Mr. Hidden's will. Other than that
bequest, William McKee died with very few possessions. He left
instructions for the distribution of his scant valuables: his stamp
collection (which he left to Dee Shaw); his pearl pin, a gift from Bessie;
and his gold watch. His boat, *Tern*, sold for $150. His $10,000 life
insurance policy had been mortgaged and only $2,250 was left of it.
After taxes and probate, what was left of his estate was shared by
Marjorie and Augustine.

---

[1] Letter to Marjorie from Gertrude Keller Johnston, July 7, 1946. Blithewold
Archives.

Chapter XVIII

BREAKDOWN OF THE FAMILY

Once Marjorie no longer had the responsibility of caring for William McKee in his last years, she was able to commit more time to her Red Cross interests and to her art. She joined the Copley Society of Boston and began to take lessons at the Museum of Fine Arts, and, privately, with Boston artist Priscilla Ordway.[1] She entered paintings in numerous juried art shows, and exhibited several times in Boston at the Copley Society and in Bristol at the Bristol Arts Museum. She also enjoyed entertaining her Boston Arts Club friends at Blithewold, where they loved to paint in the gardens.

Marjorie displaying her art at the Bristol Art Museum, July 1963[2]

---

[1] Priscilla Ordway graduated from Smith College in 1916 and taught art in Newton for many years. She exhibited her watercolors at the Boston Art Club. She visited Blithewold often, where she painted in the gardens. Many of her paintings remain at Blithewold and have been exhibited there.
[2] The painting to which Marjorie is pointing was purchased by her friend Patricia Sisson who recently gifted it to Blithewold; it is now on display in the second-floor hallway.

MARJORIE NEGOTIATES OWNERSHIP OF BLITHEWOLD

In 1946, Marjorie began negotiations to buy out her sister Augustine's share of Blithewold. The agreed price was $37,500, half the assessed value of $75,000.[1] Marjorie could keep the contents of Blithewold (including furniture, rugs, silver, and china), except for a short list of "sentimental" items that Augustine asked for. Augustine must have realized that she might have limited access to her beloved Blithewold in the future, and she asked to buy a small seven-acre strip of land to the south of Lovers Lane, for which she paid $11,000. She could thus be assured of being independent and still spend her summers in Bristol. Her property would be accessed by a narrow road that linked the land to Ferry Road. Marjorie's lawyers advised her to make it clear to Augustine that she would not necessarily always have access to her property through Blithewold.[2]

After the negotiations were completed, Augustine's husband, Bob Toland, protested that the terms were unfair and that Marjorie and George had taken advantage of Augustine.[3] Ill feelings between the sisters grew fiercer, the upshot being that the Tolands were no longer welcome at Blithewold. By now Marjorie and Augustine were barely speaking, and George had unfortunately taken it upon himself to inform Augustine that she could not come onto Blithewold property again or it would be considered trespassing.[4] Augustine put a mobile home on her part of the property at a spot overlooking Blithewold, so she could still spend the summer there without having to depend on Marjorie and George. Despite all this, Marjorie Shaw Jeffries remained close to her Aunt Marjorie. She felt conflicted, though, and she believes that her mother may have been hurt by her daughter's

---

[1] Per the valuation of Blithewold estate by Walter Channing, Inc., made in November 1932 when property values were at their lowest. Another appraisal done fourteen years later, in 1946, by John Carpenter, Inc. attached the same value to the estate.

[2] Letter from Henshaw, Lindemuth & Siegl, Counsellors at Law, to Marjorie Lyon, November 15, 1946. Blithewold Archives.

[3] Interview with Marjorie Shaw Jeffries, January 29, 2008.

[4] Ibid.

continuing closeness to her aunt, although Augustine never spoke of it.[1]

GEORGE LYON'S ILLNESS AND DEATH

Sometime in the late 1940s George Lyon began to suffer from dementia. By 1949 Marjorie was clearly unhappy and under a great deal of strain. Charles T. Hopkins, an old army friend of George's, wrote to Marjorie, sympathizing with her situation and remembering better times:

George holds a place in my affection that is shared with no other man. My feelings towards him are as alive and active now as they were back in 1917 and subsequent years. There has been so much going on in the world that has been a constant reminder of our days of adventure and close association....All during this second [world] war, in my contacts with the men in uniform, listening to their experiences, problems, etcetera, the thought was constantly with me "There but for the grace of God and a lot of dissolute years go George and I." So you see he is very much in my thoughts and they are good thoughts I can assure you. You must promise me that if anything ever occurs to you whereby I can be of the slightest assistance in this situation, you are to let me know regardless of what it is.[2]

As the years passed, George became loud and threatening, and by 1952 Marjorie's maids at Blithewold were afraid of him. They told Marjorie that they did not want to be left alone with him anymore.[3] Reluctantly, Marjorie arranged for George to be taken into care at

---

[1] Interview with Marjorie Shaw Jeffries, January 29, 2008.
[2] Letter from Charles T. Hopkins to Marjorie, January 6, 1949. Blithewold Archives.
[3] Interview with Eleanor Rae Gladding, daughter of chauffeur and estate manager, Arthur Rae, October 12, 2007.

Butler Hospital in Providence, where he died on January 17, 1954. Condolence letters to Marjorie pay tribute to her courage, loyalty, and devotion. Augustine, despite her own problems, rose above her bitterness to extend her sympathy — she wrote the ultimate family compliment: *"Mother and Father would be proud of you."*[1] Others wrote of Marjorie's *"selfless devotion"* and *"wonderful courage."*[2] Her cousin, Carl Erdman wrote, *"Priceless memories will always remain...our unbounded admiration...how gallantly you have shouldered [your burden]."*[3]

THE FAMILY CURSE

In 1953, at the age of 54, Augustine was diagnosed with manic-depression[4] (now known as bipolar disorder). She was taken to McLean Hospital,[5] where doctors prescribed lithium and Thorazine for her symptoms. Marjorie Shaw Jeffries[6] described her mother as gradually changing from a vibrant, enthusiastic woman — very active and involved with sports — to a perfectly competent but colorless personality, a common side effect of the prolonged use of Thorazine.[7]

Augustine's older daughter, Dee, was at some point also diagnosed with this disorder. Marjorie Shaw Jeffries remembers her sister, even as a child, having a bad temper. Dee was angry about her parents' divorce and did not get on with her father's new wife.[8] As an

---

[1] Augustine to Marjorie, January 17, 1954. Blithewold Archives.
[2] Letter from Frank Dexter Cheney to Marjorie, January 18, 1954. Blithewold Archives.
[3] Letter from Carl Erdman to Marjorie, January 17, 1954. Blithewold Archives.
[4] Interviews with Marjorie Shaw Jeffries, September 1, 2005, and June 11, 2007.
[5] The same hospital where Quincy's father, Quincy A. Shaw II, had spent much time.
[6] Marjorie Pemberton Shaw had married David Jeffries in 1952.
[7] Interviews with Marjorie Shaw Jeffries, June 11, 2007 and November 9, 2010.
[8] Interview with Marjorie Shaw Jeffries, June 11, 2007.

adult, although charming and adventuresome in many aspects of her life, Dee's moods of anger and depression persisted, destroying her marriage to Frances Whiting Hatch. They divorced shortly after the birth of their son Timothy, and Dee was hospitalized in Massachusetts, probably at the Austen Riggs Sanatorium in Stockbridge,[1] where her mother had been a patient. Frank Hatch's parents took care of baby Tim and raised him for the next several years. Dee later married Allan Butler and had three more children. But her illness contributed to the dissolution of this marriage also.[2] Allan Butler divorced her, leaving her hurt and angry, and she would battle manic-depression for the rest of her life.

Despite these health problems, Dee made a successful life for herself in some ways. She bought and renovated houses in Beverly Farms and Rockport, Massachusetts; she taught skiing; and she began painting in watercolors.

Watercolor of a Paris street scene, by Dee Butler

---

[1] Interview with Marjorie Shaw Jeffries, January 4, 2011.
[2] Ibid.

Once her children were grown, Dee traveled to England, Belgium, France, and Germany. Later in her life, while in Freiburg, Germany, she enrolled in German courses at the university there. She enjoyed living with the students until she started feeling ill. She traveled to England for medical advice — the diagnosis was bone cancer, and she returned to the United States for treatment. She died in 1988 at the age of 63.

Manic-depression in the Shaw family is well documented in the book *In My Blood — Six Generations of Madness and Desire in an American Family* by John Sedgwick.[1] But melancholia was also evident among the Pardee women (Bessie, Annie, Ellen, and Edith) who often went for "cures." Ellen Pardee, who died young in Paris in 1869, was said to *"have been subject to periods of despondency that almost amounted to melancholia."*[2] A strong hereditary factor is known to contribute to this disorder. Augustine would have been at risk for depression from her Pardee roots, while her daughter Dee's risk would have been multiplied through both sides of her family.

---

[1] John Sedgwick's book documents manic depression in his family, which he attributes to the merging of the Shaw and Sedgwick families in 1895. *"The Shaws were afflicted by their own line of manic depression, one that had been amplified by various intermarriages..."* John Sedgwick, *In My Blood* (Harper Collins, 2007) p. 243.
[2] C. Pardee Foulke and William F. Foulke. *Calvin Pardee.* Drake Press, Philadelphia, 1979, p. 38

Chapter XIX

THE RED CROSS YEARS

Marjorie's Red Cross Identification Card

When Marjorie first joined the Red Cross in South Carolina in 1917, she could not have known that it would lead to a lifetime of dedicated service to the organization. She would work for the Red Cross for almost 40 years, through two world wars and in peacetime. At her retirement in 1957 it was estimated that she had driven some 150,000 miles for the Boston Red Cross.

The Boston Red Cross Motor Corps at Blithewold, 1947
Marjorie Lyon far left

In the beginning, she offered help where she saw a need, and to pass the time while she was far from home. Her husband George had been sent to Camp Jackson (in Columbia, South Carolina) in 1917 to help train officers for the war in Europe. Marjorie took rooms in town to be close to him, but she soon found that she could see him for at most a few hours a week. With a great deal of time on her hands, she inquired about volunteer positions in the town — she was anxious to contribute to the war effort. Marjorie was asked to establish a new Home Services Division of the Red Cross in Columbia. She helped set up an office and managed it for more than a year, helping families whose lives had been severely impacted by the anticipated war. Later, while George was away in France, she did Red Cross service on Cape Cod, Massachusetts, and in Vermont.

After World War I, Marjorie became a Motor Corps Driver for the Boston chapter, where she would remain for the rest of her Red Cross years. Through the organization she took courses in motor mechanics, map reading, convoy drills, home nursing, advanced first aid, city driving (including driving trucks), and social services.

Marjorie's duties in Boston both between the wars and after World War II included picking up needy patients and driving them to local hospitals and clinics for outpatient treatment.[1] She befriended her patients, sometimes driving up to twenty of them a day all around the Boston area. She would later write, for her own enjoyment, essays about her experiences, and stories about the hundreds of men, women, and children she cared for, leaving a detailed record of her service.[2] One of Marjorie's Motor Corps essays reads:

> *Perhaps carrying children to and from the Infantile Paralysis Clinic is not all duty...we had four small boys (about 6 years) and two slightly older girls in the car on one trip. It wasn't a heavy load — but very energetic. Each child had a toy received at the clinic and a paper bag full of fruit. None of the boys could walk really well, but they all insisted upon carrying their toy and their bag and their cap! And then trying to race to get the front seat first!! You can imagine I was fairly busy picking up the pieces. Bless their hearts; they are so full of spirit and fun. It is interesting to note that on the day in question this driver worked 7.5 hours, drove 67 miles, carried 14 patients and made 32 calls. The ambulance did its annual tour of duty at the Marathon Run April 19th, carrying 20 injured and exhausted runners.[3]*

Many of her patients were children who had contracted polio, or infantile paralysis as it was then called. One such boy was Elmer, and Marjorie wrote of him:

---

[1] Marjorie saved her handwritten daily work schedules of her Red Cross duties, all of which are preserved in the Blithewold Archives.

[2] Marjorie's essays are in the Blithewold Archives.

[3] From essays by Marjorie Lyon. Blithewold Archives.

Elmer rode in my Red Cross car to the Polio Clinic many times in those days, and we became friends. A little fellow in a plaster cast — but always smiling. He even taught me to pitch pennies against the curbstone while we waited for other patients! I never forgot him, nor his smile. Years after I'd meet him in the street, and we were still friends.[1]

*Marjorie taking a child to the hospital for the Red Cross, 1927
"a little fellow in a plaster cast"*

---

[1] From essays by Marjorie Lyon. Blithewold Archives.

Marjorie also met the "displaced persons" ships from Europe, and assisted hundreds of refugees brought to the United States:

The Red Cross Personnel was there to meet and feed them. They were [808] people of different tongues, countries, and religions — but they had in common the loss of everything that had been theirs, and their joy at reaching America! As they filed past us, a small girl in one of the last groups seemed to typify and glorify all the others. She had golden hair, blue eyes, a big blue hair ribbon, German perhaps — tired she must have been (we all were) but on her face there was a smile of such pride and trust as she gazed at the American flag held high in her hand — the flag of her new country![1]

When World War II broke out in Europe, Marjorie helped arrange temporary homes for wartime evacuee children from England. The Red Cross would meet the ships in Boston and assign each child to a local family. It was expected that these young people would remain in the United States for the duration of the war, keeping them safe from the nightly bombing raids in London. In 1940 Marjorie took in two fifteen-year-old boys herself, welcoming Ian Wilson and Bob Sproule into her home and into her heart. They would become members of her family, the children she had never had, and she would refer to them as her adopted sons.[2] Both Ian and Bob remained in the United States after the war and later became American citizens. Bob Sproule went to college in Henniker, New Hampshire, where he met his wife Lois.[3] The Sproules and their children later spent extended time at Blithewold every summer.

---

[1] Essay by Marjorie Lyon, November 19, 1948. Blithewold Archives.
[2] Interview with Marjorie Shaw Jeffries, fall 2009.
[3] Bob and Lois graduated from New England College in 1951.

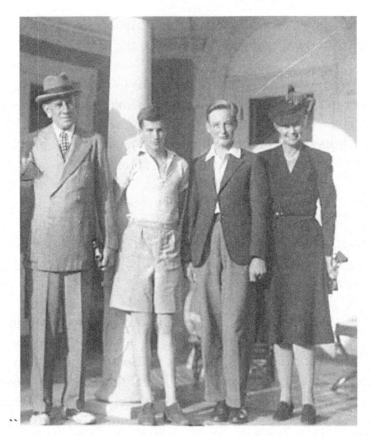

George Lyon, Ian Wilson, Bob Sproule, Marjorie Lyon, Blithewold 1940

Ian Wilson joined the U.S. Navy in 1946 and was sent to Trieste, but after his military service he returned to live in Bristol. A gifted artist and ornithologist, he lived at Blithewold whenever Marjorie Lyon was in residence. After he was diagnosed with a brain tumor in the 1950s, Marjorie supported him financially for the remainder of his life.[1]

---

[1] Interview with Marjorie Shaw Jeffries, fall 2009.

Chapter XX

MARJORIE'S LAST YEARS

After her husband George died in 1954, Marjorie realized she had no responsibilities to anyone but herself. She decided to simplify her life by selling the Lyons' home in Brookline, after which she divided her time between her Beacon Hill townhouse in Boston and Blithewold. Because for tax purposes she was registered as a Rhode Island resident, she had to spend at least six months a year in Bristol. She would spend May through October at Blithewold, working tirelessly in the gardens, painting, playing bridge and Scrabble, and entertaining local garden clubs. Marjorie had inherited not only her mother's standing as a first-class gardener, but her reputation as a generous hostess. Friends and family still gathered at Blithewold for birthdays, anniversaries, and holidays. She enjoyed entertaining the next generation of children and babies. In October, 1954, after an exhausting visit by the Sproules and their young children, she wrote wistfully:

> There's a prancing toy horse on the table,
> And a wee plastic phone on the chest.
> The house is most frightfully quiet;
> The dog lies extended at rest.
> Great Auntie's supposed to be resting,
> She's having a meal on a tray.
> But actually she just can't help thinking
> How she'd like to relive the whole day.[1]

Everyone looked forward to Marjorie's annual Labor Day Party when as many as 80 guests would gather to reflect on yet another wonderful summer on Narragansett Bay. Halsey Herreshoff, a frequent

---

[1] Poem for Bob and Lois Sproule by Marjorie Lyon, October 31, 1954. Blithewold Archives.

visitor to Blithewold, described Marjorie as *"the most gracious host you could ever imagine — and she made a great martini! She was a Great Lady."[1]* On one such occasion Halsey became the subject of family legend. He had attended a Labor Day Party as a young man, when he was still unaccustomed to the delayed effects of Marjorie's "lethal" martinis. He excused himself from the table in the middle of dinner and no one saw him for awhile. Sometime later, Marjorie's maid came to whisper quietly in her ear *"Mister Halsey is fast asleep — on the billiard table!"[2]*

In January 1956, Marjorie received a letter from William Ellery of the Trustees of Reservations of Massachusetts. He had heard that Marjorie was looking into the possibility of leaving Blithewold to a Trust: *"[I understand you are considering] leaving your beautiful property some day, to be held forever for the benefit of the public."[3]* He went on to say that were the property in Massachusetts he would certainly recommend accepting it, but since it wasn't, he suggested that she might want to consider leaving the estate to the Heritage Foundation of Rhode Island. Marjorie contacted them, and long and drawn-out negotiations between Marjorie and the Foundation began. It was not until March of 1960, however, that A. H. MacIntyre, of Marjorie's bank, the Old Colony Trust Company, was able to congratulate her, writing *"...that all the protracted plans to leave Blithewold to the Heritage Foundation were brought to fruition."[4]* With the future of Blithewold now assured, Marjorie began to open the estate for tours, hosting garden clubs from Massachusetts, Rhode Island, and New Hampshire; The Boston Horticulture Club; The

---

[1] Conversation with Halsey Herreshoff at Blithewold, October 13, 2010. Mr. Herreshoff stressed that Marjorie Lyon loved Blithewold intensely, and that he feels sure she would be pleased to know of the present stewardship of her estate and of the commitment to keep Blithewold open "in perpetuity for the enjoyment of the public."

[2] Ibid.

[3] Letter from William Ellery to Marjorie, January 22, 1956. Blithewold Archives.

[4] Letter to Marjorie from A. H. MacIntyre, Old Colony Trust Co., March 9, 1960. Blithewold Archives.

Horticultural Society of New York; Federation of Garden Clubs; The Boston Travel Club; The Rhode Island Nurserymen's Club; The Redwood Library of Newport; The Newport Naval Officers' Wives Garden Club; the Rhode Island Historical Society; and landscape architecture students. She would typically accompany the groups herself. One tree in particular that captivated all visitors was the Giant Sequoia[1] in the Enclosed Garden, and the dozen or so smaller specimens on the property that Marjorie had propagated from Blithewold's original Sequoia. The picnic luncheon that would be served after a tour (sometimes to as many as 150 people) often included produce from the vegetable garden. In 1966 the International Plant Propagators Society visited Blithewold, and wrote letters of thanks and appreciation to Marjorie.

Marjorie also now began to distribute some of these "second-generation" Giant Sequoias throughout Bristol and Newport. One was planted on the lawn of the Redwood Library in Newport,[2] and several others were given as gifts or memorials.

Marjorie continued to collect and plant trees on the property until shortly before her death. In 1972, for example, she received a Katsura tree seedling from Boston's Arnold Arboretum in thanks for her contributions to the Friends of the Arnold Arboretum. The year-old Japanese *Katsura Cercidiphyllum* seedling was propagated from trees growing on the Arboretum grounds for 94 years. The original seeds had been collected in Japan in 1878 by W. S. Clark, and sent to the Arboretum that year. Marjorie had the gift seedling planted in the Enclosed Garden, where it flourishes today. It has since been propagated by Blithewold's horticultural staff, and there are now several more mature trees in the neighborhood.

---

[1] Blithewold's Giant Sequoia (at almost 100 feet) is reputed to be the tallest of its species east of the Rockies.
[2] The Giant Sequoia at the library was subsequently replaced with a similar tree from another source.

*Marjorie on her electric cart
with flowers she collected from the garden, 1967*

In 1973, on Marjorie's ninetieth birthday, friends and relatives celebrated the occasion by planting specimen trees in her honor. These included the dawn redwood (*Metasequoia glyptostroboides*) and the franklinia (*Franklinia alatamaha*), both of which attract considerable attention today.

In her last years, Marjorie was honored in other ways, too. In 1964, she received a letter from the Museum of Science and Hayden Planetarium in Boston informing her that they were building a new wing on their facility where they would *"place the magnificent collection of heads and horns which you and George gave us."*[1] These were the "trophies" that George and Marjorie had collected on their many hunting forays into the wilderness of the American West and Canada. Other "heads" were displayed at their home in Brookline, their townhouse on Acorn Street, and at Blithewold.

---

[1] Letter from Bradford Washburn, Museum of Science and Hayden Planetarium, to Marjorie, March 27, 1964. Blithewold Archives.

The Lyons' Trophy Room at their home, 209 Newton Street, Brookline

In 1968, Marjorie heard that the Van Wickle Library at Lafayette College had become too small for the school, so a new library had been built. The original Van Wickle Library was converted into exhibit space, becoming the college art gallery. Marjorie sent one of her paintings as a gift to the college, to be displayed in the new gallery.[1]

PAINTING IN EUROPE

With complete freedom now to come and go as she pleased, Marjorie began traveling to Europe every spring, from February to April, seeking inspiration for her art work. She went to the same hotels each year where the staff knew her and would arrange transportation around the city for her. These were always painting

---

[1] Letter of thanks to Marjorie from K. Roald Bergethon, Lafayette College, June 17, 1968. Blithewold Archives.

holidays, and she enjoyed them almost every year between 1958 and 1973.

A typical painting trip included visits to London, Rome, Paris, Monte Carlo, Naples, Venice, Florence, Palermo, and Taormina. At 80 years old (in 1964) Marjorie wondered if she was losing her energy, but while in Rome at the Hassler Hotel,[1] she wrote, *"Went to Piazza Navona to paint. First day walked home up the Spanish Steps[2] — didn't think I'd ever do it this year."*

In 1965, Marjorie's niece Dee Shaw Butler[3] and Dee's daughter Ellen met her in Paris. The three went shopping to find a dress for Marjorie to wear at her eighty-second birthday celebration that was being planned for that September. They found a beautiful yellow beaded gown that Marjorie loved, and which she wore many times after that birthday celebration. Dee and Ellen were both artists and encouraged Marjorie to have an art show in Bristol to showcase all her latest paintings.

Marjorie took her last trip to Europe in 1973. She was now in her ninetieth year, but she still traveled to Rome, Taormina, Venice, Paris, and London. She painted and visited art galleries and museums every day. In Paris she wrote in her diary *"I finished the view of the flower stand."*[4] Despite her lameness and her advanced years, Marjorie managed to fit in full days of sight-seeing and theatre-going. On April 6, for example, she visited the Louvre and the Jeu de Paume National Gallery, had her hair shampooed and got a manicure, and then went to the Gallery of Modern Art. After dinner she attended *The Marriage of Figaro* at the Théâtre Français before falling into bed, justifiably

---

[1] The Hassler Hotel is at the top of the Spanish Steps in Rome.

[2] The 138 steps up a steep hill from the Piazza di Spagna to the Piazza Trinita dei Monte, Rome.

[3] By this time, Augustine's daughter Dee had been married and divorced twice: first to Frank Hatch, with whom she had a son, and then to Allan Butler with whom she had three children.

[4] Marjorie's diary, February 26, 1973. Blithewold Archives. The painting is displayed periodically at Blithewold as part of the Blithewold collection.

exhausted. The next day, April 7, she wrote, *"To Montmartre to paint"*; and on April 9, *"Off to do a sketch of the Madeleine Flower Market."*

"Bridge over the Seine" by Marjorie Lyon, Paris 1973

An admirer of Marjorie's work was Mary MacDonnell, daughter of Marjorie's cook Tilly MacDonnell. Mary lived in Paris and spent time with Marjorie there in April 1973, convincing her that she should continue to display her art.[1] Marjorie returned to Blithewold and immediately began converting her sketches into full-size paintings, preparing to show them at the Bristol Art Museum. Some of these paintings were given as gifts to family and friends.

---

[1] *"Mary MacDonnell wants me to have a show at Blithewold."* Marjorie's diary, April 9, 1973. Blithewold Archives.

Marjorie in Paris, 1973

That September Marjorie celebrated her ninetieth birthday at Blithewold, wearing her favorite yellow beaded gown (the one she had bought in Paris). It was a time of celebration and remembrance — everyone brought poems[1] to read at the dinner table, as had been the family tradition for many years. For a short while, the ongoing family differences between the sisters were overlooked. Marjorie Shaw Jeffries, who had studied music at Bryn Mawr and at Wellesley,

---

[1] These poems are preserved in the Archives at Blithewold.

played flute music that she had written especially for the occasion. (Her Aunt, she said, had always encouraged her interest in music.)

Marjorie at her ninetieth birthday celebration at Blithewold
September 12, 1973

Marjorie was diagnosed with leukemia in 1974. She needed to go to a Boston hospital for two days of treatment[1] every week during the summer, but she based herself in Bristol, wanting to spend as much time at Blithewold as possible. There she was looked after

---

[1] The treatments included blood transfusions. As evidenced in a letter to Marjorie from her cousin Kitty, June 2, 1976. Blithewold Archives.

faithfully by her cook of some 40 years, Tilly McDonnell.[1] After a time, though, Marjorie started missing her appointments. Marjorie Shaw Jeffries believes this was because her aunt could not bear to leave her gardens at Blithewold. Her health started to decline rapidly, at which point Augustine came to see her and the sisters at last reconciled. Marjorie Shaw Jeffries said:

> *This time of physical weakness and dependency of the last two years was later seen as a gift to the family, as it was at this time that Marjorie and Augustine forgot their differences and tried to make up for lost time. Augustine would go and read to her sister.*[2]

Despite her ill health, however, Marjorie prepared and presented an exhibit of new work at the Bristol Art Museum in August 1975, and still encouraged family and friends to paint and sketch at Blithewold.

Sketch of Blithewold by Marjorie Shaw Jeffries, 1975

---

[1] Interview with Marjorie Shaw Jeffries, December 2000.
[2] Ibid.

The following May Marjorie waited anxiously in Boston for arrangements to be made so that she could return to Blithewold for the summer. Two nurses were hired to provide round-the-clock care, and Tilly McDonnell supervised the running of the household, assisted by Peggy Devine.[1] In June Marjorie suffered a major setback to her health and mobility after an accident in the gardens at Blithewold. A tree limb fell on her, breaking two ribs and causing lacerations to her face.[2] After that, her strength deteriorated steadily and a hospital bed was made up for her in the Billiard Room. Marjorie Randolph Van Wickle Lyon died on November 6, 1976, several weeks after her ninety-third birthday. She is buried at Juniper Hill Cemetery with her mother, Bessie; her stepfather, William McKee; and her husband, George Lyon.

MARJORIE'S LAST WILL AND TESTAMENT

Blithewold's gardens and arboretum had matured under Marjorie's care, attracting significant interest from garden clubs near and far. In her lifetime Marjorie had welcomed gardeners and horticulturists to the estate, offering them guided tours and detailed information about the grounds and the specimen plants. After almost 80 years of work to bring Bessie's vision for Blithewold to fruition, Marjorie feared, however, that after her death the gardens and arboretum would be destroyed to make room for modern development.[3] She had seen that happen to Hanley Farm in Warren and to North Farm in Bristol. So it was that, with her family's knowledge, Marjorie had arranged to leave the entire Blithewold property to the Heritage Foundation of Rhode Island, along with a $1.2-million endowment for its upkeep.

---

[1] Taken from letters between Marjorie and her cousin, Kitty, summer 1976. Blithewold Archives.
[2] As evidenced in letters to Marjorie, June 1976, from her cousin Kitty and other well-wishers. Blithewold Archives.
[3] Interview with Marjorie Shaw Jeffries, December 2000.

When Marjorie Lyon's last will and testament was read, the bequest to the Heritage Foundation was not unexpected. There *was* an unexpected surprise in the will for the remaining family, however: the disposition of that portion of Marjorie's estate *not* included in the trust agreement. This part consisted of her home on Acorn Street in Boston, a considerable amount of family jewelry, all her personal effects, and a sizeable monetary legacy. According to Marjorie Shaw Jeffries, the family had understood that this would be equally divided between Mrs. Lyon's sister Augustine, and Augustine's two daughters, Dee and Marjorie Shaw.[1] Marjorie Lyon, however, had changed her will shortly before she died, eliminating her sister and her niece Dee from her will entirely. In the new will she left everything to Marjorie Shaw Jeffries and her husband David.[2] Marjorie Jeffries was as shocked as everyone else at this unexpected turn of events, but she duly set about the work of liquidating the estate. She invited her children to take some items from 4 Acorn Street, keeping for herself a few things of sentimental value. The bulk of the furnishings were sold or given away, but the personal papers, photographs, letters, and paintings were stored in the attic at her home in Milton, Massachusetts.

When Augustine died in Whitemarsh, Pennsylvania, a year later, she left her estate in equal parts to her two daughters, Dee and Marjorie, with the seven-acre strip of Blithewold land that she had purchased in 1946 being left to Marjorie. Still reeling from her unexpectedly large inheritance from her Aunt Marjorie and struggling to understand its implications, Marjorie Jeffries felt uneasy about her sister Dee's exclusion from the Lyon will. To assuage some of that discomfort, she gave the seven-acre strip of land to Dee as compensation.[3] (Dee later gave or sold the land to a young Bristol man, who subsequently sold it to a developer.)

---

[1] Interview with Marjorie Shaw Jeffries, December 2000.
[2] Marjorie Lyon's last will and testament, Blithewold Archives.
[3] Interview with Marjorie Shaw Jeffries, January 10, 2010.

Chapter XXI

BLITHEWOLD MANSION, GARDENS & ARBORETUM

After the death of Marjorie Lyon in 1976, the Heritage Foundation of Rhode Island, a statewide non-profit organization, immediately began to prepare Blithewold for its new role as an historic house and gardens open to the public. After forming a Board, the Foundation named the site Blithewold Mansion, Gardens & Arboretum. The entire south wing of the mansion, which had been the servants' quarters, was closed off from the rest of the house and turned into an apartment for the Executive Director.[1] Blithewold opened to the public on a limited basis in 1978. A part-time horticulturist[2] was hired, along with grounds and garden staff; and volunteers from the local communities were invited to train as gardeners' assistants, tour guides, and office support. Beginning in 1978, some changes were made to the property. A parking lot was built in the old orchard on the south side of the property, and the carriage house (part of the stable complex) was turned into a gift shop. In the mansion, rooms were arranged as they had been according to photographs taken in 1910. Public bathrooms were constructed out of the coal cellar in the basement.

The new Board offered memberships to the public, and Blithewold became a popular and desirable place to work, to volunteer, and to visit. Regular newsletters alerted members to special events — classes, exhibits, concerts, and garden parties. At the same time, a curator directed archive volunteers through the process of sorting and cataloguing letters, photographs, and diaries that had

---

[1] Donald Buma, and later Mark Zelonis.
[2] Julie L. Morris, now Director of Horticulture Emerita, thus began her long career at Blithewold. In the winters of 1979 and 1980, Julie worked on identifying the woody plants collection, and she became a full-time staff member in 1982.

been found throughout the house in drawers, trunks, and closets. In 1984, the property was listed on the National Register of Historic Places. In the late 1980s, the Northeast Document Conservation Center undertook a "Wallpaper Conservation Assessment" for Blithewold; curator Anne Shannon wrote a "Collections Management Policy"; and the Fogg Museum of Harvard University produced a "General Survey of Collections in the House." These reports laid the foundation for a systematic and professional approach to managing the Mansion's collections.

In 1987, Robert I. Goler compiled a "Collections Survey." A Visitors' Center was built in 1991 adjacent to the parking lot, its design suggested by the old Golf Clubhouse. In 1996, Ann Beha Associates completed the first comprehensive "Buildings Assessment" report which helped establish priorities for work needed on the buildings; and in 1998 the Newport Collaborative prepared a "Master Plan for the Carriage House" to explore options for reuse of the structure. Other research projects during this period included reports on "Proposed Management of the Bosquet" by Robert Rouse and Lucinda Brockway, and a "General Survey of Collections" by the Center for Conservation and Technical Studies, Harvard University Art Museum.

The Heritage Foundation (it changed its name to Heritage Trust of Rhode Island in February 1989) kept the doors of Blithewold open for 20 years, and its reputation as one of the finest garden estates in New England continued to grow. However, behind the glorious picture of success that Blithewold presented to the community, the Heritage Trust was encountering mounting financial difficulties. The Blithewold estate eventually faced the very real threat of being closed to the public forever. The endowment was almost entirely depleted, and the Trust began to explore alternative stewardship arrangements for Blithewold. When the house closed at the end of the season in 1998, the administrative staff was terminated and advised that the Blithewold estate was being offered for lease. Proposals had already been invited from interested parties, including an events-catering company, nearby Roger Williams University, and an exclusive private club — all of which had plans to severely restrict public access to the house and grounds.

SAVE BLITHEWOLD, INC.

Shocked, a small group of Blithewold supporters came together in protest at the totally unexpected news, gathering at members' homes to discuss a strategy for saving the institution. With only three weeks to go before an irreversible decision would be made, the group quickly formed a nonprofit organization and called it "Save Blithewold, Inc."[1] Each of its members went out into the community, calling on friends and neighbors, asking for pledges of support for Blithewold. Save Blithewold, Inc., in turn, pledged to take over the management of Blithewold and to keep it open to the public in accordance with Marjorie Van Wickle Lyon's wishes. The new organization tapped into an enormous wave of public concern that Blithewold might be closed down, in effect destroying the more than one hundred years of work that had created an American garden treasure.[2] They received validation and encouragement from Bill Noble, Director of Preservation at the Garden Conservancy[3] who said that, in his opinion, Blithewold was certainly worth saving.

By the time the Heritage Trust[4] called together its Board to discuss the proposals and to make a final decision about the fate of the property, Save Blithewold, Inc., was ready to come to the table with an offer of its own. The new Board members had raised firm commitments of more than $650,000 in three weeks. The Board

---

[1] This group was organized by Mary and Richard Glenn and Marty and Porter Halyburton.
[2] Bill Noble of the Garden Conservancy called Blithewold "*An American Garden Treasure.*"
[3] The Garden Conservancy is a national organization founded to preserve exceptional American gardens for the public's education and enjoyment.
[4] In August 1999, the Heritage Trust changed its name again, to Preserve Rhode Island, Inc.

pledged to run Blithewold in a fiscally responsible fashion, to ensure continued public access, and to preserve New England's finest garden estate through excellence in all areas. The astounding result was that the Heritage Trust was persuaded to give Save Blithewold, Inc. a 99-year lease.[1]

The Save Blithewold Board was a working board in the truest sense. Everyone worked tirelessly and seamlessly together with great enthusiasm and a profound sense of mission. Board members called on former volunteers to ask for their support. Site Administrators[2] oversaw day-to-day management while the new Board conducted a search for a permanent Executive Director. A carefully chosen skeleton staff was hired, to be supported by working Board members and volunteers. After three months of incredibly hard work by everyone involved, Blithewold opened for the season on schedule in April 1999. What followed was nothing short of a miracle.

In 2000, Eric Hertfelder, a well-respected preservation professional, was hired as the first Executive Director of Save Blithewold, Inc., and an ambitious program dedicated to fund-raising, horticultural excellence, and historic preservation was put into place, moving Blithewold forward rapidly into a new era of distinction.[3] Early projects of Save Blithewold, Inc. included the property survey by Scituate Surveys, relocation of the gift shop from the Carriage House to a newly expanded Visitors' Center, and refurbishing the Carriage House space for education programs. A group comprising Karen Jessup, Lucinda Brockway, Eric Hertfelder, and Julie Morris prepared a draft landscape policy.

---

[1] In 2010, Blithewold, Inc. and Preserve Rhode Island amended the lease for a period of 99 years with an extension option, so that Blithewold will be managed by Blithewold, Inc. for the foreseeable future.

[2] Philip Anderson and Constance Coar.

[3] Save Blithewold, Inc. created a mission statement, in which it pledged "to preserve New England's finest garden estate through excellence in horticulture and historic preservation, and by our example to teach and inspire others."

In 2004, the Board hired Karen Binder as the new Executive Director, and in 2006 the Board of Save Blithewold, Inc., believing that Blithewold had truly been saved, voted to change the name of the organization to simply Blithewold, Inc. as a symbol of its success and transformation into a financially and organizationally strong institution.

HISTORICAL INTERPRETATION

In 1999, two volunteer archivists[1] launched a concerted effort to further catalog, preserve, and organize the vast on-site archival collection. Blithewold secured a Conservation Assessment Program (CAP) grant to provide professional advice on how to accomplish this enormous task.[2] As per CAP's recommendations, new storage and work spaces were installed on the third floor of the mansion, and funds from the operating budget were allotted for archival preservation supplies that would provide new, safe, and accessible housing for the collection. A separate office was equipped with four computers, and a group of ten dedicated volunteers began the job of transcribing and interpreting the family letters and diaries, producing both electronic and hard copies.[3] The photographic collection was cross-referenced with the written materials, and careful identification, analysis, and cataloguing of the entire archival collection began. As a result, information retrieval became almost instantaneous and interpretation more meaningful.

Around this same time, Marjorie Shaw Jeffries began to donate to Save Blithewold, Inc. the photograph albums, letters, and personal papers she had saved from Marjorie Lyon's house on Acorn Street in Boston, as well as materials from her mother Augustine's house in

---

[1] Mary Philbrick and Margaret Whitehead.
[2] The professional CAP companies appointed were ArtCareResources of Newport, Rhode Island, and Ann Beha Associates of Boston Massachusetts.
[3] This has simplified research, and the archives are now accessible for study by serious students.

Whitemarsh, Pennsylvania. This represented a huge vote of confidence on Marjorie Jeffries' part for the new organization. From 2000 right up to the present day she has supported Blithewold emotionally and financially, as well as with the unique gift of her memories and writings about her family. Nancy Pardee Abercrombie (Frank Pardee's granddaughter) also offered new support for Blithewold, donating several boxes of letters, photographs, diaries, and documents that now form the Ario Pardee Collection. Mrs. Jeffries and Mrs. Abercrombie also donated to Blithewold paintings by Marjorie Lyon that had been gifts to them from Marjorie.

With this fresh collection of materials, research began to branch out in new directions. The new material represented the "missing pieces" of the Blithewold family history, which allowed Archivists to fill in some of the previously elusive details of life at Blithewold — the breakdown of family relationships, the devastating effects of the Depression, the change of ownership of the various properties, and an immense amount of information about what happened to the family after Bessie McKee's death in 1936.

Over the past eleven years, information from both old and new collections has made its way out of the archives to be presented in formats that inform and educate Blithewold members and visitors. There are, for example, information sheets in each room of the Mansion that include descriptions of the furniture and furnishings, and short biographies of the family members. There continue to be special historic exhibits, lectures, and presentations on various aspects of Blithewold past and present. Newsletters and the Blithewold web site disseminate new information on the estate and the family, and alert members to events and programs available.

CONSERVATION, RESTORATION, AND PRESERVATION

The management of Save Blithewold, Inc. initiated a new era of responsible fund-raising. The endowment grew from zero in 1998 to $3,800,000 in 2011. A further $2 million has been spent on restoration and conservation projects. Early major projects included stabilizing the west-facing terrace and balustrade; reroofing the Pump House; reroofing the Summerhouse in the Enclosed Garden and replacing its rotted pillars; and in 2005 completely rebuilding the old Lord & Burnham greenhouses (originally constructed in 1901).[1] Over the years the horticultural staff has planted hundreds of new trees to replace old trees as they died off. A stone bench in the Water Garden was rebuilt based on archival photographs of the original. The gravel paths that were laid out by John DeWolf in 1895 to connect the gardens were uncovered and restored. Those paths again serve to lead visitors through the grounds from one inspiring garden to the next, as they did more than a hundred years ago.

The year 2008 was a commemorative year for Blithewold. It marked the hundredth anniversary of the building of Blithewold II; thirty years of the estate being open to the public; and ten years of successful governance under the new administration. The year began with an elegant dinner in the Dining Room for seventy people on Twelfth Night, followed by a season of special exhibits, lectures, teas, and parties. A Gala Event for 400 guests on a beautiful September evening honored Marjorie Shaw Jeffries. She later wrote:

There is no end to my thoughts and memories. When my Aunt died in 1976 and the property came under the management of the Rhode Island Heritage Foundation, I thought that my association with Blithewold had also died. I knew little of the financial affairs of Blithewold beyond the knowledge that my Aunt had finally, after ten years of

---

[1] The rebuilt greenhouses were dedicated to Julia L. Morris.

searching and negotiating, found a way to preserve the property in perpetuity...She gave an enormous financial gift for endowment, which, properly handled, should have increased over the years and lasted for decades. To say that my family was shocked, horrified, and angry when we learned in September of 1998 [that plans were afoot to close Blithewold to the public] *would be an understatement. But nothing could compare with our amazement at the reaction of so very many people who came together to save Blithewold. To me it is in the realm of a miraculous undertaking. I am truly stunned that so many people have come forward with what counts: their money and their time. They are people who have no direct connection with our family, and who will receive no tangible benefit from their gift. How can I ever express to them my feeling of wonder and gratitude?[1]*

Continued successful fund-raising provides further resources for maintaining the estate. Recent projects include upgrading the fountains with recirculating water systems; reinstalling the vegetable garden;[2] stabilizing and re-shingling the Carriage House; and restoring the Loggia. Conservation professionals restored and conserved paintings, textiles, furniture, light fixtures, and original wallpapers. Return visitors to Blithewold say they have never seen it looking so pristine, well cared for, and historically authentic. The mansion's "crowning glory" (literally and figuratively) is the new slate roof, replaced in 2009. The new roof will protect the structure, and the Collections it shelters, for another hundred years. This project alone, which cost $1 million, represents the "saving" of Blithewold.

---

[1] From *Observations* by Marjorie Shaw Jeffries. Blithewold Archives.
[2] Garden volunteer Richard Philbrick planned and now manages the new vegetable garden.

THE FUTURE

In 2009, a small group,[1] with the full support of Executive Director Karen Binder, met and began to work toward an ambitious goal — of creating a Master Plan for Blithewold. The Plan would recognize the true significance of the collective estate, determine its future, and create a roadmap that would be followed by staff and Board in identifying, prioritizing, and carrying out new projects. Dedicated fund-raising for the costly Master Plan project began. When these financial goals were met, the federal Institute of Museum and Library Services (IMLS) provided matching funds, and the Board voted to proceed with Requests for Proposals. In early 2010 the Boston firm of Ann Beha Associates (ABA) was hired to begin the Master Plan process. As the year came to a close, reports from the various ABA associates (experts in their individual fields) began coming in. As of now, 2011, they are being reviewed. The reports show that Blithewold scores high in the areas of horticulture, preservation, and education, and that the foundation of responsibility and good stewardship built over the past twelve years has provided a firm basis for planning for the future.

Blithewold was indeed worth "saving," and the Master Plan will inspire the energy needed for moving forward with preserving this historical treasure. Blithewold's mansion, gardens, and arboretum will remain as a complete picture of an era gone by, safeguarded for the benefit of the public for generations to come.

---

[1] Blithewold Board members Gioia Browne and Martha Moore, staff member Margaret Whitehead, Director of Horticulture Emerita Julie Morris, and prominent landscape history professional Karen L. Jessup, Ph.D.

Members of the Founding Board of Save Blithewold, Inc.

Gail P. Davis
Robert Spink Davis
Dorothy Davison
Mary G. Glenn
Richard M. C. Glenn, III
Anne W. Hall
Robert F. Hall
Martha D. Halyburton
Porter A. Halyburton
Sanne Kure Hodges
Lynn Kelly
Sayles B. Livingston
Heather MacLeod
Nancy B. Marini
Alan B. Nathan
Alexandra O'Donnell
Virginia P. Purviance
Bruce R. Ruttenberg
Ralph L. Weaver
Margaret P. Whitehead
Shawen Williams

BIBLIOGRAPHY

Burger, Nash K. *The Road to West 43rd Street* (Jackson, MS: University Press of Mississippi, 1995).

Collinge, Constance Pardee. *Dearest Family* (privately published, 1992).

Cabot, Frank. *The Greater Perfection* (New York: W. W. Norton & Company, 2001).

Cabot, Frank. *Quatre Vents,* a DVD narrated by Frank Cabot (Cold Spring, NY: The Garden Conservancy, 2011).

Foulke, C. Pardee & Foulke, William G. *Calvin Pardee* (Philadelphia: Drake Press, 1979).

DeWolf, John. *"History of Blithewold, Bristol, Rhode Island."* Unpublished essay, ca. 1905.

Gladding, Eleanor Rae. Collected unpublished essays, 1986–1988. Blithewold Archives.

Jacobus, Donald Lines. *Pardee Genealogy* (New Haven, CT: New Haven Colony Historical Society, 1927).

Jeffries, Marjorie Shaw. *Memory Vignettes of Blithewold.* Collected unpublished essays, n.d. Blithewold Archives.

Jeffries, Marjorie Shaw. *Observations.* Collected unpublished essays, n.d. Blithewold Archives.

Johnston, Gertrude K. *Dear Pa – And So It Goes* (privately published, 1971).

Lyon, Marjorie Van Wickle. *Reminiscences of Marjorie Van Wickle Lyon in her 90th Year,* as recounted to her niece, Marjorie Jeffries. Unpublished memoir, 1973. Blithewold Archives.

Monahan, Brent. *The Jekyl Island Club* (St. Martin's Minotaur, 2000).

Moore, Honor. *The White Blackbird* (New York: W. W. Norton & Company, 1996).

Morris, Julie L., and Margaret Whitehead. *Blithewold Mansion, Gardens & Arboretum.* Privately published, 2004.

Nicolson, Adam, *Sissinghurst — An Unfinished History* (New York: Viking, 2008).

Nicolson, Juliet. *The Perfect Summer* (New York: Grove Press, 2006).

Nicolson, Juliet. *The Great Silence (New York:* Grove Press, 2009).

Pardee, Alice DeWolf. *Blithewold* (Providence, RI: Heritage Foundation of Rhode Island, 1978).

Sedgwick, John. *In My Blood* (New York: Harper Collins, 2007).

Skillman, David Bishop. *The Biography of a College* (New York: The Scribner Press, 1932).

Standiford, Les. *Last Train to Paradise* (New York: Three Rivers Press, 2002).

Wharton, Edith. *A Backward Glance* (New York: D. Appleton-Century Company, Inc., 1934).

CPSIA information can be obtained at www.ICGtesting.com
Printed in the USA
BVOW04s1354080916

460823BV00005B/3/P